ON SOLID

STRATEGIES FOR TEACHING READING K–3

GROUND

ON SOLID

STRATEGIES FOR TEACHING READING K–3

GROUND

Sharon Taberski

Foreword by
Shelley Harwayne

HEINEMANN

Portsmouth, NH

Heinemann
A division of Reed Elsevier Inc.
361 Hanover Street
Portsmouth, NH 03801-3912
www.heinemann.com

Offices and agents throughout the world

© 2000 by Sharon Taberski

The author and publisher wish to thank those who have generously given permission to
reprint borrowed material:

Cover illustration and text from the poem "A Birthday Wish" in "Could We Be Friends? Poems for Pals,"
written by Bobbi Katz and illustrated by Joung Un Kim, from Mondo's BOOKSHOP Literacy Program.
Text © 1997 by Bobbi Katz and illustration copyright © 1997 by Joung Un Kim, reprinted by permission
of Mondo Publishing, One Plaza Road, Greenvale, N.Y. 11548. All rights reserved.

Text and illustration for the poem "Words" from "Could We Be Friends? Poems for Pals," written by
Bobbi Katz and illustrated by Joung Un Kim, from Mondo's BOOKSHOP Literacy Program. Text © 1997
by Bobbi Katz and illustration copyright © 1997 by Joung Un Kim, reprinted by permission of Mondo
Publishing, One Plaza Road, Greenvale, N.Y. 11548. All rights reserved.

Excerpts and illustration from "Friends," written by Mon Hong and illustrated by Winson Trang, from
Mondo's BOOKSHOP Literacy Program. Text and illustration copyright © 1995, reprinted by permission
of Mondo Publishing, One Plaza Road, Greenvale, N.Y. 11548. All rights reserved.

Excerpt from *Snaggle Doodles* by Patricia Reilly Giff. Illustrated by Blanche Sims. Copyright © 1985
by Patricia Reilly Giff. Illustrations copyright © 1985 by Blanche Sims. Used by permission of Dell
Publishing, a division of Random House, Inc. and Patricia Reilly Giff.

Credits continue on p. 221

Library of Congress Cataloging-in-Publication Data
Taberski, Sharon.
    On solid ground : strategies for teaching reading K–3 / Sharon Taberski.
      p. cm.
    Includes bibliographical references and index.
    ISBN 0-325-00227-4
    1. Reading (Primary)—United States. 2. School children—United States—Books and
reading. 3. Reading (Primary)—United States—Language experience approach. I. Title.
LB1525.T32 2000
372.41'6—dc21   00-020275

Editor: Ray Coutu
Production service: Patricia Adams
Production coordination: Abigail M. Heim
Cover design: Judy Arisman
Cover photo: Donnelly Marks
Manufacturing: Louise Richardson

Printed in the United States of America on acid-free paper
06 05 04   EB   13 14

To my father James D'Ambrosio and my husband Ted,
for years and years of love

Contents

PART TWO **Assessing Children to Determine Their Strengths and Needs 35**

PART THREE **Demonstrating Strategies: Whole Class, Small Group, One-on-One 79**

Epilogue   *182*

Appendices   *183*

Works Cited   *205*

Index   *209*

Foreword

WHEN MY CHILDREN WERE YOUNG, THEY attended a Montessori preschool. I recall being very impressed when they explained how they had learned to wash their hands ever so carefully. They could demonstrate how to select the best water temperature as well as the right moves to lather, rinse, and pat dry. They had learned to wash their hands as effectively as any medical professional. What surprised me most was the realization that I had never thought about these procedures, nor whether there was a better way. I simply did it.

Hand washing, of course, has nothing to do with teaching reading, but when I think about Sharon Taberski, and what I've learned from her over the last seven years, I am reminded of the difference between doing things on automatic pilot and pausing to examine our practice, searching for the better way. Sharon Taberski eloquently reminds us that there is no room for automatic pilot in the teaching of reading. We can no longer blindly follow steps in a manual or dish out prescribed dialogue from a teacher's edition. Nor can we simply fill our classrooms with the best children's literature and believe children will magically learn to read.

Sharon Taberski's greatest gift to the Manhattan New School community has been the gift of thoughtfulness. She has taught all of us to pause and think deeply about the teaching of reading and then proceed with clarity and expertise. With this book, Sharon is now able to share this gift with school communities throughout the world.

Sharon's classroom has been just across the hall from my office at the Manhattan New School. I can think of no better way to start the day, take a break, or get a surge of energy than to stop by, especially during the teaching of reading. At first glance, Sharon seems to make literacy teaching look so easy. Her classroom is elegantly designed, voices are hushed and respectful, the children are on task and cooperative, and Sharon is always teaching. To the first-time visitor or prospective parent, Sharon does indeed make the teaching of reading appear to be so easy. But these folks haven't spent hours learning from Sharon at staff meetings, listening to her deliver keynote addresses at conferences, or watching her wonderful videos, *A Close-Up Look at Teaching Reading*, over and over again. They don't know how passionate Sharon is about the teaching of reading and how much of her personal and professional time is devoted to researching and rethinking it. Quite simply, Sharon makes the teaching of reading look so easy because she knows exactly what she is doing.

Sharon would be the first to admit that the teaching of reading is no easy matter. To do a really fine job requires a great deal of know-how. Teachers need to know how to engage whole classes in real acts of reading, so that they can confer individually with students. They need to be able to do running records, then analyze children's strengths and needs so that they can design supports to help them grow as readers. They need to be able to browse children's literature and select books that match each and every child in their class. They need to know how to organize classroom libraries so that all children know how to find the books that will best support their growth. They need to know how to turn such labels as "independent, shared, and guided reading" into effective and practical teaching moments. They need to become intimate with the most powerful reading strategies and be able to convey those strategies to students sensibly. They need to know how to model fluent reading each time they read aloud. They need to know how to invite children to respond to the texts they read, as well as to their own process of reading. They need to know how to explain to family members the role of phonics, spelling, and word study in the acquisition of literacy.

I have seen Sharon do all of these things and more in a crowded New York City classroom, filled with a beautiful mosaic of children speaking dozens of languages. Each year I marvel at the progress Sharon's students make as they proudly and joyously read fiction, informational texts, songs, and poetry. No, the teaching of reading is not easy, but with this book, Sharon graciously shares the solid ground from which she proceeds. If more politicians and the press were to spend time in her classroom, there would be no media frenzy nor great debate between whole language educators and the phonics folks. Sharon knows how to teach children to read in ways that will last a lifetime. There is no controversy about the teaching of reading in Room 201 at the Manhattan New School.

Sharon not only teaches with voice, she writes with voice. *On Solid Ground* was written with the same care and attention to detail that Sharon brings to her classroom. She has organized its contents as logically and thoughtfully as she arranges the furniture and supplies in her classroom, eliminating clutter and ambiguity. She anticipates her readers' questions as she does the needs of her students. She presents big ideas as explicitly and precisely as she creates goals for each of her students. She shares practical suggestions in the same straightforward way she prepares her daily agenda. Sharon is the consummate teacher across the hall, willing to share her best practice, her materials, her management, and most of all the wisdom she has acquired from years of devotion and study.

At the end of every school year, parents thank me for placing their children in Sharon's capable hands. Readers will feel likewise, grateful to have been touched by her eloquence and expertise.

Shelley Harwayne

Acknowledgments

MAKING CONNECTIONS LIES AT THE HEART of all teaching and learning. And so I'd like to acknowledge those colleagues, friends, and family to whom I'm connected and so deeply grateful.

First and foremost on my list are Shelley Harwayne, Diane Snowball, and Sue Slaven, all talented educators and good friends. Working with Shelley at the Manhattan New School has been a glorious dream-come-true. Visitors often remark that she has created a sort of "teacher heaven," and she has. I thank her for the knowledge she so generously shares, for her brilliance and creativity (she never runs out of ideas), and for her friendship. It's Shelley who started me on the path to writing this book and who continues to encourage me every step of the way.

Diane Snowball has taught me so much and has been generous in so many ways. She deeply understands the reading/writing process—I'm convinced that just being in her presence makes me smarter. Di has always made me feel that I had a professional contribution to make, even in times when I didn't. Di is truly a great lady, a great educator, and a great friend.

Sue Slaven (until very recently, Sue Smith) and I have spent many long hours sharing ideas about good teaching practice. Sue, a literacy consultant in high demand in Community School District 2 and other school districts throughout the country, knows first-hand the challenges teachers face as we try to make changes in our teaching. I'm inspired by Sue— by how much she knows and how hard she works to support teachers in their efforts to support children. She's a model teacher and a model friend.

I'm fortunate to work alongside talented and dedicated colleagues at the Manhattan New School. Judy Davis, Joanne Hindley Salch, Joan Backer, Paula Rogovin, Isabel Beaton, Carmen Colon, and Renay Sadis, long-time friends and colleagues, make coming to school fun. I thank them for years of generosity and insight. At times I have to pinch myself when I walk into school. It's hard to believe that so many talented and dedicated educators share the same schoolhouse: Tara Fishman, Eve Mutchnick, Mindy Gerstenhaber, Hillary Fertig, Elissa Eisen, Lorraine Shapiro, Pam Mayer, Layne Hudes, Debby Yellin, Regina Chiou, Karen Ruzzo, Kevin Tallat-Kelpsa, Mary Anne Sacco, Amy Mandel, Pat Werner, David Besancon, Sharon Hill, Doreen Esposito, Janet Williams, Roberta Pantal Rhodes, Denise Rickles, Constance Foland, Christine Mulligan, Michael Miller, Diane Lederman, Pam Saturday, Jordan Forstot, Michelle Warshaw, Susan Arias, Valerie Radetzky, Michael Latto, Adeline Pirinea, and Anita Lee. A special thanks to Lisa Siegman, our esteemed science teacher, for starting me thinking about systems. I also want to thank Barbara Santella, Judy Klein, Rachele Lisi, Dora Cruz, and Beatrice Zavala, our dedicated office and school aide staff, who hold us together. This professional community we create and continually recreate at MNS is one that never ceases to amaze and excite me.

I want to thank Herb Shapiro for the lovely black-and-white photographs he took of my class when I was just beginning to imagine what this book would look like.

Many thanks to Anthony Alvarado, Elaine Fink, and Bea Johnstone, Community School District 2 superintendents, for supporting Shelley's efforts and mine. They've understood the importance of ongoing professional development and have given us the green light to try out new ideas. We can be creative and effective because of their support.

I'd also like to thank the wonderful MNS parents and children. To the parents, thank you for sharing your beautiful children and for the hours you spend helping out at school and in our classrooms. And to the children—a big hug and endless gratitude for continuing to remind me of what's truly important.

I'd like to thank colleagues from the Teachers College Writing Project for years of support and comradery. To Lucy Calkins for recognizing the need for teachers to come together to share ideas and for providing the structure for it to happen. She challenged us all to question our long-held beliefs. To Artie Voigt and Mimi Aronson for their humor and insightful thinking. To Bonnie Uslianer and Ellen Goldberg for hours and hours of dinner conversations about best teaching practices.

Thank you to all my friends at Mondo Publishing—Mark and Diane Vineis, Maggie Thurston, and Tony Stead. They've been consistently generous in their support, and I thank them for including me in their publishing family.

A special thanks to all my friends at Heinemann, especially Ray Coutu, my editor. I thank him for always being there with smart and honest feedback. Many a time he helped me change direction, reassuring me that we'd be in a much better place. Without Ray this book would not have happened. Thank you to Mike Gibbons, general manager, for working so hard to make a difference in teachers' lives and for taking such fine care of his authors. And to Leigh Peake, editorial director, Renée Le Verrier, managing editor, Patty Adams, production editor and copy editor, Maura Sullivan, marketing manager, and Lynne Mehley, promotions coordinator for their talent and hard work. And to

Roberta Lew, Janine Duggan, Charna Ethier, and Christine Monahan for their help in securing permissions from publishers. Also many thanks to Toby Gordon, the editor of my video series, *A Close-Up Look at Teaching Reading*, for getting me started. Knowing each of you leaves me in awe of the publishing field.

Thank you to all the teachers I've met and worked with along the way. Your questions help me formulate my own. Your comments inspire me to continually revise and refine my teaching. I look forward to many more workshops, gatherings, and dinners in the future.

I want to thank my father, James D'Ambrosio, for a lifetime of support and love. He always told me there's nothing I can't do if I try. And even though he is still not always sure what I do when I take off on weekends to do consulting work, or why, when he visits my class, he sees children reading and loving it. He encourages me to keep going and to have fun.

I want to thank my beautiful children Ann, Matt, and Dan for their humor, insight, and encouragement. Thank you for understanding my all-too-frequent absences at family gatherings and for cheering me on. It's every parent's dream to have children who are brighter, more talented, and more generous than they are. Thanks for making Dad's and my dream come true.

And finally, I want to thank Ted, my partner and first-reader through it all, who makes me happy. He grounds me. I count on him for fun, for patience, for respect, and for love. He never lets me down. He's forever encouraging me to try new things and because of his love, I do.

Introduction

ON SOLID GROUND IS AN ACCOUNT OF how I teach reading. More than a list of activities or description of strategies, it's about how all the parts of our teaching can work together. It's about helping children see connections and make new ones. It doesn't advocate a lock-step progression through a set of pre-defined skills and strategies, but calls on teachers to be systematic in our thinking so that we can be wise in the ways we interact with children. What I'm sharing in this book is the result of how I've rethought my practice over the last ten years.

I began teaching at the Manhattan New School the year after it opened. I knew founding faculty members Shelley Harwayne, Joanne Hindley Salch, and Joan Backer from our years at the Teachers College Writing Project, where we had come together regularly in study groups, at literacy institutes, and at site-facilitator meetings to discuss our staff development work in New York City classrooms. We read and discussed the best professional books and were privileged to hear many renowned researchers share their thinking. By going to MNS, we had all returned to what we loved most—working with children. We wanted to put our ideas into practice.

Those first few months were hard. There were times I would have killed for a class set of books and a script. I even secretly longed for the children's desks to be bolted to the floor just as they were when our beautiful schoolhouse opened its doors almost 100 years earlier. I had forgotten how challenging it can be to keep twenty-six children engaged in meaningful work from 8:40 to 3:00 each day. But under Shelley's gifted mentorship, and with the support of colleagues like Joanne and Joan, I found my footing and continued my life-long journey to refine my teaching.

The title of this book, *On Solid Ground*, grew out of conversations with Sue Slavin, my close friend and fellow literacy consultant. Sue and I would frequently meet for coffee after school to share classroom experiences, both good ones and bad. One afternoon, I was particularly excited by the progress my children were making. "Sue, you should see how serious Mikey is about his reading. He wants so much to learn to read. And Tiffany—her eyes just sparkle when she sees she's getting better. She practically skips back to her seat after a conference." Sue, wanting to know why, kept prodding. What was happening in my classroom that made these children and me so willing to take risks, so confident that we were on the right path? After several attempts at an explanation, I finally said, "It's like we're on solid ground." Sue looked at me and I at her. She knew I'd been racking my brains for months trying to come up with a title. *On Solid Ground* was it. It described what I strive for in my teaching: a firm, reliable, rooted foundation for the children's work and mine.

The children and I are on solid ground every day, every moment because my teaching is systematic. I understand how all the parts of my day, the classroom environment, the components of my reading program, and my teaching practices work together to support my teaching and children's learning.

Part One of this book describes how being clear about my role as a teacher and having realistic goals help me focus on what's important. Then I discuss how I set up my classroom, provide materials, and organize my day to support my efforts with children to reach these goals.

Parts Two, Three, and Four describe facets of my teaching. Specifically, they show how assessing children's reading, demonstrating effective strategies and skills, and providing opportunities for practice and response play out in whole-class, small-group, and one-on-one teaching sessions. By conferring with children regularly throughout the year, I can assess their strengths and needs as readers and match them with books. I then customize my read aloud, shared reading, and guided reading demonstrations to meet their needs. I can explain to children why I've selected a particular strategy to show them and how to apply it when they go off to read on their own. By providing children with just-right books for independent reading, I'm encouraging them to combine meaning, syntax, and phonics to figure out words they don't know, and to use strategies to understand texts that give them trouble. I can be precise in addressing children's needs and encourage them to reflect on their reading, get responses from classmates, respond orally and in writing, and use writing to give shape to some of the things they've learned. My teaching is systematic because my thinking is.

Teaching reading and learning how to read are complex endeavors. But because my practices are purposeful and connected, the children and I can think wisely about reading. This helps us assess, reassess, and refine our efforts so that we're doing more of what's working and less of what isn't. Shall we begin?

PART ONE

Understanding Our Role and Goals

1

From Where Are You Thinking?

JOHN STEINBECK IS ONE OF MY LITERARY heroes. For years I've been enchanted by his ability to describe the most commonplace events in the most profound ways. In *The Log from the Sea of Cortez*, for example, he comments on how perspective affects our view of waves rolling to the shore, ". . . where the last wave, if you think from the sea, and the first if you think from the shore, touches and breaks." Where we stand—on the deck of a ship looking toward shore, or on the beach itself—determines whether we call the same wave last or first. As Steinbeck muses, ". . . it is important where you are thinking from."

In a way, I have embraced Steinbeck's musing as my own mantra in working with children. I understand that my views about how children learn and the research supporting those views determine my effectiveness in teaching reading. They shape the reading goals I set, how I define my role in helping children achieve those goals, my interactions with children, and my teaching practices. Take the following story.

The Story of Billy

Billy was referred to the Manhattan New School for tutoring by his mother, who knew our principal and many of the teachers. She hoped we might help her son, a first grader at a private school across town, overcome some difficulties he'd been having with reading.

After several weeks of working with Billy, I received a phone call from his teacher who wanted to share some helpful information. She told me that he was the weakest reader in his group. He knew how to blend letters and substitute middle vowels. He had trouble with letter formations, specifically, he mixed up lower-

and uppercase letters. His self-esteem fluctuated. He was starting to be critical of other children in his group. He wanted to be the best.

She explained what she'd been doing to help Billy. She said that the school stressed phonics and the children in Billy's group read stories that incorporate all the short vowels. They had done short vowels, digraphs, and blends. After vacation, they would do long vowels and "magic e."

I was troubled by this teacher's description of Billy's reading, because it failed to take into account Billy as a whole person. I had discovered that Billy loved to listen to scary and funny stories, and he talked incessantly of fishing trips with his dad. He also loved books about lizards. But Billy had also confided in me that there was nothing he liked about reading. He counted the pages as he read and asked painfully, "How much longer do I have to read?" Billy lacked strategies, other than phonics, to figure out words he didn't know, and as his teacher pointed out, he lacked self-confidence.

I described the goals I had set for him and what I was doing to help. I wanted to help Billy acquire a variety of reading strategies so that he need not rely so heavily on phonics. Instead, I wanted him to combine meaning, language structure, and phonics to make sense of text. I wanted to match Billy with books about topics and experiences he could relate to, books written in a language approximating his aural and spoken language, always being careful to provide him with enough support to successfully meet the challenges he faced. More than anything, I wanted Billy to love to read.

Although his teacher and I shared the best intentions for Billy, we were coming at the teaching of reading from opposite directions. But what did these obvious differences in practice convey about our theories of how children learn to read? What made us teach so differently? First and foremost, we were thinking about the teaching of reading from very different places.

I don't doubt the sincerity of Billy's teacher's point of view. However, I sensed a mechanical approach to her teaching that lacked any allusions to literature she loved and wanted to share, any questioning of why her approach wasn't working, or curiosity about alternative approaches she might try. Her gravest error, I believe, was not that she taught letter-sound relationships (for I do that, too), but that she overdid it. She used one method—phonics— and was blind to approaches that might work better for Billy, and I dare say, for many of the other children under her care.

The Child's Role in Learning to Read

Learning to read involves implementing a complex set of attitudes, understandings, and behaviors. It is not stimulus-response learning, as when small children learn to keep their hands off hot stoves. Nor is it acquiring narrow skills, such as tying shoelaces. Children learning to read are active agents, initiating and assuming responsibility for their learning. They continually integrate new findings into their framework of knowledge about language and texts, replacing what no longer works with revised theories and fresh information.

Hypothesizing about how children learn to read, and then conducting controlled experiments to prove or disprove them, is one way to gain a better understanding of this complex process. Another equally valid approach is to be in the classroom day after day, year after year, actually teaching children to read, all the while reflecting on your practice and assessing which methods work best.

My experience, seen through the lens of Marie Clay's research documented in *Becoming Literate: The Construction of Inner Control*, has taught me that when children are encouraged to use all the information sources available as they read—meaning, structure, and graphophonics—they approach reading as a meaning-making activity. And most importantly, the children are the meaning makers.

Rest assured that I highly regard the teacher's role in supporting children in this process. In fact, that's what this book is

about—what teachers can do to help children learn to read. But first, here's "where I'm thinking from" regarding how children acquire fluency and independence in reading.

Experiences and Background Knowledge

Children use their own experiences and background knowledge to figure out words and comprehend text.

Children expect text to make sense. The closer the content is to their own experiences or a subject they know a lot about, the more capable they are at anticipating what will happen next —even which words might be used—and drawing implications for their own lives.

For example, when a child knowledgeable about dinosaurs reads a book about them, she expects to find information that affirms and extends what she already knows. She anticipates, often with prompting from the teacher, that words like "triceratops," "tyrannosaurus rex," "meat-eater," "plant-eater," "millions," "extinct," and "huge" will probably appear in the text. When she comes to confusing parts, she uses her background knowledge, combined with her knowledge of how language works and letter-sound relationships, whether working at the word level (that is, figuring out how to read a word or understand what it means), or at the text level (trying to comprehend the whole).

When she comes to the word "triceratops," she might, because of how it fits with what she already knows:

- Start to sound it out and look through to the end, realizing that the ending letters "t-o-p-s" would exclude "tyrannosaurus" as a possibility.
- Use information in the pictures, if there are any, and realize what the word must be if she recognizes the dinosaur in the picture.
- Use what she knows about dinosaurs and what the text has stated to figure out the word.

Each of these attempts at learning succeeds to the extent that it fits with what she already knows.

In Edward Fry's *Ten Best Ideas for Reading Teachers*, David Pearson affirms that the adage, "Learning proceeds from the known to the new," is at the heart of all comprehension and learning. He says it "explains how children learn, why they fail when they don't, how we should arrange experiences to facilitate new learning, and what makes a good teacher." Relating the old to the new, or what is known to the unknown, is a powerful tool for readers of all ages and stages in development.

Knowledge of How Language Works

Children use their knowledge of how language works to figure out words and understand text.

When children read, they consider which words sound right together. Therefore the closer book language is to the language they speak, the easier it will be for them to cue into syntax.

Children who use structural cues wouldn't read, "My father *down* our car in the country." They'd know that *down* isn't the type of word that fits grammatically in the sentence—It wouldn't sound right to put a preposition where a verb should go. If they substituted the wrong type of word, they would correct themselves (or be prompted by the teacher to reconsider what they'd said) because it just didn't sound right. Young children make these grammatical decisions without even knowing what a preposition or a verb is. Although they will learn these terms later, it is important for us to understand that they don't need to define them to use language structure to make sense of a text.

Jasmin and Danny were first graders. One morning I noticed them working hard reading a book with a simple story line. I saw them rerun sentences to give themselves a fresh start and use pictures to get help with difficult words or confirm what they'd read. I heard them mutter to one another things like, "It's not 'fish' because that starts with /f/ and this doesn't," or "What would make sense?" after they'd skipped the word and then returned to it to try sounding it out again.

When they finished, Jasmin ran up to me saying: "Sharon, we read the book. We finished it. But we just couldn't get these 'blue pages.' They were too hard." The "blue pages" were perforated flash cards inserted in the book by the publisher so children could practice the words in the story and, presumably, become better at reading. But although Jasmin and Danny could read these words in the context of the story, they were unable to read the very same words out of context on the cards. (They didn't know that I had watched them go from left to right along the top row of cards, and then down the left column, like one might read

Chinese. But neither way worked.) Jasmin and Danny expected text to make sense and sound a certain way, but this didn't. However, when they had read the story, the context itself had actually scaffolded their reading of individual words.

English-language learners will obviously have more difficulty using meaning and structural cues than those whose first language is English. But this shouldn't lead us to assume that these students need a different kind of reading instruction. All learners need to be immersed in the language they're trying to acquire, regardless of whether it's their second language or their first, with many opportunities to speak, read, and write it themselves. Only then can they detect which word usage sounds right.

Knowledge of Letter-Sound Relationships

Children use their knowledge of letter-sound relationships to figure out words and comprehend texts.

When children read, they usually ask what sound is represented by the letters in the words they're trying to read. This is done most effectively by also considering what makes sense and sounds right.

After each reading workshop, as my children gather at the meeting area to share reading strategies that worked for them, they often recall how they figured out words they didn't know. One time, Jeffrey, a second grader, shared how when he came to the word "heart" —a demon of a word by any standard—he didn't know it. But he knew that "h" said /h/ and that the final "t" said /t/. Then, when he reread the sentence, he knew the word was "heart." Although Jeffrey didn't know the word at first, he figured it out by combining graphophonics, meaning, and structure. By rereading the sentence, he tried these sounds in light of what made sense and sounded right.

Barbara Foorman, an advocate of children learning phonics first using decodable texts, and later, after they've become more proficient readers, using trade books, cautions in that "the approximately 75–100 phonics rules typically taught are nothing more than probable hints as to how letters might be pronounced in a given word. In reality, over 500 rules are needed to program a computer to convert English text to speech." In the last example, when Jeffrey was trying to figure out "heart," for all he knew the "ear" spelling pattern might have represented the sounds in "h*ear*," "*earth*," or "b*ear*." How could he have gotten the word using phonics alone? He had to use other strategies as well.

While I don't subscribe to the "phonics first" approach where children's reading material is limited by the letter sounds the teacher has formally introduced, I do think it's important for children to learn letter-sound relationships and use them to figure out new words. How could it be otherwise when English is an alphabetic language? But, it's because of its importance that I don't believe it should be applied in isolation. These three cueing systems—meaning, structure, and graphophonics—work best together as a cadre of strategies, rather than alone.

Learning Through Analogy

Children learn in large part through analogy, using what they already know about words to learn new ones.

In *Science and Human Values*, Jacob Bronowski writes that, "the discoveries of science, (and) the works of art are explorations—more, are explosions, of hidden likeness. The discoverer or the artist presents in them two aspects of nature and fuses them into one." The same is true of learning, which involves making connections between things that were once unconnected in the learner's mind.

Children who read and write their own names have learned to associate the letters in their name with the sounds the letters represent. For example, in kindergarten (or maybe even earlier) when Sam saw his name written, he began to associate the letter "s" with the /s/ sound. While initially he may have learned to recognize his name wholly, as he had "McDonalds" and "Mommy," he later associated the letters with the sounds they represent. Then, when he observed this same letter in other words, he could use that knowledge to figure them out.

One morning when a visitor stopped by our classroom, the very same Sam, now in first grade, bombarded her with all the connections he'd been making between words. "Did you know I can spell 'other'? 'O-t-h-e-r' And because I know 'other,' I can also spell 'brother.' 'B-r-o-t-h-e-r.' And 'another.' And 'mother.' Wanna hear me . . . ?"

In *Beyond Traditional Phonics: Research Discoveries and Reading Instruction*, Margaret

Moustafa gives a detailed analysis of Usha Goswami's 1986 research on the use of analogy in reading. Goswami uncovered important information about how children learn words. She gave five-, six-, and seven-year-olds pairs of words, such as "hark" and "lark," and "hark" and "harm" to read. She told them one word in the pair and not the other. Across the age levels, children figured out many of the words by using what they knew about the word they were told. Younger children did this as well as their older counterparts.

This led Goswami to conclude that children use what they know about words to learn new ones, thus explaining how children's knowledge of words increases exponentially the more words they know.

Real Reading Experiences

Children learn to read by engaging in real reading experiences.

Although giving children abundant opportunities to read might seem too obvious to mention, it's a facet of their learning that's easily overlooked. Children need large blocks of time at school and at home to read. Not to fill in workbook pages or answer comprehension questions to reinforce or check skills they're being taught, but to read whole texts and apply the strategies while reading.

Becoming a Nation of Readers, the 1985 federal document, reported much research on this, such as Fielding's and Stanovich's finding that second- through fifth-grade students who are better at reading read significantly more than their "non-reading" counterpart, and therefore become even better readers, in an upward spiral of achievement and proficiency. I also believe that reading practice leads children to *acquire* the basic skills more effectively.

In 1994, Richard Allington pointed out in that although American children read more in school than they did ten years earlier, they still spend less than 10 percent of the school day actively engaged in actual reading and writing: "We continue to organize the school day in such a way that children have little opportunity to read and write."

When children have daily extended periods of time to read books that are appropriately supportive and challenging, they get practice in the whole act of reading and experience how all the parts work together. Workbooks and practice sheets, intended to strengthen a specific skill or concept, tend to focus on an isolated component of reading and fail to actually engage students in reading.

In his book *Learning All the Time*, John Holt presents a paradigm about education that he laments is prevalent in far too many school systems throughout the country. This is the metaphor of an assembly line in a bottling plant or canning factory:

> Down the conveyor belts come rows of empty containers of sundry shapes and sizes. Beside the belts is an array of pouring and squirting devices, controlled by employees of the factory. As the containers go by, these workers squirt various amounts of different substances—reading, spelling, math, history, science—into the containers.

Holt asks the obvious question: "How come so many containers, having had these substances squirted at them for so many years, are still going out of the factory empty?" Yet despite this sad fact, Holt notes that so many teachers cling to the notion of the more taught, the more learned. He is referring to the type of teaching that fits the factory metaphor, where the learner is a passive receptacle; the one that assumes that by telling children information, we can make them learn.

Children (and teachers) must understand that the same kind of curiosity and risk-taking that enabled them to learn so effectively from the time they were born to the time they entered school is also expected and encouraged in school as they learn to read. The teacher's ongoing demonstrations, along with many, many opportunities to practice reading—monitoring their reading, cross-checking one information source against another, and self-correcting when necessary (Clay, 1991)—allow children to become strategic readers. The effective teacher not only imparts information, but sees the children as active learners and helps them find ways to learn for themselves.

As teachers, our time with children is limited. To make the best use of it, we must know which things are smart to do and which are better to avoid, which lead to learning and which just take up time. These judgments can only be made when we understand how children learn to read. This enables us to select some things and reject others—whether these be activities, ideas for classroom organization, books for the classroom and for the individual reader, or assessment practices. We need to make informed decisions, based on how we believe children learn to read.

Our Role in Teaching Children to Read

Up to this point, I haven't said too much about the teacher's role. Which might surprise you, given that this is a professional book for teachers! I did this deliberately, starting with Billy, the learner, and some theories about children's reading, because I wanted to highlight the active role readers must assume.

But now, just as emphatically, I'll describe key facets of our role in helping children learn to read. I used to think that telling children what to do, assigning pages from phonics workbooks, and following the progression of activities outlined in the teacher's guide was teaching reading. Now I know that, just as learning to read is complex, requiring children to problem-solve and make meaning, teaching children to read is complex, involving a *series of interactions* with learners. I know my role is to:

- assess children's reading
- demonstrate effective reading strategies
- provide children with opportunities to read and practice a variety of approaches to text
- respond to their reading, and encourage them to reflect on their reading process orally and in writing

Assessing Children's Reading

When we assess a child's reading during a conference to decide if his book is too hard, when we record the substitutions he makes as he reads orally, and when we analyze the strategies he uses so we can show him others—we're teaching reading.

Assessing children's reading and then using these assessments to inform my work lies at the center of my teaching. It's an on-going process and differs significantly from the testing and evaluation which typically come *after* teaching.

Years ago, I frequently tested children but seldom assessed them. I referred to teaching manuals for what to do and say instead of observing what the children were doing as they read and listening to their words. Now I determine how each child's attitudes, understandings, and behaviors support or impede his growth as a reader, and I intervene to recommend additional strategies and materials to help him become more effective.

Several months ago, Kiko, a student I taught the year before, returned to the Manhattan New School for a visit. In June, his family had moved to Iowa, and it had taken them a while to adjust. His mother reported that for the first few weeks of school, Kiko followed his teacher around asking, "When's my conference? When am I having a reading conference?"

At first, his teacher didn't understand what Kiko meant. It wasn't until his mother brought to school his last year's reading folder and assessment notebook that his teacher realized how central reading conferences were to Kiko's learning to read. Kiko couldn't understand how to become a better reader without meeting with his teacher so she could listen to him read, suggest strategies he could try, and recommend new books.

And likewise, I can't imagine teaching children to read without meeting with them one-on-one to assess their reading. It's my chance to direct readers to more effective practices, gather information to help me plan further instruction, and match children with appropriate books. Kiko and I both need reading conferences!

Demonstrating Effective Strategies

When we work with children in a guided reading group and demonstrate how they can monitor their reading, when we read aloud from a factual text and highlight its unique features, and when we show children how to figure out words by recognizing familiar spelling patterns—we're teaching reading.

In order to demonstrate reading strategies effectively, I need to be close to the children—both physically, and in the sense of knowing what each of them does as they read. I can't hide behind a desk and *tell* children what to do. I need to sit alongside them and *show* them. I used to think I taught a class of students. Now I know I am teaching twenty-six individual children to read. This lesson was a long time coming, but one well worth learning.

One Tuesday when Ray Coutu, my editor at Heinemann, was visiting, I asked if, during my children's writing time, we might discuss my draft of a chapter for this book. I wanted to *demonstrate* that we all need demonstrations!

The children listened as Ray showed me how the examples he'd jotted in the margins might strengthen the points I wanted to make. They listened when he suggested I move paragraphs around, and as he read aloud the revised version to show what he meant. They got the point I wanted to make because I showed them, I didn't tell them. In life, we often learn first-hand from those who know more about a particular topic or have greater mastery of a skill than we do.

Providing Opportunities for Practice

When we provide independent reading sessions each day so that children can practice their reading and use the strategies we've demonstrated, when we leave reminder notes in their assessment notebooks of what they should do when they read, and when we match children with books that support their independent work—we're teaching reading.

Years ago, I'd cringe if a principal walked into the room when the children were reading silently. I felt that if they were "just reading," I wasn't doing my job. Now I know that providing time for children to read *is* a critical part of my role. But just sending them off to read independently doesn't necessarily provide the kind of practice they need.

The independent reading opportunities I provide now are far more purposeful than before. In fact, from the first day of school, my children read independently for extended periods of time, using "just-right" books—books that support their growth. If a child is reading a book that's so hard she can only use letter-sound relationships to figure out unfamiliar words, how can she invoke meaning or language structure when the words no longer make sense?

Children need to understand that when they are reading independently, they're working at their reading. I demonstrate this by showing them strategies they can use when they can't recognize a word or understand the text. They know it's every reader's responsibility to make sense of what the author has written. Over the course of the year, when children in my class read "silently" each day for extended periods of time, they're consolidating their strategies and skills.

Responding

When we respond to what children do well and to what they might do better, when we provide time at the end of each workshop for them to reflect on strategies, and when we encourage children to respond orally or in writing to text they've read—we're teaching reading.

Children need to know how they're doing and whether their practices are bringing them closer to their goal. But it would do little good if the only responses they received were those that compared them to other students. Children need to measure their growth primarily against what they themselves did last year, last month, yesterday. I show them the records I make of their oral reading, and how, for example, the "SC" notation means they've self-corrected. They know this means they're progressing as readers and so they try to repeat this behavior. I explain that, although I understand they want to read harder books, doing so sometimes works against them.

Each day at the end of the reading workshop, I ask the children to think about what they did that worked well for them. In sharing their successes, the children realize that what worked well today is a strategy they can add to their repertoire for the future, that these are tools to use again and again.

It's a question I ask myself, too—What did *I* do well today? What worked so well that I want to build it into my repertoire of teaching? Just as I ask children to reflect on their reading and learning, I reflect on my teaching. It's how we all get better at what we do. It's how we reach our goals.

Postscript—Billy Revisited

In the experience recounted earlier, Billy's teacher was using a bottom-up approach to teaching reading. She taught phonetic skills sequentially, building one skill upon another—from letter sounds to short vowels to long vowels to "magic e," in the hopes that eventually the children would be proficient enough at decoding to progress to more naturally written text.

One problem with this approach is that it often loses sight of the ultimate goal. It's tempting to focus on details because it's easier than keeping sight of the big picture: helping children become proficient readers who love to read.

In learning to read, it is the whole story (its message and structure), children's understanding about how language works, and the life-experiences they bring to the texts that provide the framework they need to be successful. This is the foundation upon which phonetic and grammatical skills develop. When children understand the whole, they can successfully attend to the finer features of text and language, and in that way come to a fuller appreciation of the whole.

In teaching, it is the attitudes, understandings, and behaviors that our children have and strive toward that guide our decisions about which skills and strategies to teach. When we recognize the complexity of this process and the extent to which children are driven to make sense of things, we plan activities that are responsive to their needs. We teachers, like the children we teach, need it all—the "big picture" to guide us and the methods to ground us.

Eventually, Billy became a full time student at the Manhattan New School, enrolled in my second-grade class. That year I worked one-on-one with him during reading conferences, trying to identify the skills and strategies he needed. I encouraged him to consider what makes sense, sounds right, and matches the sounds the letters represent. We met in guided reading groups to work on strategies he and other children needed to use more. And I planned whole-class instruction to further demonstrate strategies for better comprehension and dealing with text.

By June, Billy was reading "Goosebumps" books and was our in-house expert on lizards. He loved reading poetry and wanted to read a lot of it since he dreamed of being a poet himself.

Eight-year-old Billy discovered that the magic in reading actually lies in discovering the mysteries of the world. He learned that beavers built 1,000-foot dams in Colorado. He learned that one "favorite" book has a way of leading you to others. (At last count, he had sixty-two books in the "Goosebumps" series to look forward to!) And he learned that you can "read" the emotions of chameleons by the colors they turn. In the language of chameleons, green means something like, "I am a calm and peaceful lizard." That year Billy had become a calm and peaceful boy, for that was the year he became a reader.

Defining Your Goals

My Goals for Teaching Children to Read

Over the years I've found that it's as important to know *for what I'm striving* as it is to know *from where I'm thinking*. In fact, having clear goals is one of the most important steps I can take to more effective teaching. Without these, it's too easy to let the daily decisions I make—those that will eventually lead to the achievement or demise of these long-term goals—be overly influenced by the unexpected and often distracting issues that come up daily in the classroom. So at the beginning of each year, I consider what I want to accomplish and how to make it happen.

I want children to:

1. Become strategic readers, with a full range of strategies for figuring out words and understanding text.
2. Read a variety of genres and appreciate the different purposes for reading.
3. Use writing as a tool to make sense of what they read and extend the quality of their reading.
4. Appreciate the power that reading can have in their lives, motivating them to become life-long readers.

I try to be realistic about the goals I set and hold myself strictly accountable for helping children achieve them. It's counterproductive to have too many goals and later abandon them because I'm overwhelmed by the inevitable demands of the classroom. So I limit the number of goals I set, and work seriously and purposefully on each one.

Helping Children Become Strategic Readers

My primary goal is helping each child acquire a self-improving system for reading. Marie Clay explains that self-improving readers have reached a level of independence and fluency that enables them to use the skills they've acquired to become better readers each time they sit down to read. In *Reading Recovery: A Guidebook for Teachers in Training*, she describes what self-improving readers do as they read. They:

- *Monitor* their reading to see if it makes sense semantically, syntactically, and visually—that is, in relation to meaning, sentence structure, and letter-sound relationships.
- *Search* for semantic, syntactic, and visual cues.
- *Discover* new things about text.
- *Cross-check* one cueing system against another to ensure that their reading is accurate.
- *Self-correct* their reading when what they've read doesn't match the semantic, syntactic, and visual cues.
- *Solve* new words using multiple cueing systems.

Self-improving readers use a variety of strategies to establish meaning. When their reading is going well—when they know the words and understand the text—they're working successfully (albeit subconsciously) at maintaining meaning. When they meet unfamiliar words or fail to understand what they've read, they have ways to work things out. (See Figure 2–1 for a list of strategies I demonstrate and remind the children to use as they read.)

The children in my class understand that becoming a strategic reader is a long-range goal within their reach. When I confer with children, I explain that I'm trying to determine what they do when they read and show them other things to try. As they read independently, they know to refer to the reminder notes I've made in their assessment notebooks for strategies to practice.

During read aloud, shared reading, and guided reading, I demonstrate strategies and encourage children to practice them as they read independently. And at the end of the reading workshop, the children share what worked for them that day.

I remember a time I visited Lorraine Shapiro's first-grade classroom to watch her teach. It's always a thrill to see her at work. Although she's a veteran teacher, Lorraine is always celebrat-

---

FIGURE 2–1A Some Strategies for Figuring Out Words

- Look at the beginning letter(s). What sound do you hear?

- Look at the pictures. Do they help?

- Look through the word to the end. What sound do you hear in the middle? At the end?

- Think of what word would make sense, sound right, and match the letters.

- Start the sentence over, making your mouth ready to say the word.

- Skip the word, read to the end of the sentence, and then come back to the word. How does what you've read help you with the word?

- Listen to whether what you reading makes sense and matches the letters (monitor). Correct it if it doesn't (self-correct).

- Look for spelling patterns you recognize.

- Look for smaller words within the word.

- Think of where you may have seen the word before.

FIGURE 2–1B Some Strategies for Understanding Text

- Stop to think about the text. Predict what you think is going to happen. Why do you think this? Read to prove your prediction.

- Make a story map. How does knowing the story elements, i.e., characters, setting, problem, main events, and resolution, help you think about the whole story?

- Make a character map. How does the way the character "usually acts" help you predict what he or she might do?

- Write about what you're reading to understand it better.

- Use your own experiences to understand what you're reading.

- Reread the sentence, paragraph, or chapter.

- Read on a little, and then come back to the part that confused you.

- Select a book that's part of a series. Once you read one book, the others will be easier.

- Select a book on a topic you're interested in.

- Read the same book a friend is reading. Discuss it.

- Review the front and back cover and table of contents to help you understand where the book is headed.

- When reading factual texts, examine the chapter headings, illustrations, captions, and charts before, during, and after reading.

- Create a "picture" in your mind of what you're reading.

- Think about "who's talking."

ing something new she's learned about the art of teaching and approaches each new situation as an interesting problem to solve.

That afternoon, as Lorraine and I chatted for a moment in a corner of her classroom, an argument erupted between two children who were reading together. Joan was visibly upset as she ran over to Lorraine complaining: "She gave me the fish! She gave me the fish!" I was puzzled, but Lorraine knew exactly what Joan meant. After Lorraine settled the children down, she explained that she's been working hard all year to make sure the children understand the importance of giving classmates the opportunity to solve, on their own, the problems they encounter while reading. Instead of telling their partners the words (giving them the fish), she wants them to encourage one another to use strategies to solve their own problems (teaching them to fish). And Lorraine's children would settle for nothing less.

Encouraging Children to Read a Variety of Genres

It's not enough that children become proficient readers of fiction if they avoid other genres. Fiction is wonderfully satisfying and engaging, but reading it exclusively fails to prepare children for the informational texts they'll read most frequently throughout their later school years and their lives outside of school. They would miss the intensity and pleasure of poetry. And exposure to all three genres, in turn, influences what children choose to write, as well as the quality of their writing.

As adults, most of our reading involves practical informational texts: newspapers, professional journals, magazine articles, work-related texts, how-to manuals, museum publications, travel brochures, cookbooks, and catalogues. We need to prepare children by introducing factual genres in the early grades while also providing opportunities for them to explore texts that interest them.

My students love reading about animals, inventions, space, dinosaurs, and the "olden" times (i.e., anything prior to twenty years ago). They pore over maps, atlases, dictionaries, and other reference materials. When Billy, whose reading experiences I described in Chapter 1, transferred to our school, he didn't have to postpone reading about lizards and salamanders until he became a better reader. He immediately read whatever parts he could of

"Eyewitness" books and "Look Closer" books, anticipating the time when he'd be able to read them in their entirety. In fact, a "friendly" feature of factual texts is that, unlike fiction, they don't need to be read from cover to cover. You can start wherever you like to suit your purpose and interest.

Occasionally, I survey the children for the titles of the book they select during the first independent reading session. (See Chapter 3 for our daily reading and writing schedule.) Invariably I find that in addition to our Big Books, most are reading factual texts. I encourage this, because I know that during the reading workshop much of what they'll read independently will be fiction. (I believe this is true because there are so many more fictional texts available for beginning readers, and the narrative style matches children's oral language more closely.)

The children know that during our class meeting, which immediately follows the first independent reading session, I'll ask them to share things they brought from home or books they've read that relate to what we're studying in class. So they're "looking for" information that will enhance our studies of beavers, eagles, Native Americans, inventions, New Amsterdam, and New York City. It involves them in reading factual texts, helps them understand some of its features, and allows them to learn some fascinating information to support topics we're investigating. Did you know that merlins, predatory birds, can pluck small birds from right out of the sky? Or that the bald eagle got its name, not because its white head makes it appear bald, but from the old English word "balde," which means white? Interesting, isn't it?

I also encourage children to read a lot of poetry. Because of its brevity, it's at once appealing and complex. In just a few lines, children might learn something big about life or just get a big laugh. At first, as we read poems together during shared reading, the children simply enjoy their rhythm and repetition. They frequently join in with clapping and body movements. Later, as they're introduced to a wider range of poetry, they appreciate the fresh or deeper perspective it gives to everyday things. Each genre offers children a different peephole from which to view the world.

As children develop as readers, reading becomes more of a tool to learn about science, social studies, and literature, and less a skill in and of itself. Where once their reading was primarily literal, focusing on an accurate reading of text, it later becomes increasingly interpretative, with children more purposefully bringing their own perspective into play.

Using Writing as a Tool to Deepen Their Understanding of What They Read

I want children's written responses to books to enhance their understanding of what they read. As children move through the emergent, early, transitional, and fluent stages, my expectations for how they respond in writing changes. (These developmental stages are discussed later in this chapter and throughout the book.)

I generally ask emergent and early readers to respond in writing less frequently than transitional and fluent readers. Once I'm confident that this is a good use of their time, I'll ask them to do it more frequently and in greater detail.

Transitional and fluent readers respond in writing more easily. Since they are generally more skilled in both reading and writing, their written responses can be made quickly enough to leave ample time for reading. And their responses are more likely to help them understand or interpret what they've read. They can relate books to other experiences they've had—both life-experiences and experiences reading other books.

Reading is what children need to do most, regardless of their stage. Far too frequently, written responses are assigned to keep children busy while teachers engage in small-group or individual work with students. I know: I used to assign writing for this reason. But now I'm very careful to make sure that I request written responses for the right reasons.

Jerome Bruner is another one of my heroes, right up there with John Steinbeck. Several years ago, shortly after his book *Acts of Meaning* was published, Bruner was addressing students at Teachers College. I brought my copy of the book for him to autograph. This was most unusual for me; I can't think of another autograph I'd ever sought. But I just wanted a chance to exchange a word or two with him. He asked me what I taught and I explained that I was a staff developer helping teachers set up writing workshops in their classrooms. The inscription he wrote—"For Sharon Taberski, in the hope that teaching to write is also teaching to think"—embodies what I believe to be true of writing. And to this day, it has guided my practice.

When I ask children to respond to books, it's never just to keep them busy. It's to push their thinking, help them clarify what they're reading, and promote their appreciation of books.

Motivating Children to Love to Read

The books I provide for children must be enjoyable and my teaching methods engaging to be effective vehicles for developing children's reading skills.

When Billy was first learning to read, he didn't love it. He didn't even like it. Reading was presented in a way that saved the best for last. The plan was that after he'd built-up enough skills, he'd then be able to appreciate what books have to offer. Imagine using this same approach with a child learning to play baseball. Imagine making your child work at the batting station until he got really good, and only then letting him enjoy the excitement of playing in a game!

When Billy first came to my class, I worked very hard to help him understand how reading could affect his life—immediately. Later, I gave him books about salamanders and lizards. I took him seriously when he said he wanted to be a poet, and directed him to our poetry collection. Billy and all the children in my class need to engage in reading—seeing it as something they want to do, a skill they want to acquire. With this in mind, I'm careful to select books for read aloud, shared reading, guided reading, and independent reading that entice children to want more. Unless I offer children the very best of informational texts, poetry, and fiction, my efforts to help them read strategically will be undermined.

At the risk of being misinterpreted, I must clarify an important point. In saying I offer children the very best literature, I don't suggest or recommend giving a beginning reader a copy of *Charlotte's Web*, for example, and sending her merrily on her way. But I do seek out predictable, supportive texts with good story lines, rich language, and engaging pictures. Books that can be matched appropriately to children's stages and needs as readers. How could I accomplish my other goals if I didn't? How could I ask children to use a variety of reading strategies if the only texts I gave them were too hard or, conversely, "decodable," that is texts that were written to let children practice phonetic skills. How could I ask them to respond meaningfully to books if the books I provided weren't at all that interesting? And imagine what decodable factual texts and poetry would be like? (Dr. Seuss excepted, of course.)

Several months ago I received a most unusual offer—a chance to purchase a set of seven 32-page books, including a 24-page test booklet. It was promoted as a way to "start your students on their way to meeting the Chancellor's new Educational Standard of reading 25 books a year . . . *and* prepare for the CTB testing at the same time." The questions accompanying the literature would (so they said) help children make inferences and draw conclusions, recall information and note details, understand the theme and main idea, understand cause/effect . . . and on and on.

This "killing two birds with one stone" approach would certainly do just that—kill both birds. What child would long to read books while anticipating the comprehension questions to follow? You know the kind I mean: Johnny didn't like to read because (a) the books weren't interesting, (b) the books were too hard for him, (c) he had to answer comprehension questions after reading each book, or (d) all of the above. In this case, the answer is (d) all of the above. The only sure way I know to prepare a child for a reading test is to teach him to read. If a child is equipped with strategies to use when he comes to words or passages that give him trouble, coupled with a few brief preparation sessions to familiarize him with test-taking procedures, then he should be quite successful on any reliable reading test he takes.

Setting Goals According to Children's Stages in Reading

As in most primary-grade classrooms, the children in my combined first and second grade range from emergent to fluent readers. Those at the emergent and early stages are just beginning to acquire a network of strategies and skills to help them establish control over print and develop as readers. Transitional and fluent readers are consolidating these strategies and skills, and acquiring others to handle more complex text and a wider range of genres. Therefore, the reading goals I set for each reader depend on where he is on this developmental continuum and where he needs to go next.

Victor, Kathy, Clive, and Theo are children in my class whose attitudes, understandings,

and behaviors exemplify those of readers at the emergent, early, transitional, and fluent stages in reading. (See Figure 2–2 for characteristics of readers at different developmental stages.) These labels are not intended to pigeon-hole children, but to assess their progress along a continuum of growth. In fact, it's likely that children will exhibit behaviors from the adjacent stages along with those from their predominant stage. The following sections describe these varied readers and present sample pages from their assessment notebooks and books they're reading. (Assessment notebooks are discussed in length in Chapters 3, 5, and 6.)

Emergent Readers

Victor is an emergent reader.

He has a good working knowledge of concepts about print, and knows he should point to each word to help him keep his place and focus on the print. When Victor can't get a word, he tries the first letter and then supplies a word that matches only that letter, as he did on his running record when reading *Friends* by Min Hong. He substituted "look" for "like," "run" for "ride," and "play" for "pull." His substitutions usually make sense. (See Figures 2–3 and 2–4 for his running record in his assessment notebook and the text he read.)

Although Victor is eager to learn to read, he doesn't fully appreciate the problem-solving nature of reading. Even though he senses his reading isn't accurate, he doesn't give each word the attention he should. (And just looking more carefully at the picture would have helped him realize that the girl was "riding" not "running," and the friend was "pulling" not "playing.") Except for reading "look" for "like," his substitutions made sense, but he needs to attend more closely to the letter-sound relationships at the middle and end of the word. And I need to provide opportunities for him to do so throughout the reading and writing workshop. Each time I learn what a child can and can't do, it directs me to what I need to do as well.

Although Victor skipped the word "name" after trying the initial sound and then came back to it, it was with my prompting. Looking back, it might have been wiser to encourage him to reread the previous line, giving himself a larger context in which to work.

I need to make sure the books for Victor and other emergent readers provide the kinds of support they need to be successful. Their books

FIGURE 2–2 Some Characteristics of Readers at Different Stages

Emergent Readers:	Early Readers:	Transitional Readers:	Fluent Readers:
understand that print contains a consistent message	recognize most high-frequency words and many simple words	recognize an increasing number of words, many of which are "difficult" or content-related	identify most words automatically
recognize some high-frequency words, names, and simple words in context	use pictures to *confirm* meaning	integrate meaning, syntax, and phonics more consistently	consistently monitor, cross-check, and self-correct reading
use pictures to *predict* meaning	can figure out most simple words using meaning, syntax, and phonics	have a variety of ways to figure out unfamiliar words	read chapter books with good understanding
attend to left-to-right, top-to-bottom directionality and features of print, e.g., lines of text, words, and letters	use known spelling patterns to figure out new words	can generally read independent-level text with fluency, expression, and proper phrasing	offer their own interpretations of text, based on personal experiences and prior reading experiences
identify some initial and ending sounds in words	are becoming more skilled at monitoring, cross-checking, and self-correcting reading	are beginning to handle longer, more complex text with short chapters and more interesting characters	read for a variety of purposes
can be prompted to check for accuracy and sense	are gaining control of reading strategies	can summarize texts they've read	may read a variety of genres independently
use prior knowledge and their own experiences to make meaning	use their own experiences and background knowledge to predict meaning	are growing more aware of story and text structures, and can use mapping strategies to help organize their thinking	may respond to text by offering examples from their own lives, or by making connections to other books they've read or books by the same author
use repetitive story patterns and language to help with fluency and to support their efforts to attend to unknown words	can retell a story or recount things they've learned		respond to the author's craft and may try to mimic it in their own writing
	occasionally use story language in their writing, especially at the beginning of a piece		

(For additional sources on characteristics of readers at different developmental stages, see Fountas and Pinnell's *Guided Reading: First Good Teaching for All*, 1997, and *First Steps Reading Developmental Continuum*, 1994.)

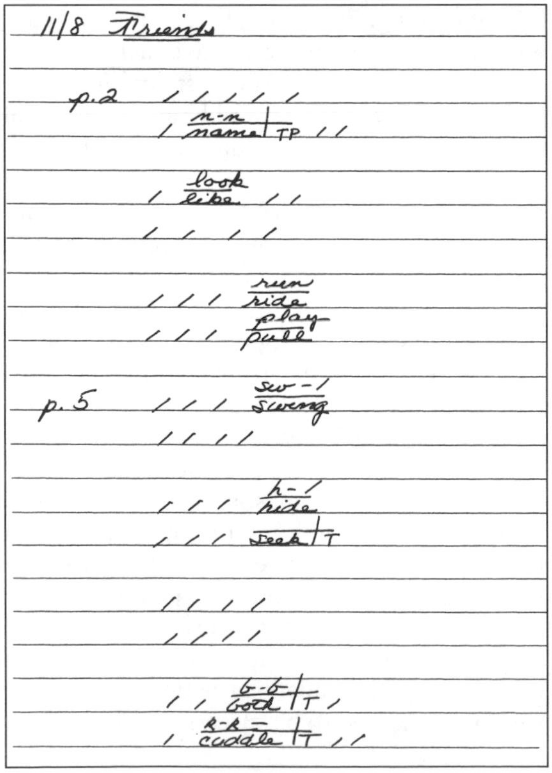

FIGURE 2–3

Victor's Running Record in His Assessment Notebook

should reflect their oral language, contain a strong match of pictures to text, and relate to experiences they've had or to subjects they can relate to. *Friends*, the book Victor read during our conference (see Figure 2–4), was a good one because:

- children can relate to the experience
- pictures closely match the texts they illustrate
- lines of text are placed consistently on each page
- spacing between the words and lines make them easier to distinguish
- sentence structures are simple and repetitive
- language patterns reflect ones children might use
- words such as "I," "she," "likes," and "to" are repeated throughout the text so that children can focus on figuring out unfamiliar words

Like all the children in class, Victor keeps the five-to-ten books he's reading in his book bag, a large zip-lock bag. Frequently, they're titles he's read during guided reading groups or smaller copies of Big Books I've read with the class. They might also be books I've introduced during reading conferences. His book bag allows him to keep his books together so they're available when it's time to read.

Early Readers

Kathy is a an early reader.

She uses a variety of strategies for words she doesn't know and is growing confident in handling whatever comes her way. When she doesn't know a word, she usually tries to sound it out. If she can't, she often reads past the word to the end of the sentence and then comes back to try it again.

She generally uses pictures to confirm, not predict, what the text says. When reading *Silly Willy* by Anne Hanzl (see Figure 2–5), she hesitated on "coins," but then got it, explaining that she looked at the picture and remembered that "the other word is 'paid,' like someone is paying him with coins." Kathy used picture cues (meaning) and context to figure out the word. (See Figures 2–5 and 2–6 for Kathy's running record in her assessment notebook and the text she read.)

Kathy appreciates the problem-solving nature of reading. She understands that what she reads must make sense, sound right, and match the letters, and usually works at words she doesn't know until she gets them right. She consistently monitors and self-corrects her reading. For example, she corrected her reading of "silly" for "lazy" when she realized that "'silly' doesn't match the sounds of the letters."

"Just-right" books for Kathy and other early readers are those that offer just the right amount of support so they can successfully meet new challenges. *Silly Willy* is a good book for early readers because:

- the story pattern is predictable, e.g., Silly Willy tries repeatedly (but inappropriately) to apply his mother's suggestion for how he should carry what he's bought
- there's simple story language to cue the child that this is a folk tale, e.g., "Once upon a time," and "And they all lived happily ever after."
- there's enough easily recognizable words to allow children to apply a variety of strategies to words they don't know
- the vocabulary is challenging but not intimidating, e.g., "cross," "trouser," "crisp," "staggered"

FIGURE 2–4

Page and Text from *Friends* by Min Hong

FIGURE 2–5

Kathy's Running Record in her Assessment Notebook

FIGURE 2–6

Page and Text from *Silly Willy* by Ann Hanzl

FIGURE 2-7

Clive's Assessment Notebook

> 5/14 I asked Clive for a conf.
> S: How're you doing?
> C: Great! I really like these books — they're funny — the kids do funny things.
> (He's reading *Snaggle Doodles* — on p. 26 — Started this morning)
>
> S: How many have you read?
> C: Eight. After this I'll go back to #2 — *Candy Corn Contest* and then *Purple Climbing Days*
> S: Don't need to read them all.
> C: I like to — helps me understand them better.
>
> S: Any way for me to help?
> C: I got to a word and I got it — "invitations" — and I knew it. I know /shuns/. It has four syllables — then got to "inventions" — a lot like it.

FIGURE 2-8

Page from *Snaggle Doodles* by Patricia Reilly Giff

Chapter 2

"Spring is a time for new things," said Ms. Rooney. "Leaves on the trees. Spring jackets."

Emily reached into her desk. She pulled out Uni, her little rubber unicorn. She galloped him across her desk.

Then she looked out the open window.

"New fresh air," she said. She took a deep breath.

"Right," said Ms. Rooney. "And new inventions. Did you know that the safety pin was invented in the springtime?"

"And Coca-Cola," said Ms. Vincent, the student teacher.

"And erasers on pencils," Ms. Rooney said.

"And baseball bats," said Beast.

"Really?" asked Ms. Rooney.

11

- there's a balance of narration and dialogue
- the humor is appealing to children
- it's a story they'd enjoy reading again and again

Transitional Readers

Clive is a transitional reader.

At the time of his conference, Clive was reading books from the "Kids of the Polk Street School" series—each and every one of them! (See Figure 2–7 and 2–8 for Clive's assessment notebook and a page from the book he was reading.)

He'd already read eight books in the series and planned to read two others. When I reminded Clive that he needn't read them all and that he certainly didn't need to read them in order, he insisted he liked doing it this way. He said it helped him understand the stories better because sometimes things that happen in the earlier books are mentioned again in later stories. While this strategy was working for Clive, I noted I would need to encourage him to use some of the other comprehension strategies I had demonstrated during read aloud and guided reading. (See Chapters 7 and 8 for a description of these strategies.)

Clive reads at a good pace. He'd started reading *Snaggle Doodles* by Patricia Reilly Giff that morning and was already on page twenty-six at the time of our conference. Reading rate is one indicator of a child's over-all comprehension. When they read too slowly, it may mean their books are too hard. They're having to place too much attention on figuring out words, leaving little to handle more complex comprehension issues. And if they do this day after day (because their books are long), it will be difficult to hold on to the story line and the different characters while working hard at the words. At the transitional stage, although children generally have strategies to figure out most words they don't know, they still need help understanding what they're reading.

When I asked Clive if there was any way I could help him, he indicated that he was doing fine by himself. And, as if to prove it, he said: "I got to a word and I got it—'invitations'—and I knew it. I know /shuns/. It has four syllables. Then I got to 'inventions,' and it was a lot like it." Clive used his knowledge of spelling patterns and syllables to figure out these new words. And even more importantly, he used what he knew about one word to help him figure out another.

Children at the transitional stage read a lot of "series" books. Through their shared characters, settings, and events, these books support transitional readers' development just as the repetitive language and structure of emergent and early texts supported them when they were starting out.

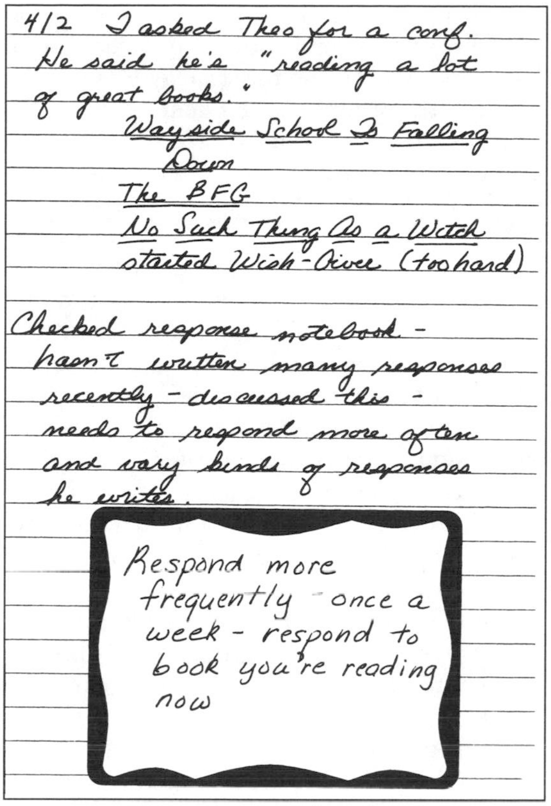
4/2 I asked Theo for a conf.
He said he's "reading a lot of great books."
Wayside School Is Falling Down
The BFG
No Such Thing As a Witch
started Wish-Giver (too hard)

Checked response notebook - hasn't written many responses recently - discussed this - needs to respond more often and vary kinds of responses he writes.

Respond more frequently - once a week - respond to book you're reading now

FIGURE 2–9

Theo's Assessment Notebook

Fluent Readers

Theo is a fluent reader.

He enjoys reading and talks enthusiastically about all the great books he's reading. His comments reflect a genuine understanding and appreciation of the stories, and he's quick to tell anyone who'll listen about all his favorites.

During a recent conference, I learned that Theo had recently read *The Wayside School Is Falling Down* by Louis Sacher, *The BFG* by Roald Dahl, and *No Such Thing As a Witch* by Ruth Chew. (See Figures 2–9 and 2–10 for Theo's assessment notebook and a page from *No Such Thing As a Witch.*) He'd also started reading *The Wish-Giver* by Bill Brittain but stopped after two days because he didn't understand it. Theo no longer needs the support that series books provide, so most books he reads are unrelated. He can even keep two going at the same time.

When I looked through Theo's reading response notebook, I learned that he had written fewer responses than I would expect from a fluent reader. I pointed this out and wrote him a reminder in his assessment notebook to try to respond to books at least once a week. And instead of only summarizing the books, he should try to show the connections he's making between books, and between the books and his life-experiences.

When I asked Theo if there was any way that I could help him with his reading, he declined my offer. I reminded him that earlier in the day he'd asked if the word "stalks" in James Howe's *Celery Stalks at Midnight* meant plants, and that, in fact, he frequently asks what words mean. I wondered if he had strategies for figuring out the meanings of words he didn't know. Theo admitted that even though he could pronounce almost any word, he might not always know what it means. He said he should probably use a dictionary. I proposed that in addition to using a dictionary, there are other strategies to try, and that we would discuss some during read aloud and shared reading. (I knew that read aloud would enable us to consider textual

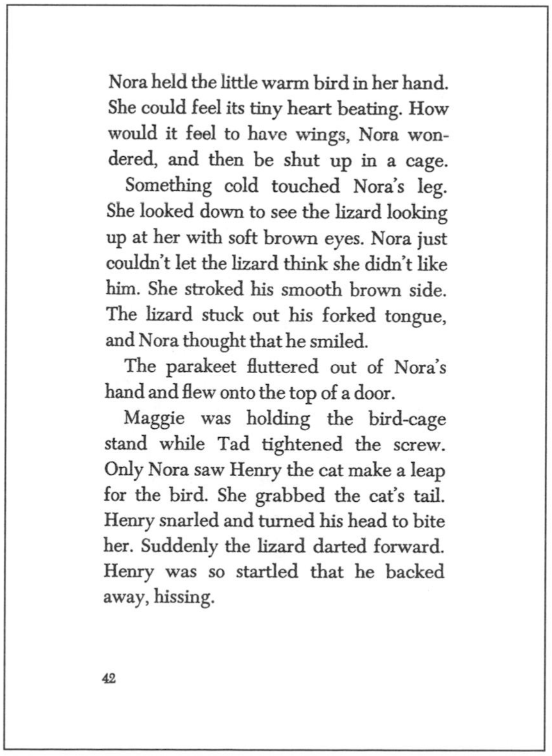
Nora held the little warm bird in her hand. She could feel its tiny heart beating. How would it feel to have wings, Nora wondered, and then be shut up in a cage.

Something cold touched Nora's leg. She looked down to see the lizard looking up at her with soft brown eyes. Nora just couldn't let the lizard think she didn't like him. She stroked his smooth brown side. The lizard stuck out his forked tongue, and Nora thought that he smiled.

The parakeet fluttered out of Nora's hand and flew onto the top of a door.

Maggie was holding the bird-cage stand while Tad tightened the screw. Only Nora saw Henry the cat make a leap for the bird. She grabbed the cat's tail. Henry snarled and turned his head to bite her. Suddenly the lizard darted forward. Henry was so startled that he backed away, hissing.

42

FIGURE 2–10

Page from *No Such Thing As a Witch* by Ruth Chew

cues to figure out the meaning of words, and shared reading would allow us to actually *look at* the text while using the strategy.)

Since transitional and fluent readers like Clive and Theo have already acquired the basic reading skills, their needs are often less apparent than those of children at the emergent and early stages. Nonetheless, I still need to guide them to new levels of proficiency and independence. They need to read different genres and apply their self-improving systems to these new genres. As they read informational texts, they'll encounter tables of contents, indexes, captions, sidebars, diagrams, and glossaries—all requiring demonstrations of their use. In addition, they need to learn to use chapter titles and subtitles to locate information and make predictions. They need to acquire research and study skills, learn how to take notes and organize information, and write factual pieces about what they've read. (Emergent and early readers are exposed to this too, but in a less extensive way.)

Transitional and fluent readers also need strategies for dealing with longer, more content-specific words. When reading about air pollution, for example, they're likely to meet words like "exposure" and "radiation," and need strategies to help read them and understand their meaning.

Children at all stages of reading development need to become more familiar with different types of poetry and the ways in which poetry anthologies are organized. Sometimes all the poems are written by one author, and at other times, they're collections of poems by several authors. My children love to hear how I decided on the overall theme for my poetry anthology, *Morning, Noon, and Night: Poems to Fill Your Day*, and then selected the poems for that volume. This prompted many of them to try writing their own anthologies.

Conclusion

The range of readers represented by Victor, Kathy, Clive, and Theo need appropriate intervention and guidance from teachers who can identify their current reading stages and the behaviors they're working toward. Although each child reaches a different level of proficiency by the end of the year, all children, regardless of where they started, must acquire more strategies to figure out words and understand text, and know how and when to use them. They need to become comfortable reading a variety of genres, use writing to help them understand what they're reading, and love to read—reading not only because they have to, but because they want to. To achieve this, I attend to the behaviors and needs of each child in class in light of the goals I have set.

Creating a Purposeful Environment and Daily Schedule

I N REGGIO EMILIA, A CITY IN NORTHERN ITALY where preschools are renowned for their quality of education, the two teachers in each classroom refer to the environment as the "third teacher." They recognize the importance of their classroom's physical setup and take great care in its preparation. I share this view. And since I work alone with my children (with no aides or parents to lighten my load), I appreciate how a purposeful environment makes it feel like there's an extra pair of hands helping me succeed.

How I set up my classroom, the way I organize my day, and the materials I provide can either "make or break" my efforts to work effectively with children. I take to heart Don Holdaway's advice in *Independence in Reading*: "Much of our teaching energy is spent on compensating for an unfavorable environment. It would be far more sensible to use our energies first on the environment itself." I try to. Let me show you what I mean.

The Organization of My Classroom Space

Visitors to my classroom are surprised by its homey appearance. There are carpets and area rugs on the floor, bookcases and baskets full of books, a sofa with pillows, and plants hanging from baskets, in window boxes, and on table tops. Some say it looks more like a living room than a classroom; others think it looks like a library. I'm pleased when I hear this since our classroom is where the children and I live and work from 8:40 to 3:00 every school day. (See Figure 3–1 for my floor plan.)

There are those who might initially be taken aback by the informal appearance of rooms like

mine. They need to be assured that while the environment appears informal, it doesn't indicate a casual attitude toward either teaching or learning. In fact, quite the opposite is true. This is a studied informality that invites children to experience, share, practice, and learn. These classrooms are organized with specific purposes in mind. They provide opportunities for rigorous teaching and reflect high expectations about children's learning. And most importantly, they usually don't exist in a vacuum. They thrive in school environments that foster creativity and respect for each teacher's individuality. (For more about how the larger school environment supports classroom setup see Shelley Harwayne's *Going Public: Priorities and Practice at the Manhattan New School* and *Lifetime Guarantees: Toward Ambitious Literacy Teaching*.)

Perhaps my classroom's most telling feature is the absence of a teacher's desk. I had one years ago and found it took up too much space and conveyed an unfortunate, though unintended, message about how I viewed the children's and my role. Young children in my classroom, who naturally equate size with worth (often thinking that taller people are older than shorter people and that larger coins are more valuable than smaller ones) may have mistakenly thought that my giant-sized desk, compared with their smaller workspace, reflected the relative importance of their place in the classroom. And think of the valuable space it actually took up!

While we're unable to expand the physical area of our classroom, we *can* make decisions about what goes into it! Now instead of a teacher's desk, I use a small table by the door for piling papers and notices that need to go home.

The children don't have individual desks and chairs either. When I first started at MNS, I

FIGURE 3–1

Floor Plan of My Classroom

Adapted from an illustration
by John Lavoie

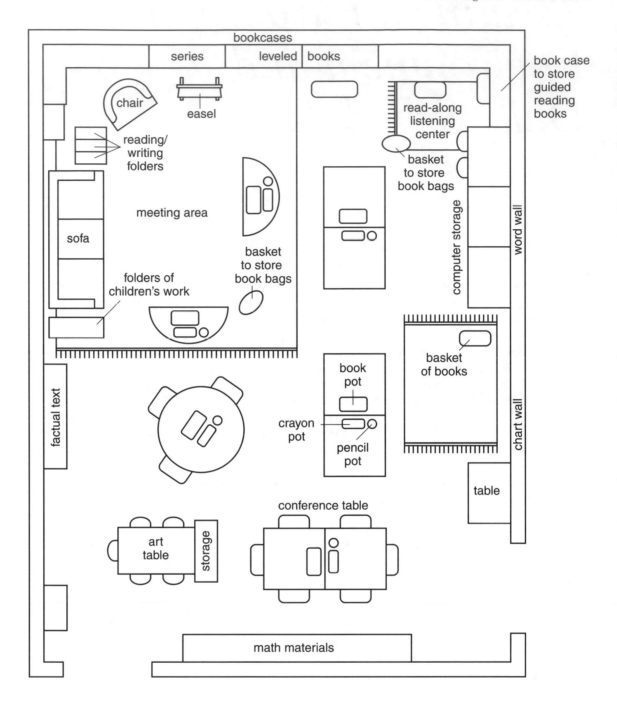

designated a place at a table with a chair for each child. But soon I realized that all that furniture left little space for the children and me to meet in small groups or just "get away" from the others to work alone. I noticed that Joanne Hindley Salch, a colleague and author of the highly acclaimed *In the Company of Children*, had adjusted the leg height of her tables so her children could sit on the floor and use the tabletops as writing surfaces. I immediately saw the value of this but, I initially resisted doing the same thing with my tables, not wanting to "copy" her idea. Fortunately, this foolish reluc-

tance was short-lived. After a couple weeks, I couldn't tolerate bumping into chairs or being unable to settle into comfortable spaces with small groups of children. So I embraced a good thing, and asked our custodian to adjust the height of my tables and put half of my chairs in storage. (There are still several tables of standard height in my classroom.) Instantly, we had more room. And to think it was there all along!

Since my children don't have desks, they keep their homework folder and any small items they bring from home (keys, bake sale money, books) in personal 12″ × 9″ × 2″ trays in a small storage unit near the coatroom. They put their completed homework in a wire basket on top of this cabinet and any notes from their parents or office correspondence into a second basket.

The children don't bring pencils, erasers, markers, or crayons from home since they're available in our "community" pots in the center of each table. These supplies are provided by the school and supplemented by funds I collect from the parents at the start of the year. Their reading, writing, and math folders are stored together in plastic bins at the meeting area, and each child's individual bag of books is kept in one of two wicker baskets set in different areas of the room.

Having children store their materials like this, instead of in desks, which can become terribly messy and unmanageable, enables them to direct less attention to materials and more time to learning. It stops those heated debates about whose yellow "Dixon Ticonderoga" Number 2 pencil is whose!

The Meeting Area

The 10′ × 10′ meeting area is the hub of our classroom. We gather here at the beginning and end of each reading and writing workshop and during read aloud, shared reading, and shared writing sessions to read, write, and discuss texts. Here I demonstrate strategies children might try, and highlight features of print, text, and books. And here the children share strategies that worked well for them each day.

The children sit on the sofa, on the carpet, and on low tables along the edge of the carpet; I sit on the rocking chair alongside the easel, which is the focal point of the meeting area. I sit facing the door—while the children have their backs to it—so I can acknowledge visitors with minimal distractions. The sofa and low tables are the children's favorite places to sit and the only ones I need a seating schedule for. Although I forget this every September, I'm soon reminded that the reason the children are racing up to the classroom each morning is to get these coveted seats.

It's essential that the seating in the meeting area be comfortable, stationary, and intimate. Children need to be up close so they can see what's going on and focus their attention on the work at hand. I've learned that this holds true for adults as well. When working out my consulting plans in school districts, I always ask about the seating arrangements, because it's exceedingly hard to engage participants—and for them to remain engaged—when they're uncomfortable, off to the side, or so far away from the speaker that they can't make eye contact or see the overhead transparencies.

Teachers who rearrange furniture throughout the day frequently become frustrated with the transitions, which are always problematic but unduly so when there are desks and chairs to move around. It's much easier in the long run to designate a section of the room as the gathering place, and then organize the rest of the classroom around it.

The Conference Table

On days that I've scheduled reading conferences, I pass out all the reading folders at the end of our 9:00 to 9:30 meeting and I gather the four or five children with whom I'll confer one-on-one at the back conference table. (See Figure 3–8 for a daily reading and writing schedule.) They bring their reading folder and book bag (more about these materials later in this chapter) and work here from 9:30 to 10:20 while awaiting their conference. The other children in class read independently. I sit at one end of the table, at an angle facing the classroom, so I can monitor the children who are working on their own.

I prefer to confer with children *at this table* instead of moving to meet with each of them wherever they happen to be sitting. I used to do the latter, but looking back, I realized I wasted a lot of time moving from child to child. It was all too easy to spend a disproportionate amount of time with one or two children who happened to be particularly needy or engaging that day and to miss others altogether. My conferences are much more purposeful and efficient now.

I've assembled two trays of supplies, stored in the unit behind my seat, to use when demonstrating reading strategies during conferences. The trays contain a small magnetic board and letters, a chalkboard and chalk, sentence strips and scissors, index cards, and blank books. They also hold an assortment of colored-dot stickers for leveling books and adhesive labels for writing reminder notes to the children about strategies to practice. When I need something, I turn and reach for it in the tray. Gone are the days when I'd have to walk across the room to get scissors or markers and interrupt my teaching. Materials should be stored close to where they're used, even if it means having several pairs of scissors and staplers available in different parts of the room. It's much more practical to anticipate what you'll need and have it on hand.

The Classroom Library

LEVELED BOOK POTS

During the first independent reading session from 8:40 to 9:00, the children select books from the table book pots (which are not leveled), from those propped against the easel, or from our nonfiction library. Then during the second independent reading session from 9:30 to 10:20, they read texts from the leveled book pots that are stored on the bookcase shelves (see Figure 3–2).

I store these books in pots with their front covers facing out, instead of on shelves library-style with their spines out. This makes it easier for the children and me to look through the pots and find books they're interested in and can read independently with the right degree of word accuracy. It's hard for young children to bend their heads to read book titles written

along the spines of books squeezed into shelves. When children can see the cover, they are more likely to flip through the books until they find an appealing one and then read a little to see if it's "just right." If it isn't, children can easily return the books to the pots, and I can help them select others.

Children need "just-right" books to read independently when they aren't meeting with me for a reading conference or guided reading group. I match children with books during conferences, often sending them over to the book pots to look for books on their own for a minute or two before I join them. More fluent readers often select their own books, especially when they're reading books in a series.

Sorting books by stage, and level of difficulty within each stage, helps me and the children select the ones that will be most helpful in practicing the strategies they're acquiring. I closely monitor the books children read. Although I have a strong hand in the selection of books they read, my goal is to help children know which books are "good for them" so that they can eventually choose their own.

The books are leveled with blue-, yellow-, red-, and green-dot stickers at their upper right-hand corners to indicate, respectively, the

FIGURE 3–2

Books Grouped by Stage and Series

emergent, early, transitional, and fluent stages of reading. They're kept in book pots with other "blue," "yellow," "red," and "green" books. Each dot is numbered "1," "2," or "3" to show its level of difficulty within that stage, making it easier for me to help children select new books for their bags, and helping them know where to look when I recommend they try to find books themselves.

As children consolidate their reading skills, they start reading series books like "Nate the Great," "Kids of the Polk Street School," and "Triplet Trouble." I'm thrilled when this happens: first, because it means the children are well on their way to becoming fluent readers; and second, because it's easier for us to find new books for them to read and for them to independently select their own. If they can read one book in a series, they can usually read them all! Series books, with their predictable characters, settings, and story lines, support developing readers, just as repetitive and rhyming texts supported these same readers when they were starting out.

I also keep a supply of books from Reading Recovery lists on hand in a separate basket to use at the beginning of the year with children at the emergent and early reading stage. These books are leveled in smaller, more discrete increments than most other books in my classroom. I keep Fountas and Pinnell's *Guided Reading: Good First Teaching for All Children* and *Matching Books to Readers: Using Leveled Books in Guided Reading, K–3* on hand for reference. But I'm careful not to abdicate my responsibility for knowing which books are good for each child.

Knowing how to match children with books is a critical part of my role (see Chapter 11). In order to keep refining this skill, I continually consider and reconsider the characteristics of the books I use to teach reading, not only their level, and the characteristics of readers at different stages. It's of little value to know a child is reading "level 10" books or that the books in his bag are "red 1" without knowing what this means and how it relates to the child's reading behaviors. Therefore, I often use books like *Guided Reading* and *Matching Books to Readers* or Barbara Peterson's chapter, "Selecting Books for Beginning Readers," in *Bridges to Literacy*, not so much for their mention of specific titles and levels as for their insights into the characteristics of books that support and challenge readers at different stages. My responsibility, after all, is to become more in-

formed so I can make these kinds of decisions myself.

NON-LEVELED BOOK POTS

Nonfiction Library

Although there are factual texts in our leveled book pots in addition to fiction and poetry, we also have a nonfiction library that includes reference books (e.g., atlases, travel books, dictionaries) and informational text on a variety of topics. Instead of one set of a particular dictionary, I have five or six copies of several titles. What better way to help children understand how to use a dictionary than to encourage them to compare different versions of this reference tool?

I try to select some factual tradebooks that specifically support our science and social studies investigations and others that relate to children's interests. These books are in pots, but they aren't leveled. Although I always say I'm going to tackle this, I never seem to get around to it. When I finally do, however, I expect the process to be quite challenging.

Aside from enlarging type size to support readers—and in fact, this is often overdone making the text disproportionately large and cumbersome—many nonfiction texts fail to help young readers process information more effectively. They pack too much on a page or into one paragraph. Often key concepts aren't identified by bold type, and many don't have appropriate clarifying pictures, charts, or graphs. Formatting and page design are just as critical in factual text as in fiction—perhaps even more so—since by nature these texts lack many of the features that support readers of fiction, such as narration and oral language structures. Despite these problems, I'm always on the lookout for books to support the children in learning to read informational text effectively and enthusiastically. And I'll get to leveling them—soon.

Table Book Pots

There's a pot of books on each table in the classroom, each containing a variety of genres as well as books for readers at different stages in reading. The children select books from these pots during the first independent reading session and throughout the day as the need arises. I frequently grab a book from one of these pots during a writing conference to demonstrate a convention of writing (e.g., paragraphs, quotation marks) or highlight an author's style.

BIG BOOKS

At the start of the year, I go through my supply of Big Books and decide on the ones I'm likely to use within the next several months. I keep these at the meeting area for easy access and store the rest in a closet. I try to vary the genres and levels of difficulty of the Big Books I use and select ones with accompanying songs on tape. Children love to sing, and it's a sure-fire way to help them engage with text.

BOOKS FOR GUIDED READING

I keep my books for guided reading in a separate bookcase on four shelves according to the emergent, early, transitional, and fluent stage of reading (see Figure 3–3). I'm particular about which books I use, making certain they support my demonstrations of strategies the children need to practice. I bundle six copies of each title and organize them on the shelf so they're ready for distribution. I don't put the titles I use for guided reading into the leveled or table book

pots because I prefer that the children read them for the first time in their group.

MY PERSONAL LIBRARY

Some books in the classroom are off limits to the children. I keep books that I'm particularly fond of reading aloud, or use to demonstrate specific reading or writing strategies, in a bookcase behind my rocking chair so they're there when I need them. Then, after I've shared them, I place them on the easel for the children to borrow. The children understand that they should return these books to the easel, so I can reshelve them, instead of placing them in their book bags or tray. (Sometimes I purchase one or two extra copies of their favorites to have on hand for the children to borrow for their book bags.)

Chart Wall and Word Wall

CHART WALL

On the long wall across from the sofa, I display poems, chants, and songs the children and I have read together, as well as experience and skills charts that grow out of our shared literacy experiences. I also post editing checklists and charts demonstrating ways children might respond to books along this wall. (See Figure 3–4.)

When we're finished working with a chart at the easel, I clasp it onto one of the four-tier skirt hangers that hang on hooks along the chart wall. This way I can hang several charts on each hanger and rearrange them when I want to refocus the children's attention on a specific strategy or skill. The children frequently refer to these charts as they read and write.

I also refer to the charts as I confer with children. If I notice a child having trouble reading or writing words that contain spelling patterns we've studied, I might direct him to the chart that would help. It's not enough to just post the charts without giving explicit and repeated demonstrations of their use. Charlotte Montgomery, a colleague from Fairfax County, Virginia, once expressed her concern to Diane Snowball, a good friend and mentor to us both, that her children seldom refer to charts. Di's simple, but incisive response, "Well, do you?" drove home the importance of showing children throughout the day how these charts might help them as they read and write. That age-old advice to writers, "Show, don't tell," rings true in teaching as well.

FIGURE 3–3

Where I Store My Books for Guided Reading

WORD WALLS

High-Frequency Word Wall

I list commonly used words the children and I find in our shared reading and writing texts on our high-frequency word wall, a 4′ × 6′ wipe-off board at the center of the chart wall. (Early in the year when most of my readers are at the emergent or early stage, I use the long bulletin board across the back wall of our classroom. This allows me to make the word cards large enough for the children to easily see.) At the end of each week, after we've finished working with a shared reading or writing text, we read through it one more time, listing the words we expect to meet again and again as we read and write in the future. Later in the day, I write several of these high-frequency words (the exact number depends on the children's stage in reading) on oaktag cards. The following Monday, I tape them to the wall as the children direct me to place each word under its correct beginning letter.

In *Phonics They Use*, Patricia Cunningham describes several types of word walls, and emphasizes the importance of involving children in activities that actually require them to *use* the "wall." I learned that lesson several years ago when, during a conference, I reminded Nina that the word she was having difficulty writing was on our word wall. Nina's reply, "What word wall?" demonstrated that unless I refer to the word wall throughout the day and remind children to do the same, they may not learn to use it or even remember it's there.

At the end of each month, the new high-frequency words we've added to our word wall go into the children's spelling folders and become part of their spelling words. It's important to foster this natural connection between reading, writing, and spelling since each supports the development of the others and are all essential facets of children's literacy learning.

Spelling Pattern Word Wall

I also have a spelling pattern word wall (see Figure 9–1 on page 119), made from a 3′ × 5′ piece of butcher block paper stapled to a bulletin board. Around the border, I've thumbtacked the thirty-seven "dependable" spelling patterns, written on oaktag cards so that I can move them around as needed. (These spelling patterns represent Richard Wiley and Donald Durrell's thirty-seven *rimes*, which are sounds the spelling patterns represent, not the patterns themselves.)

FIGURE 3–4

Chart Wall and Small Meeting Area

Whenever I highlight a dependable spelling pattern during shared reading or writing, I "feature" it on the word wall. I tape the "spelling pattern card" on a 1′ × 3′ sheet of white butcher block and have children list words containing that pattern under it. We can feature four spelling patterns at a time and add new sheets of spelling patterns on top of the old ones as needed. We usually initiate these investigations and add words to the sheets during shared reading or writing and then pin it to the word wall when we're done.

The Materials

Over the summer, I purchase the folders and notebooks the children will need for reading, writing, and spelling. I don't want to send home a supply list on the first day of school and then have to wait several days, sometimes longer, until everyone has what they need. I want to begin our classroom routines on day one.

So on the first day, I send a letter to each family listing the supplies I have already bought and asking them to reimburse me. Parents are happy to do this since it saves them the hassle of tracking down hard to find items. Many parents even send thank-you notes.

Those of you who prefer not to purchase school supplies yourselves, or who work in school districts that don't permit it, might want to be more specific with parents about what to buy and even where to shop. You might make arrangements with a local stationery store to stock the materials and then ask parents to buy in those stores.

I purchase the following items for each child:

- a red plastic double-pocket reading folder
- a blue plastic double-pocket writing folder
- a four-sectioned pressed board spelling/poetry folder
- a 4″ × 6″ assessment notebook for reading
- a 4″ × 6″ assessment notebook for writing
- a reading response notebook (sixty-leaf)
- a handwriting notebook

The Reading Folder and Its Contents

Each child has a reading folder containing the assessment notebook, the reading response notebook, a Weekly Reading Log, and any response (Appendix F) or strategy sheets she may be using (see Appendixes G, H, and I and Chap-

ter 8 for a description of how they're used). Figure 3–5 illustrates the contents of a reading folder.

I use red plastic folders for reading and blue plastic folders for writing. Unlike the paper folders that fall apart after a few weeks, these plastic folders last all year. Having a different color folder for reading and writing helps keep them organized. I store the folders in a bin alongside my rocking chair in the meeting area.

THE ASSESSMENT NOTEBOOK

I almost feel like there should be bells ringing and lights flashing as I describe my assessment notebooks. For without a doubt, they're my most important teaching tool. During reading conferences, I use the child's personal assessment notebook to record running records (i.e. notations of the child's oral reading), her retellings of stories, and entries summarizing discussions we've had about her reading. (See Figure 2–5 on page 15 for a sample notebook page and Chapters 5 and 6 for how the notebooks are used.)

At the end of the conference, I return the notebook to the child's folder where she can refer to it for strategies she should practice

FIGURE 3–5
Reading Folder
Contents

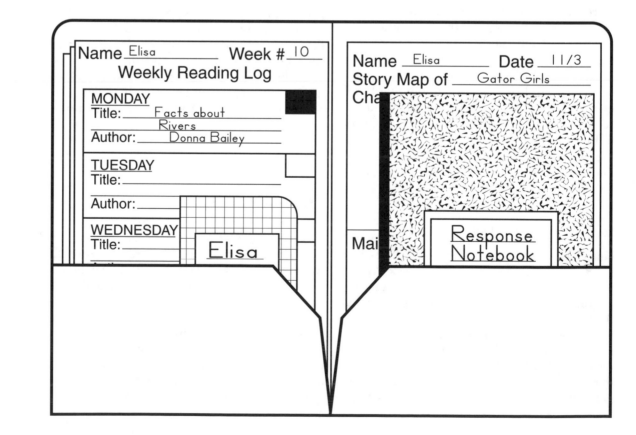

while reading independently, or until I use it during guided reading to record the title of the reading book and the strategy the group is working on.

Over the years, I've tried several other methods of keeping track of my assessment notes, but none of them worked for me. I wrote notes on adhesive labels with the intention of later transferring them to each child's tabbed section in a looseleaf binder. But most of the time, I never got around to attaching the labels, or I misplaced them altogether. Then I tried recording my notes directly onto pages of a large notebook, but the notebook became too awkward to carry around and eventually disappeared under a pile of papers.

The assessment notebooks I use now do just what I need them to do. Each notebook provides enough space for me to document a child's reading growth from the beginning of the school year to the end, complete with:

- strategies she's using well and others she needs to use more effectively
- running records, retellings, and reading discussions
- guided reading groups in which she's participated
- the titles of some books she's read
- reminder notes to the child of what strategies she should practice

The notebooks fit neatly into the children's reading folders, which are returned to the storage bin at the end of each reading workshop. I never lose or misplace them, and neither do the children.

THE READING RESPONSE NOTEBOOK

The reading response notebooks are composition notebooks the children use to respond to some of the books they read. Transitional and fluent readers begin using these notebooks early in the year, while emergent and early readers start the year with response sheets (described in the following sections), and then later move into the response notebooks as their skills develop.

I prefer these thinner sixty-leaf notebooks, which I buy at a teacher supply store, to the thicker notebooks found in most neighborhood stores, because they fit better in the children's reading folders. Most children don't need more than 120 pages (two pages per leaf) to respond to books, and if they do, they're probably responding too frequently and not devoting enough workshop time to reading.

RESPONSE SHEETS AND STRATEGY SHEETS

In designing the separate response sheets for emergent and early readers (Appendix F), I leave the top half of the sheet for a picture and give them a few lines at the bottom to write a sentence or two about the book. Children at these early stages of development can take a long time to write a lengthy response and it's often a challenge for them to try. The response sheets allow them to convey their ideas about a book through their drawings and one or two sentences (see Teddy's response sheet in Figure 13–3 on page 168.

A child might use any of the variety of reading strategy sheets I make available as the year unfolds to help him focus on a specific strategy (Appendixes G, H, and I). While response sheets are used *after* the child has completed reading the text, strategy sheets are used *as* he reads. (I discuss strategy sheets at length in Chapter 12, "Independent Reading.") Copies of blank response sheets and strategy sheets are stored in metal filing shelves for the children to take as needed.

WEEKLY READING LOG

Each Monday, when I pass out the children's reading folders at the start of the second independent reading session, I give every child a new Weekly Reading Log. On it, he records the title and author of the main book he's read each day during the reading workshop and indicates whether it is fiction, factual, or poetry by color-coding the corner box (described in the following section). Children reading longer books might only read part of a book each day, and record the same title and author for several days. Others may read several shorter books in a day. (See Figure 3–6 for Alexis' Weekly Reading Log.)

Kindergarten children just starting out would have a hard time doing this, so I recommend waiting to introduce this log. But in my combined first and second grade, I start the year with this log and ask the children to fill in the parts they can. Sometimes all they do is record the title of a book and draw a picture—and that's fine. It's a tool they'll grow into.

The children indicate whether their books are fiction, factual, or poetry by coloring the box at the upper right-hand corner of each day's record red, blue, or yellow. Red means the book is fiction; blue means it's factual; and yellow means it's poetry. As the year proceeds, the children and I can see at a glance whether they're reading a variety of genres. One day when I asked which children needed to meet,

FIGURE 3–6

Alexis' Weekly Reading Log

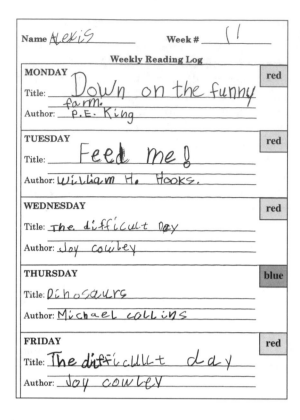

Name __Alexis__   Week # ____1____

Weekly Reading Log

MONDAY   red

Title: __Down on the funny farm.__

Author: __P.E. King__

TUESDAY   red

Title: __Feed me!__

Author: __William H. Hooks.__

WEDNESDAY   red

Title: __The difficult Day__

Author: __Joy cowbey__

THURSDAY   blue

Title: __Dihosaurs__

Author: __Michael collins__

FRIDAY   red

Title: __The difficult day__

Author: __Joy cowley__

It's important for children to reflect on their reading. This weekly stock-taking gives them one more opportunity to think about what has worked and is therefore worth repeating.

Book Bags

Each child in my class has a 10″ × 12″ book bag (a heavy-duty freezer bag) with his name on it for keeping from three-to-ten books he's "working on" during the second independent reading time. (Kindergarten teachers may want to provide larger bags to accommodate the larger size of many of their children's books.)

I play a very strong role in helping children select books, especially at the earlier stages of reading. Although they can read whichever books they want during the first independent reading time, during the second independent reading time, I want their books to provide just the right kinds of supports and challenges. (See Chapter 11 to learn how I match children with books at the start of the year and change the books in their bags as needed.)

During September, I devote all of our reading and writing conferences to getting to know my children as readers and matching them with their first set of books. Having a bag to hold their books is especially helpful for emergent and early readers who read shorter books. If they don't have several books close by that are just right for them, then they're likely to spend much of their time looking for books and chatting with friends along the way. And if the children aren't working, then I can't work either. These bags are a critically important teaching tool, enabling me to hold purposeful conferences or lead guided reading groups while the rest of the class is engaged in meaningful reading experiences.

Emily was desperate for a conference, waving her hand in front of my face. When I asked what she wanted, she said: "I need to get 'true' books. I checked my boxes and they're all red!"

This color-coding method leads us to discuss characteristics of fiction, factual text, and poetry throughout the year. Children do get confused about these distinctions, but it's part of their growth process. For example, Itamar was surprised to learn that "some things in fiction are true." He'd been reading *The Beast in Ms. Rooney's Room* from the "Kids of the Polk Street School" series, and discovered that "the Polk Street School was named after a *real* president"—James J. Polk.

Each Friday at the end of the reading workshop, the children take five or ten minutes to record on the back of the log (Appendix B) what they did well that week and their plans for the following one. Figure 3–7 shows two different types of responses children made.

Samantha's response was very detailed, identifying specific strategies she used and could use again, while Lauren's was from the heart: "This week I was successful at reading and every time I read I get better. Next week I plan to 'read like I never read before.'" Of course, Lauren needed to become more specific, but for the time being, her attitude toward reading would take her far.

The Writing Folders and the Spelling/Poetry Folders

Although the focus of this book is reading, I will occasionally refer to writing because of the fundamental ways in which they're connected. Miles, an eight-year-old in my class several years ago, gave his astute perception of these complementary processes as he was interviewed for my video series, *A Close-up Look at Teaching Reading*: "When I'm reading, I'm reading writing. And when I'm writing, I'm reading."

He understands that both activities involve "composing" text.

When we write, we're shaping our own ideas, and continually reading them back to be sure they make sense. And when we read, we're reconstructing what someone else has already written, again attending to the sense it makes. Each process supports the other. And perhaps that's why when I'm teaching writing (and spelling), I also feel I'm teaching reading. Let me describe some of the materials I use to teach writing and spelling.

THE WRITING FOLDERS

Each child has a blue plastic double-pocket *writing folder* where she keeps an assessment notebook, "working" pieces of writing, a word book of high-frequency words, and a handwriting notebook.

I use an individual *writing assessment notebook* to record observations I make about a child's writing. I record what she does well and what she needs to do more, types of genres she's writing, and guided writing groups in which she's taken part.

The children keep *several pieces of writing* in their folders at a time. When they finish a piece or no longer want to work on it, they put it into a cumulative folder in a storage wall unit. I generally keep all their writing in school, and then send it home at the end of the year. It's satisfying and fun for the children to compare pieces they've done in March, for example, with pieces written in October. And it's an excellent way to drive home the point that they're actually working to become better than they were in the past, not to do better than classmates or to meet my expectations.

They also have a *handwriting notebook* in their writing folder. I purchase these at a teacher supply store because the lines are the appropriate height, with a middle dotted line to support their handwriting.

Our school provides a beginning *word book* for each child, which she keeps in her folder. (I use Mondo's *Word Book*.) I like having these in the writing folders because they contain commonly used words, helping the children become more independent in finding the correct spellings of frequently used words.

SPELLING/POETRY FOLDER

Spelling helps children focus on the sequence of letters in words and learn more about how

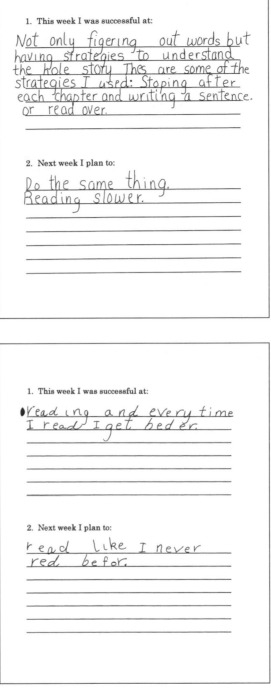

1. This week I was successful at:

Not only figering out words but having strategies to understand the hole story Thes are some of the strategies I used: Stoping after each chapter and writing a sentence. or read over.

2. Next week I plan to:

Do the same thing. Reading slower.

1. This week I was successful at:

•reading and every time I read I get beder.

2. Next week I plan to:

read like I never red befor.

FIGURE 3–7

Back of Samantha's and Lauren's Weekly Reading Logs

words work. The spelling/poetry folders are pressed board folders with four sections, each with a brass fastener at the top to attach: (1) copies of poems, songs, and language-experience charts (2) "If I Can Spell" sheets, (3) high-frequency word lists, and (4) "Words I Want to Learn to Spell" sheets. (See Appendix C for a sample page of each of these sections and a description of how they're used.)

The Daily Schedule

In order to work effectively with individual children, small groups, and the whole class, I need large, uninterrupted blocks of time and a predictable structure. All the components must work together as part of one system. When I confer with Lauren during a reading conference, I need to know that she can go back to her reading and practice the strategies we've discussed. When I demonstrate ways to figure out unfamiliar words during shared reading, I need to know that the children can try these strategies on books that will support their efforts. When I identify children with similar needs during writing conferences, I must have structures in place to assist them. I need time and opportunities to teach children to read and write; the children need time and the opportunity to learn.

My Reading Schedule

Reading starts at 8:40 and continues until 10:30. We begin with our first independent reading session, from 8:40 to 9:00. Then, during the meeting time from 9:00 to 9:30, we do read aloud, shared reading, and/or shared writing. (Early in the year or when most of my children are emergent or early readers, our meeting lasts until 9:45 to provide additional time for shared reading and writing.) The reading workshop—with its conferences, guided reading, and independent reading—begins formally at 9:30 (or 9:45), and is followed by the writing workshop, which lasts until 11:20 when the children go to lunch. (See Figure 3–8 for my reading and writing schedule.)

8:40–9:00 FIRST INDEPENDENT READING SESSION AND WORD STUDY GROUPS

First Independent Reading Session

After the children put away their homework, coats, and school bags, they select books from our nonfiction library, the table book pots, and those propped against the easel. Many of them choose books beyond their independent reading levels. If so, they just read the parts they can or enjoy the pictures. They often browse through them looking for interesting information to share with their classmates during the meeting time (described in the following section). Many

FIGURE 3–8 Schedule for Reading and Writing	
8:40–9:00	**First Independent Reading/Word Study Groups**
9:00–9:30	**Meeting** (Whole-Group Session)
	Read Aloud, Shared Reading and /or Shared Writing with a Strategy or Skill Focus
9:30–10:30	**Reading Workshop**
	Reading Conferences *or* Guided Reading
	Second Independent Reading
	Reading Share (10:20–10:30)— "What did you learn about yourself as a reader? What worked so well today that you might try do it again and again?"
10:30–10:40	**Writing Mini-lesson or Children Sharing Pieces of Writing**
10:40–11:20	**Writing Workshop** (includes spelling and handwriting)
	Writing Conferences *or* Guided Writing
	Independent Writing
	Writing Share (11:10–11:20)— "What did you learn about yourself as a writer? What worked so well today that you might try to do it again and again?"

read Big Books we've read previously in shared reading.

Children who choose books from the table book pots, which contain books from a range of genres and levels of difficulty, are more likely to select texts that are a closer match to the types of books they can read well on their own. Many even choose easier books. It's as though they consider this first independent reading session a time to warm-up for the more rigorous reading that follows during the workshop, much the same way that athletes and musicians warm-up before they play.

I schedule two independent reading sessions daily to address two needs: first, children need to browse and savor interesting books even if they end up being too difficult to comprehend completely on their own, and second, they need to do serious strategic reading of books that closely match their capabilities as readers.

Word Study Group

In my early teaching years, I used to put up board work first thing in the morning for the children to do as soon as they arrived in class. This gave me time for the clerical work I felt I needed to do (e.g., collecting milk money, responding to parent's notes, checking homework). But as I reflected on the parts of my day that were "adding up" and those that weren't, I realized that I was using the best time of day—the morning when everyone is fresh and alert—for secondary work that could be done later.

Now I start teaching as soon as the children arrive. Three or four mornings a week, I meet with a group of four-to-six readers for a word study group at the small meeting area alongside the chart wall. Usually these are children who need to pay closer attention to the relationship between spelling patterns and their corresponding sounds. I don't group the children formally. I just take a quick inventory of their needs at the start of the week by referring to my Guided Reading Planning Sheets (see Figures 8–2, 8–3, and 8–4) and pull together children who would benefit most from this additional time with me.

I might meet with a group on two consecutive days to do a Making Words activity as described in Cunningham and Hall's book *Making Words*. We "make the words" on the first day, and then sort them on the second. On one or two other days, I might also meet with a second group to focus on inflectional endings, prefixes and suffixes, common spelling patterns, or whatever skill needs practice.

Although I occasionally meet with transitional and fluent readers, I tend to view this early morning time as a "found" opportunity to give additional attention to children at the emergent and early stage who are just acquiring basic reading skills. And so it may happen that I meet with the same children again and again to help them jumpstart their reading.

On days that I don't work with a word study group, I might confer informally with one or two children, help a child find some new books for the second independent reading session, or step back to observe how things are going.

9:00–9:30 READ ALOUD, SHARED READING, AND/OR SHARED WRITING

Read Aloud

I frequently read books aloud and provide opportunities for the children to respond orally. Whether fiction, factual texts, or poetry these are generally books that most of the children can't read on their own.

As I read aloud, I sometimes introduce and demonstrate reading strategies that I plan to reintroduce during guided reading and reading conferences later in the year. I might demonstrate "Stopping to Think" to help children pause to reflect on what they're reading and to think about what may happen next. Or I might show them how to organize parts of a longer book into a story map to help them better understand and "get a handle on" a book that may take several days to read.

I always provide opportunities for children to respond orally to the books I read aloud. Their oral responses prepare them for their written responses they'll later be asked to make on their own.

Shared Reading

The children and I share in the reading of poems, songs, chants, and Big Books, blending our voices into one. All readers, regardless of their reading stage, can join in without the fear of making mistakes. As needed, they learn important concepts about print, text, and books and can initiate or extend their explorations of letter-sound relationships. Children practice reading with expression. They get ideas for their own stories or examine the structure of a text. Thus, shared reading allows readers at different stages to read together, and serves as a springboard for further learning.

Shared Writing

During shared writing, the children and I compose text together. We might recount a class trip we took, innovate on a text we read together, or write our own story or poem. The children tell me what to write, I scribe it on chart paper, and together we work out the conventions of print, spelling, and grammar.

At the end of the meeting time, before I give out the children's reading folders, I take a few minutes to highlight a skill or strategy related to the read aloud, shared reading, or shared writing we just completed. Then I remind them to practice it as they read.

9:30–10:20 READING CONFERENCES, GUIDED READING, AND THE SECOND INDEPENDENT READING

Reading Conferences

I meet with four or five children for reading conferences two or three days a week to assess their reading, match them with books, and demonstrate strategies one-on-one. Early in the year, I meet with children three times a week to learn as much as possible about them as readers and match them with books they can read independently. As the year progresses, and I know more about the children, I confer with them less often—two days a week instead of three.

Guided Reading

I meet with guided reading groups on days I'm not holding reading conferences. I group three to six readers with similar needs to work on specific strategies and guide them through multiple copies of the same text—one that would be just a bit too hard for them to read on their own. The groups remain together as briefly as two days or as long as two weeks—depending on how long it takes me to effectively demonstrate the target strategy and for the children to practice it.

Second Independent Reading

While I hold reading conferences or lead guided reading groups, the rest of the children read independently. They might read alone or with partners—sometimes working on strategy sheets as they read, listening to and reading along with books on tape, working on extension activities that grow out of guided reading groups, or responding to texts they've read. It's critical that children spend this independent reading time engaged in real reading experiences with whole texts, not in activities that break language into small units that are often too fragmented for them to understand.

I work hard to make sure that the children are matched with books that appropriately support and challenge them during this time. If they aren't matched with the right kinds of books, then their independent reading time will be less productive.

10:20–10:30 READING SHARE

At the end of the reading workshop, the children return their folders to the bins and reconvene at the meeting area. I ask: What did you learn today about yourself as a reader—what did you do that worked so well that you might try it again and again? It's the same question I ask every day from the first day of school to the last. Then two to three children take turns sitting on the rocking chair, sharing what they learned with the class. This daily ritual provides opportunities for children to hear what strategies their classmates have found most helpful, and for me to respond to them about how they're doing.

The flow from independent reading to read aloud and shared reading, to reading conferences, guided reading, and independent reading, and finally to sharing reading strategies at the end of the workshop provides a meaningful structure that supports my assessments and demonstrations. It also gives children time to practice and opportunities for reflection and response. And just as the components of the reading workshop flow into each other, my reading workshop flows into my writing workshop.

10:30–11:20 HOW THE WRITING WORKSHOP PARALLELS THE READING WORKSHOP

I try to keep the reading and writing schedules similar, beginning each with a *focus lesson* that directs the children's attention to strategies or skills they need to acquire. In reading, these focus lessons occur at the end of the read aloud and shared reading or writing session just before the children go off to read. In writing, they occur during the mini-lesson.

During the writing workshop, I either meet with several children for *writing conferences* or I hold guided writing groups. I assess their writing, offer support and advice, recommend books they might read as models of effective writing, help them find words for their spelling lists, or show them how to form troublesome letters.

On days I'm not having conferences, I meet with children for *guided writing groups*. When several children have a similar need, I form a group to address it. Sometimes children have trouble finding a topic to write about. Sometimes they're having trouble correctly using periods or quotation marks. Sometimes they want to try a new genre, but don't know where to start. Whatever the issue, these small groups help children acquire strategies and skills to address them.

During the workshop, the children *write* and keep their pieces of writing in their folder. Each day they resume working where they left off the day before. The children don't progress through a "five-step" writing process in sync, that is, brainstorming topics on Monday, writing a first draft on Tuesday, revising on Wednesday, etc. . . . Children are at different points in the process. While some children are deciding on a topic, others are finding the correct spelling of words, or copying over edited pieces of writing in their very best handwriting. Because they write every day—and have written every day since starting kindergarten—they appreciate the very personal and organic nature of writing.

Occasionally at the end of the writing workshop, I *ask the children what they learned that day about themselves as writers.* And as they share, it's often possible for them to note (with my assistance at first) the parallels between their work as readers and as writers. If Jena shared that she got a lot of writing done because she sat in a spot where children were working quietly, I try to relate that to an earlier reading share where a child learned the same thing about reading. If Alex shared that he remembered to put periods at the ends of his sentences, another child might recall that stopping at periods helped him to better understand the story he was reading. Reading and writing are truly two sides of the same coin.

By keeping my schedule predictable, and the structure and materials for the reading workshop and the writing workshop parallel, I'm able to support the children's and my work so we attend to the truly complex issues involved in both reading and writing. I assess children's work and use what I learn about them to address their needs. Children continue to work at making sense of whole texts and integrate strategies to increase their fluency and independence in both reading and writing. When environments are simple and their structures predictable, children direct their energies to the task at hand. They are creative in the connections they make as they read and write, in ways that really count.

Conclusion

The organization and look of our rooms, the materials we use, and the way we structure the day send a powerful message to children and parents about our attitudes toward teaching and our expectations for our children. When we create classroom environments that are attractive, comfortable, and purposeful, providing materials that support our work with children, structuring our time to support our goals, then we'll surely reap the results of our efforts.

Our classrooms should reflect our goals. If we *want* certain things to happen, then we need to *do* what's necessary to make them happen. There's a direct "if–then" relationship between our goals as teachers and the classrooms we create. If we want children to become strategic readers, then we create classrooms that reinforce the strategies we've demonstrated and allow children to practice on books that match their needs.

If we want children to read a variety of genres, then we need to bring these genres into our rooms and make them accessible. Read aloud, shared reading, guided reading, and independent reading should include the various genres we want children to become more familiar with, demonstrations of how to read the different genres, and then time for children to practice this themselves.

If we want children to respond to books they've read in ways that will deepen their understanding, then we must provide the tools, opportunities, and demonstrations of how to do this. And last of all, if we want children to love to read, then we must provide the kinds of books that will encourage this life-long relationship. This won't happen because we will it. It happens by knowing what we want to achieve and by setting up our classrooms, materials, and schedules to make it happen. And now, on to the teaching.

PART TWO

Assessing Children to Determine Their Strengths and Needs

CHAPTER 4

Reading Conferences: Creating a Context for Assessment

ONE DAY LAST YEAR I WAS RETURNING TO my classroom after dismissing the children, and found Sameer, a former student, sitting on a bench outside my door. He was holding a large white envelope. "It's for you," he said, looking up shyly and handing it to me. Inside was a thank-you note:

> Thank you Shron for haveing reading conferences it really helped my reading. Thank you again. And whit my writing. A lot of people thank my reading because of you. If another kid was in your class he would learn a lot form you.

> Love

> Sameer

When Sameer was in my class, he had recently arrived from India and was having difficulty learning to read. It struck me how, of all the read alouds, shared reading sessions, and guided reading groups in which he'd participated, Sameer singled out reading conferences, our one-on-one time together, as most beneficial. He clearly appreciated what had taken me years to learn.

In my early years of teaching, I seldom met individually with children to learn about their attitudes toward reading, their understandings about print, and the genres and topics they enjoyed most. I didn't take running records throughout the year to learn what strategies they used so I could help them use more effective ones. And I seldom talked with them about what they read to see how well they understood it. I never needed to—or so I thought.

Instead, I simply referred to or, more precisely, *deferred to* the teaching guide in my basal reading program to find out which stories to read, which questions to ask, and which follow-up activities to assign. The prescriptive "cookbook" nature of the program created the illusion that I could teach without assessing for myself what each of my children needed and then plan instruction to meet those needs. But I now realize that teaching must be based on more than a generic, one-size-fits-all program.

It's important for me to know that Vicky is desperate to read the "harder" books that Lauren and Sarah are reading. She needs reassurance from me that by practicing the easier books, she'll soon be reading chapter books along with her friends. Many conferences end with a hand on her shoulder, promising: "You're almost there Vicky, you're almost there. Just stick with it a little longer."

I need to know that Ben seldom monitors his reading. As I analyze the miscues in his running records, I find that he generally continues right on reading even when what he says doesn't make sense or match the letters. I need to help him attend to print and meaning by restating what he says and asking, "Does that match the letters?" or "Does that make sense?" and then help him work toward initiating his own corrections.

I need to know that Victor has just begun using spelling patterns in familiar words to write new ones. This breakthrough occurred during writing, but affects my work with him in reading as well. I need to show Victor that he can make similar connections between words he already knows how to read and words he's trying to figure out.

What better time than during our one-on-one reading conferences to help Vicky, Ben, and

Victor, and each of the other twenty-three children in my class, to use strategies and skills that will make them better readers? What better time to see how well they understand what they've read? And what better time to match them with books that are just right for their independent reading? Reading conferences are at the center of my teaching. They provide information and inspiration for my work and allow me to keep my finger on the pulse of each child's reading.

Scheduling Reading Conferences

Allowing for Schedule Changes to Meet Changing Needs

During the reading workshop from 9:30 to 10:30, I either confer with children individually or hold guided reading groups. The number of days I set aside for reading conferences each week decreases from three to two as I get a better handle on what children need. Conversely, the number of days I meet with guided reading groups increases from two to three so I can address children's needs in small groups. However, the first month of school is slightly different.

THE FIRST MONTH OF SCHOOL

At the start of the year, when I'm just beginning to learn about my children as readers and gathering that first set of "just-right" books for their book bags, I schedule reading conferences five days a week from 9:30 to 10:20. I even use my writing conference and guided writing time from 10:30 to 11:20 to confer about reading. (Chapter 12 addresses what the other children are doing while I'm conferring with readers individually.)

These initial conferences help me assess each child's stage in reading, identify some skills and strategies to focus on, and find the books best suited for independent reading. All this takes time. If my teaching is to be better than it was years ago, if I now believe that I teach not a *class* of twenty-six, but twenty-six *individuals*, then I must learn about each one of them specifically, and find ways to address their individual needs one-on-one, in small groups, and in whole-class settings. To do this, I begin conferring with children the first week of school and continue throughout the year.

THE REST OF THE YEAR

During the second and third month, I schedule reading conferences three days a week and guided reading groups two days a week. There's still a lot to learn about the strategies each child uses and the level of text that is most appropriate for independent reading.

From the fourth month on, I reverse this schedule and hold reading conferences two days a week and guided reading groups three days a week. By then I know more about the children as readers and can address some of their common needs in small groups. I also continue to work with them individually and plan whole-group instruction based on my assessments of their reading.

Scheduling Conferences with Individual Children

We gather at the meeting area each day for read aloud, shared reading or shared writing (see schedule, Figure 3–8), and review our plans for the day. On conference days, I tell them who I'd like to meet with and/or ask who needs a conference. I don't automatically confer with every child once and then start over for another round. Instead on each conference day, I select the four or five children based on their current needs and mine. (The number of children I confer with each day depends on the stage at which most of readers are at. If most are at the emergent and early stage, I may only be able to confer with three or four children since their assessments typically involve taking running records and direct help finding books.)

I don't give each child in my class equal time, but I try to give each of them what they need. At the start of the year, kindergarten teachers have children who aren't yet ready for more formal reading instruction. These pre-emergent readers need lots of experience handling books and many demonstrations throughout shared reading, read aloud, and individual conferences on how print works. Conferences provide the time and opportunity to observe how they handle books. You may want to administer Marie Clay's Concepts About Print (CAP), a five-to-ten-minute assessment that provides valuable information to help plan instruction for our youngest readers.

Emergent and early readers need regular and direct intervention as they begin to use meaning, structure, and graphophonic cues to make sense of print. They need to make connections between words and spelling patterns they know and others they're trying to figure out. They also need to monitor and self-correct their reading. Given these multiple and more basic areas that require my help, I generally confer with emergent and early readers more frequently than transitional and fluent readers.

Transitional and fluent readers don't need help figuring out most words, but they do need me to show them ways to figure out the *meaning* of unfamiliar words and to fully comprehend longer stories and new genres. They don't need me to remind them that what they read has to make sense and match the letters. But they do need help integrating the different story elements and organizing their thinking at the whole-text level, and guidance with their written responses to books so that they think more deeply. I give each reader the amount and kind of help she needs.

TEACHER-INITIATED CONFERENCES

I look forward to my reading conferences with children. Our time alone gives me the chance to get to know them better and to plan instruction to meet their needs.

Rotating Conferences

Alex has just returned to school after a week-long bout with the flu. I want to meet with him to find out what he's reading and learn where to go from here.

I often request a conference when I haven't met with a child recently and want to see how he's doing. He may have been home sick or out of town for a few days. Or he may be too shy to initiate a conference himself. I can identify these children by referring to the Guided Reading Planning Sheets I keep on my clipboard. (See Figure 8–4 for sample Guided Reading Planning Sheets.)

At the start of each month, I write the name of each child in class on one of four planning sheets, labeled "emergent," "early," "transitional," or "fluent." By listing children monthly according to their stage in reading, and writing a brief description of their reading alongside their names, I can identify children I still need to meet with. The absence of a note is a signal to me that a child may need a conference.

Learning Which Cueing Systems and Strategies Children Use

For the past several weeks, I've been helping Norma attend to graphophonic cues, especially at the ending of words. While she usually gets the beginning sounds, she doesn't pay enough attention to the rest of the word. She often says words that don't match the letters or leaves endings, such as "s" or "ed," off altogether. I want to see if she's making progress.

Regardless of their stage in reading, I need to know which strategies children use at the word and text level. By taking and analyzing running records, I assess how well emergent and early readers use semantic, syntactic, and graphophonic cues, and how effectively they monitor their reading and self-correct. By *referring* to Norma's running records for instances where she needed to pay closer attention to these cueing systems, I explicitly showed her the times she hadn't paid enough attention to the endings of words (see Figures 4–1 and 4–2). I hoped this conference and the note I wrote in her assessment notebook would remind her to attend to this more in the future. (See Chapter 5 for more on running records.)

FIGURE 4–1

An Excerpt from Norma's Running Record

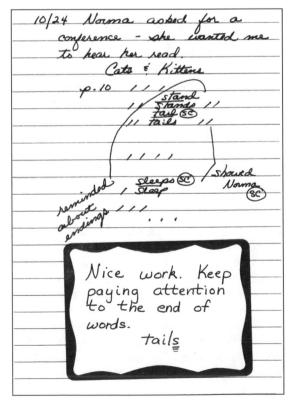

FIGURE 4–2 Text from *Cats and Kittens*

Cats get mad.
Their fur stands on end.
Their tails puff up.
Kittens get mad too.
Cats sleep.
Kittens sleep too.

Since transitional and fluent readers already have ways to work out most unfamiliar words, they should be directing more attention to understanding how elements of stories, factual texts, and poems work together as wholes. I learn how well they understand what they've read by talking with them during conferences and asking them to retell the story or parts of it. If they're reading factual texts, I might ask them to tell me some things they've learned. (See Chapter 6 for more on retellings.)

Learning How My "Most Fluent" Readers Are Doing

Other than occasionally asking for a conference to get new books, Frannie seldom needs help during independent reading. Since she's read most of what interests her from our class library, she frequently goes next door to Joan Backer's fourth-grade class for new books. I want to see what she's reading.

I confer less frequently with my most fluent readers than I do with the other children. These children have actually moved beyond the fluent stage, being able to read even young adult novels. But being able doesn't mean they *should*.

So besides making sure that these children have enough books to read, I also examine the content of their books to see whether they are appropriate for their age and emotional maturity. Seven-, eight-, and nine-year-olds don't need to be reading about a teenager caught in a love triangle with her best friend and the boy of her dreams. It's my responsibility to guide their selections to more appropriate choices.

I also direct them to new genres and new topics within those genres. While these readers are "over the top" in terms of the fiction they read, most haven't yet explored the range of possibilities within factual texts and poetry. "Story" is one way to make sense of the world, but learning how the natural world works and enjoying poets' fresh perspectives on it are others. Children need to discuss newspaper and magazine articles, marvel over biographies of famous people, interpret poems, and use informational text to answer questions. Factual texts and poetry add essential dimensions to children's literary lives and should be promoted early on.

Making Sure the Books in Children's Bags Are Right for Independent Reading

Anna walked into class one day announcing she was reading the "M & M books." "Taryn is reading them," she explained, "and I'm as good a reader as she is. So I brought some of my sister's old 'M & M' books from home for my book bag. I think I can read them too."

Although the children understand that the books we select for their book bags are ones they can read within a 95 percent or higher word accuracy rate, they occasionally try to slip in a harder book, hoping I won't notice or, at the very least, won't object. (This happens a lot when there's been a substitute teacher in the room; I return to find the most unlikely books in the children's bags!)

When this occurs, I ask the child to meet with me so I can take a running record. I can see if the books are "just right" or not, but, more importantly, she can see it too. After taking a running record, all I need to do is turn the assessment notebook toward the child to show her the times she's substituted words (that is, the times she's deviated from the text). This makes our selection process less a matter of me holding a child back from reading the books she's dying to "get to," and more one of her assuming responsibility for choosing books that she can read with acceptable accuracy.

And then again, if the child's reading is reasonably close to the 95 percent word accuracy rate I seek for independent reading—let's say 92 percent—I may let her keep the book. However, I make certain that she understands that she must work extra hard at this book, perhaps rereading it several times and getting help when she can't work out problems herself.

Figure 5–3 on page 50 lists some guidelines I use to determine the level of text accuracy required for different teaching situations. These are adapted from Marie Clay's levels of text difficulty in *The Early Detection of Reading Difficulties.* While I propose the same accuracy rate as Clay for independent reading (at least 95 percent), I recommend that word accuracy for instructional-level text be between 92 percent and 97 percent. (Clay recommends that it be between 90 and 94 percent.) The reason for this difference may be that Clay presumably has in mind the assistance children receive in one-on-one Reading Recovery situations, while I'm referring to a small-group guided reading model.

Making Sure Children Read a Variety of Genres

At the end of a reading conference, I checked Griffin's Weekly Reading Logs and learned that he'd read only fiction for the past couple months. I want to help him find factual texts about topics in which he's interested.

When I notice children aren't reading enough factual texts and poetry, I intervene to help them select some. During the conference, we talk about topics they're interested in, and go to the leveled book pots together to see what we can find.

Although informational texts often have fewer lines of text on a page and many more illustrations and diagrams than fictional text, they are often more challenging. Whereas fiction is written in a narrative style and contains language and experiences most children can relate to, factual texts contain concepts, vocabulary, and organizational features that are less familiar. Therefore, I'm careful when helping children select informational texts and poetry.

Helping Children Select a Range of Books in a Particular Genre

Joan's a fluent reader who enjoys reading and generally selects books on her own from the "green" book pots. During a reading share, she mentioned that for the past two weeks she'd only been reading books from "The Box Car Children" series, sometimes even two at a time, just in case she gets bored with one. I want to introduce Joan to some other chapter books she might enjoy as much.

Just as it's important that children read a variety of genres, it's also important that they read a range of material within a genre. Although it's quite normal for a child to fall in love with a particular series or author and want to only read those books, I need to familiarize her with other titles and series. There's so much literature out there—so many authors with diverse styles, writing about so many interesting characters and time periods—that I'd be remiss not to help her broaden her horizon. I'd never recommend that children stop reading altogether the particular books that they love, unless of course, they were somehow harmful or inappropriate. But I do encourage them to vary the books they read. And it's fun to watch as "new books" become "old favorites."

CHILD-INITIATED READING CONFERENCES

Once a child gets over his initial apprehension about meeting with me for a conference, he's generally willing and eager to meet. When he sees that he alone is the star, and that my purpose is not to criticize but to show him ways to improve, then he wants to meet—sometimes too often. The children ask for conferences when:

They Want New Books

Jasmin thought the books in his book bag were too easy so he asked for a reading conference to "give his books up." For the past few weeks, he'd been working hard practicing "Henry and Mudge" and "Nate the Great" books to become more fluent. He realizes he's close to being able to try some early chapter books, a goal toward which he's been working for a long time.

Children most often ask for conferences to get new books because they've read the books in their bags—often several times—and now think they're too easy. Occasionally they want to give them all back, but usually they ask to replace only the "easy" ones. I love watching them decide which to keep and which to put back, making a pile of "books that are too easy" and a pile of "books they want to practice more." And it's amazing to see how well they know themselves as readers.

My children understand the importance of practice and rereading, and consequently, seldom read books only once. In fact, emergent and early readers often read books over many times until they get really good at them. As I conferred with Jasmin, I said I hoped he wouldn't be disappointed if the chapter book he tried was too difficult. He said he wouldn't be. It would just mean he'd have to practice more. "It's like you always say: 'Jasmin, if you don't practice, you won't get better.' And so I read and read and read and read." What's hard to read the first time becomes easier the second, third, and even fourth time.

They Get a Reminder Note in Their Assessment Notebooks

Because of the note I left for him at the end of our last conference, Jeffrey asked for a conference when he finished reading *Mummies in the Morning*.

At the end of each reading conference, I write a note to remind the child of a reading strategy he should practice, or action he should take. (See Figure 4–3.) Sometimes it reminds him to ask for a conference after he's read a particular book so I can check his comprehension or his written response. This practice helps the children follow through on the work we decided upon during their conference.

In addition, if I discover that I haven't met with a child for a while or that there's something about his reading I want to examine more closely, I write a reminder note asking for a conference on our next scheduled conference day. They're always better at remembering than I am, and the notes serve as an extra reminder.

Leaving notes for children who can't read yet presents a challenge at the beginning of the year. I had to find a way to let these children know what to practice during independent reading. So I draw a picture on the stickers in addition to a brief note. Figure 4–4 shows a variety of notes I might leave for emergent readers.

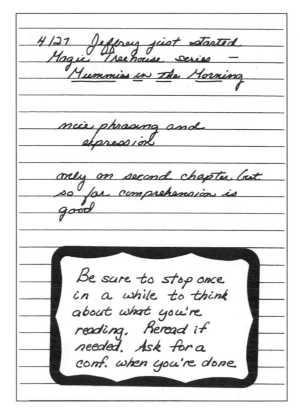

FIGURE 4–3

Reminder Note to Jeffrey

They Want Me to Hear Them Read

Lily raised her hand when I asked who wanted a reading conference. When I asked "why," she shrugged her shoulders and said: "I just want to read for you."

We all enjoy an audience sometimes, and children are no different. Often children ask for a conference because they want me to hear them read, usually a text they've read before. They know they're making progress, and want to be sure I know it too.

In addition to making sure the book is an appropriate match for the child, I may also listen for fluency and expression. If I notice a child unnecessarily pointing to words, I ask her to read without pointing. If I notice her reading word by word, I encourage her to try chunking words into phrases that mimic her speech.

FIGURE 4–4

Picture Reminders

They Want Help Finding Poetry or Factual Texts

When Jessica checked her Weekly Reading Log, she saw she hadn't read any poetry or factual texts for the past several weeks and asked me to help her find some.

When children are at the beginning stages of reading, it's not uncommon for most of their reading to be fiction. But as they move into the late early and transitional stages, they're able to handle different genres and more complex text.

After a few weeks of reading only fiction—it's quite obvious from the page upon page of red boxes on their Weekly Reading Logs—they see that they need to read more poetry and factual texts. I tell them that over a period of several weeks, these boxes should be as colorful as the foods on their plates when they're eating a balanced diet. A diet of fiction alone isn't enough.

Children, especially younger ones, don't always know for sure if their books are fiction or factual. They realize that fairy tales and other fanciful stories are "not true," but get confused with realistic fiction, where the story "could have happened, but didn't." This leads to discussions about the difference between fiction and factual text throughout the year until they grasp this distinction more fully.

Managing Reading Conferences

The predictability of the workshop structure underpins both the children's work and mine. The children know that if they're not having a conference, they should read independently. They know that at the end of each workshop, I'll ask a couple of them to share with the class what they learned that day about themselves as readers. Because they know the routines, they settle right into their reading and stay on task longer.

Likewise, the workshop structure—in fact, the organization of my total literacy program—helps me remain focused on assessing children's strengths and needs during reading conferences. Since I design my teaching to include opportunities to assess children's reading and address their needs, I can more adeptly attend to the assessment issues at hand, confident that I've also built in additional times for demonstration, practice, and response. I'm constantly striving to become more aware of how each part of my teaching supports and extends the others.

Distributing the Reading Folders and Settling In

At 9:30, at the end of the meeting, I begin the transition to the reading workshop. I remind the children to find a quiet spot to sit, alongside someone who won't distract them from their reading. I also remind them to check the reminder notes in their assessment notebooks.

Before I hand out the reading folders, I select one folder to check. (See Chapter 3 for more information on reading folders.) I always ask

"And who's the lucky one today?" I "think aloud" as I check how well the child has kept up his Weekly Reading Logs and whether or not he's reading a variety of genres. I also check that he's responding as frequently as he should, but not too much, at the expense of reading. Looking through one folder and commenting on what I find serves as a gentle reminder to the other children of what they, too, should work on during the reading workshop.

Then I take the first three folders and read off the child's name on the front of each. The child whose name I read first takes all three folders from me—while the other two children leave the meeting area. He distributes their folders. I continue to give out the rest of the folders, three at a time, until each child has his.

I wait a minute or two for the children to settle into their reading. Since the workshop structure is set in September, and the children are matched with books for independent reading, I can hold thoughtful, focused conferences while the rest of the children read books that appropriately support, interest, and challenge them.

Orchestrating the Conferences

The children bring their reading folders and book bags to the conference table. With four or five children sitting around a table awaiting their turn, I'm compelled to move through each conference quickly, and there are immediate consequences if I don't. Who wants a disappointed child complaining that he didn't get the help he needed finding new books, or that I broke my promise to meet with him? This system helps to ensure that I carry out the conferences I've scheduled.

As I confer with the child to my left, the others practice reading their books as they await their turns. At the end of the conference, the child with whom I've already conferred changes seats with the child directly to his left (see Figure 4–5). Then, that child takes his assessment notebook from his folder, opens it to the next page, and sets it facing me to signal the start of the conference.

Once reading conferences begin, I don't allow interruptions. Barring an emergency, the rest of the class works independent of my help.

Being Explicit Throughout the Conference

THE START OF THE CONFERENCE

I begin each conference by asking the child why he wanted a conference or explaining why I wanted one. By establishing the purpose at the onset, I'm better able to focus on the child's specific needs and my goals, making our meeting more productive.

- I explain to Amelia that I want to see if she's self-correcting when what she reads doesn't make sense or match the letters. I'll pay close attention to this as I take a running record of her reading.
- Samantha asked for a conference because she wants help finding a new series of books. She finished the "New Kids of the Polk Street School" series, reading four of the six books. She started the other two, but didn't like them.

DURING THE CONFERENCE

During each conference, I share with the child what I'm noticing about her oral reading, how well she seems to be understanding what she read, and her reading habits in general. I try to show her what she did well and which practices need improvement.

- I show Amelia her running record and point out the times she self-corrected to make sense and match the letters. By circling her self-corrections, I highlight her effective use of this strategy, encouraging her to use it more.
- Although I keep in mind Samantha's request for a new series and eventually help her find one, her comment at the start of the conference led me to wonder why she didn't finish two of the six books she started. Could it be that she didn't understand them as well as the others? Or that she didn't give them enough of a chance? Or was it because, as she said, she genuinely didn't like the stories, which is a legitimate enough reason for any reader to abandon a book? When I'm convinced that she was able to understand the stories, but just didn't enjoy them, I help her find a new series. (Please note that my children aren't required to read every book in a series before starting a new one.)

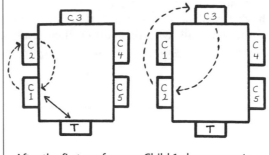

After the first conference, Child 1 changes seats with Child 2, and after the second conference, Child 2 changes seats with Child 3. This exchange of seats continues until I've met with each child.

FIGURE 4–5

Diagram of How Children Rotate Their Seats for Reading Conferences

THE END OF THE CONFERENCE

At the end of each reading conference, I'm explicit with children about what they are to do when they return to their independent reading.

- I remind Amelia to continue monitoring her reading so that it makes sense and matches the letters, and self-correct when necessary. I write a reminder note in her assessment notebook.
- I ask Samantha to request a conference when she has finished the first book in the new series. I want to make sure she understands it. I remind her that—while she's excited to finally be reading chapter books—reading without comprehending is not really reading at all. The most important thing is that she understand and enjoy what she reads. The note I leave reminds her to ask for a conference.

Conclusion

Our resolve to assess children's reading must be coupled with an environment and structures that make it possible. In Chapter 3, I described how I create a supportive environment, and in this chapter, I outlined the schedules and routines of successful conferences.

Most important to me are having assessment notebooks and set times and places to confer with children. These allow me to take running records of their reading to learn more about strategies they use and find ways to help them read more effectively. I ask them to retell stories they've read to see how well they understood them, and I talk with them about their reading to see what they like and dislike, how they feel about themselves as readers, and the goals they've set. The assessments that occur during reading conferences truly underpin my teaching. I am a better teacher because of them.

Taking Records of Children's Oral Reading

SARAH ASKED ME FOR A READING CONFERENCE. She'd found a book during our day's first independent reading session that she said she'd like to try. As we sat for our conference, she opened her assessment notebook to the next clean page, then turned it toward me so I could take notes on her reading. She knew I'd want to. All my children know I like to keep a close watch on the strategies they use.

As Sarah read, I listened for how closely her reading matched the text. When it did, I made a check for each word she read accurately. When her reading digressed from the text, I used one of several notations to indicate what she'd done (see Figure 5–1). Without taking running records of her reading, I could never remember how Sarah read on any given day and put it together with what she'd done over the course of several days and weeks.

Simply stated, a running record is a graphic account of a child's oral reading. Unlike writing, where the written pieces themselves become the records of growth, reading is a process that occurs in the brain without tangible and permanent evidence of a child's activities. Therefore, running records provide the information I need to make wise teaching decisions. They help me:

- decide whether the book a child is reading is matched to her stage of reading development
- analyze a child's miscues to see which cueing systems and strategies she uses and the ones she might learn to use more effectively
- track a child's reading progress over time

First we'll take a brief look at how running records came into being and a description of how to take them, then review the three benefits they provide.

A Historical Perspective

Ken and Yetta Goodman were among the first researchers to extensively analyze the cues children take from text. They wanted to learn more about children's reading processes by observing their reading behaviors, specifically their miscues. Ken Goodman coined the term *miscue* to describe any deviation the reader makes from the actual words of the text, recognizing that these are not random occurrences, but logical, systematic representations of how children understand the reading process and the cueing systems they use.

Ken Goodman's research, described in "A Linguistic Study of Cues and Miscues in Reading" (1965), demonstrates that, in addition to taking visual cues from print when they read, children also cue into the flow of language—its structural similarities to oral language and its meaning. The teacher needs to look closely at children's reading behaviors and help them revise their "theory of reading" to take more fully into account *each* of these textual cues—letter-sound relationships, meaning, and structure.

Marie Clay developed the running record, outlined in *An Observation Survey of Early Literacy Achievement*, which is a method of observing and recording a child's oral reading using any text he happens to be reading. Because of Clay's work with running records, a teacher no longer needs to prepare in advance copies of text for recording her observations of a child's reading. She just takes a piece of paper (in my case, a notebook), sits alongside the child, and makes notations to describe his reading.

Running records can be taken with relative ease, allowing teachers many more chances to record children's oral reading than if they were preparing text beforehand or relying on a publisher's pre-packaged assessment tools. Years ago when I used a basal reading series, I gave each child an informal reading inventory (IRI) at the start of the school year using different levels of text within the basal series; I needed to find their instructional levels so I could group them for guided reading. My focus, however, was only on counting errors, not analyzing them. Although IRIs have improved since I first used them, they often fail to provide enough insight into children's reading strategies and are impractical for on-going classroom use.

In contrast, running records provide greater flexibility and many more opportunities for assessment since they can be taken "on the run" using *any* text a child is reading. Being able to take and analyze frequent running records of children's reading throughout the year provides distinct advantages. First of all, they become more of a *tool for teaching* rather than an instrument to report on children's status in class or stages in reading. The explicit information running records provide directs students to appropriate texts and reading strategies. While it may be argued that this is also possible with informal reading inventories, it's unlikely, because of the preparation and planning they require.

Second, running records can be taken frequently, allowing teachers to learn about a child's *pattern of errors*. There's a critical difference between appraising a child's reading of a single text and analyzing her reading of several texts over time. The latter provides more insight into what the child usually does, making instruction more targeted and effective. As noted in Peter Johnston and Marie Clay's chapter on "Recording Oral Reading" in *Knowing Literacy: Constructive Literacy Assessment*: "An individual error is less informative than a pattern of errors, and the clearer the pattern, the more helpful it is for informing teaching."

Third and simply, as with any method of measurement, the *more samples* you take the more likely you are to get an accurate picture of the child's reading. Running records allow me to collect and analyze dozens of samples of a child's reading throughout the year to inform my teaching.

Taking an Oral-Reading Record

When children ask for conferences, as Sarah did, or when I ask a child to meet with me, it's because there's a payoff. Children who request conferences need me to affirm what they're already doing well, suggest new reading strategies to try, or help them find better books to read. When I ask for a conference, I want to make sure they're reading appropriate books and learn which cueing systems and strategies they use as they read so I can reinforce them and demonstrate others. Running records are an integral part of my teaching, leading the way because they express what children are doing.

I take running records in children's assessment notebooks when I confer with them at the back conference table. Either the child decides on the book from her bag or I select one because I want to see whether or not what she's reading is a good match for her stage in reading. Conferences that include running records may take ten minutes, a little longer than when I ask children to retell a portion of the text they've read or talk with them about their reading. They also take longer at the beginning of the year when I'm trying to match children with their first set of books for their book bags and still getting to know them as readers.

That's why on any given day, I try to include a range of readers at different stages to confer with. This helps me to get to all the conferences I've scheduled, rather than meeting with one novice reader after another. Even in kindergarten classes where most children are just learning to read, I try to include one or two more skilled readers in with the others.

Notations to Record Children's Oral Reading

With few exceptions, the notations I use to record children's oral reading are the ones described in Marie Clay's book *An Observation Survey of Early Literacy Achievement*. We owe a debt of gratitude to Clay for making this assessment procedure so accessible to classroom teachers. (See Figure 5–1 for a chart of notations I use to record children's oral reading.)

I've taken the liberty to adapt some of her notations and procedures to suit my classroom needs. For teachers interested in a detailed

FIGURE 5–1 Notations to Record Children's Oral Reading

Accurate Reading	$\checkmark$ (or) / *text word*
Substitution	*spoken word* *text word*
Attempt	*attempt* *text word*
Self-Correction	*spoken word* (SC) *text word*
Insertion	*spoken word* *spoken word* ∧ (or) —
Omission	— *text word*
Repetition	*text word* R
Skip and Return	SK *text word* // …
Asks for Help	A *text word*
Told the Word	*text word* T
Try Again	[*spoken word* *spoken word…*] TA [*text word* *text word…*]
Teacher Prompt	*text word* (TP)

analysis of running record procedures, I highly recommend Clay's *An Observation Survey of Early Literacy Achievement.*

All notations written *above* the line represent actions the *child* has taken. All interventions *I* make are written *alongside* the text word I've recorded, with the exception of the "R" notation for "Repetition," which is written to the right of and just a little below the notation for the word or phrase the child is repeating. When two notations are described together in the following section, for example "Substitutions and Attempts at Words," an example of the first is on the first line and an example of the second is on the next line.

The following is a description of the notations I use.

ACCURATE READING

Text:	Child's Reading:	Running Record:
We went to the store	We went to the store	/ / / / /
to buy some ice cream.	to buy some ice cream.	/ / / / /

I record each word a child reads accurately with a check (✓) or a tick mark (a slanted line "/"). I keep my eye on the child's text as I record my notations so they follow the same format as the text the child is reading.

SUBSTITUTIONS AND ATTEMPTS AT WORDS

Text:	Child's Reading:	Running Record:
We went to the store	We want to the store	*want* / went / / /
to buy some ice cream.	to buy so-me ice cream.	*so-me* / / some / /

When a child comes to a word he doesn't know, he naturally stops to figure it out. He might substitute an incorrect word for the word in the text. If he does, I record the text word, draw a line above it, and write the substitution above the line.

I also record all his attempts (with letters representing the sounds he makes) on the line above the text word. Then if the child gets the word, I make a check or tick alongside his initial attempts. An attempt may be considered a substitution when, through his intention, the child represents it as his reading of the text.

Some experts advise writing the miscue as the child says it, and then coming back when the child has finished reading to record the actual text word on which he miscued. Although this does allow the teacher more time to closely observe and record the child's attempts at the word, I prefer to make *all* my notations—both the miscue and the text word—as I go. Even if it means putting my hand on the child's arm to let her know she needs to pause for a moment so I can catch up. I also find that my record of words a child hesitates on (even if she eventually gets the word)—indicated by the text word and line above it—gives me additional information about her facility in reading the selection.

SELF-CORRECTIONS

Text:	Child's Reading:	Running Record:
We went to the store	We went to the story store	*story* (SC) / / / / store
to buy some ice cream.	to buy some ice cream.	/ / / / /

When the child substitutes a word for one in the text and then corrects himself, I write "SC" alongside the substitution. Self-corrections are important indicators that the child is monitoring his reading, cross-checking his information sources (cueing systems) against one another, and using additional sources of information to make corrections as needed.

INSERTIONS AND OMISSIONS

Text:	Child's Reading:	Running Record:
We went to the store to buy some ice cream.	We went to the big store to buy ice cream.	/ / / / ^ / big / / some / /

When a child inserts a word, I indicate this with a caret (^) and write the word the child has added above it. Or I record the word with a line under it and a dash below it to show there is no match for the word in the text, for example, (big̲).

When a child omits a word, I record the text word with a dash above it to show he left the word out. I use the same symbols to represent times when children fail to stop for "end of sentence" punctuation marks (omit— ꞊), or pause inappropriately (insert— ꞈ).

REPETITIONS AND "SKIP AND RETURN"

Text:	Child's Reading:	Running Record:
We went to the store to buy some ice cream.	We went we went to the store to buy [skipped "some"] ice cream [returned] some ice cream.	/ / R / / / / / some SK / / ↓

When the child repeats a word, I record an "R" just a little below and to the right of the check or tick that indicates the word she's repeating. If she repeats an entire phrase or sentence, I make an "R" and draw an arrow back to where she started repeating. R₂ and R₃ means she's repeated it two or three times.

When the child tries a word but is unsuccessful, she might skip the word and read on a little, often to the end of the sentence, before coming back to try the word again. I show this with an "SK" and a bi-directional arrow pointing to where she read to and where she returned to before trying the word again. (I've added this notation myself because I find it's a helpful strategy for early readers. They, unlike most emergent readers, are usually willing to skip a word and then come back to it.)

ASKS FOR HELP

Text:	Child's Reading:	Running Record:
We went to the store to buy some ice cream.	We went to the [child asks for help] to buy some ice cream.	/ / / / store │A / / / / /

When the child tries to figure out a word but can't, he may ask for help. If he does, I record the text word, make a vertical line to separate his first attempt/s from his appeal, and write "A" above the line to the right of the vertical line to show the child asked for help.

TOLD THE WORD

Text:	Child's Reading:	Running Record:
We went to the store to buy some ice cream.	We went to the store to buy some [he is told the word] cream.	/ / / / / / / / ice │T /

If after trying a word the child is unable to get it, I tell her so she can continue reading. I record a "T" next to the text word.

TRY AGAIN

Text:	Child's Reading:	Running Record:
"Willy," said Tom "Where are you going?"	Willy and Tom were going	⎡ and ⎢ / said / ⎢ were going ⎣ Where are ⎤ TA

When a child reads a sentence and makes miscues that are likely to compound themselves as he continues to read, I sometimes intervene to ask him to go back to the beginning of the sentence, paragraph, or page to try again. I bracket the section he's retrying and write the notation "TA" alongside it.

TEACHER PROMPTS

Text:	Child's Reading:	Running Record:
We went to the store to buy some ice cream.	We went to the store to get some ice cream. [teacher prompt]	/ / / / / get ↰ / buy / / / TP

When the child attempts a word or makes a substitution, but is unable to self-correct, I sometimes prompt her to help get the word. I write "TP" in the margin, circle it, and then draw an arrow to the notation to which it refers. In this instance, I might prompt her to look at the letters in "buy" and think about what sounds they represent.

On other occasions, I might recommend she think about what would make sense and/or sound right, recall what happened so far in the story, or check the illustrations. My intent is that the child will eventually internalize these prompts and use them to get the word or self-correct on her own. (See Chapter 10, "Teaching Reading Strategies One-on-One.")

* * *

Depending on my purpose for taking a running record, I may or may not intervene as the children are reading. If I want to match children with books or determine their stage in reading, I try not to intervene at all—or as little as possible. If it's later in the year and I want to demonstrate a strategy or remind children of practices they should be initiating on their own, I may intervene occasionally with teacher prompts or suggestions that they try again.

Counting "Errors"

As the child is reading or when I'm analyzing her reading to learn how she perceives text, I refer to her deviations from the text as *miscues*, but later, when estimating her rate of accuracy,

I call them *errors*. I prefer this to only calling them errors because it highlights the fact that they are more than just mistakes. They give us a sense, however incomplete, of the child's understanding about text. Later, when I'm counting them to figure out a child's percent of word accuracy, I call them errors. (See Figure 5–2 for some guidelines for counting errors.)

I determine a child's accuracy rate with a text by counting her "errors" and comparing this to the total number of words she's read altogether. For example, if a child miscues on 6 words out of 100, her accuracy rate is 94 percent.

Generally, a child needs to read at least 100 words to provide a large enough reading sample for me to determine how well she can read a text of comparable difficulty. However, if she's reading an emergent level book that contains fewer words, it's sufficient for her to read it through just once. At other times, the sample may be longer.

If the child makes between 1 and 5 miscues every 100 words and has a satisfactory understanding of the text, I feel confident that she'll be able to read this and comparable books successfully on her own, and will use a variety of strategies when she comes to words she doesn't automatically know.

Estimating the Rate of Accuracy

When determining a child's accuracy rate with a book, I don't use an algorithm to compute the percentage of errors. It's enough for my purposes to *estimate* the rate of accuracy from the

---

FIGURE 5–2 Some Guidelines for Counting a Child's Errors

- Each substitution (except for proper names) is counted as one error.

- If a child fails to supply the correct word, his combined attempts at the word—regardless of how many—are counted as one error. (If a child gets the correct word after several attempts, it does not count as an error.)

- A self-correction is not an error.

- Insertions and omissions are counted as errors.

- Repetitions and "Skip and Returns" are not considered errors.

- When the child asks for help or is told a word, it is counted as an error.

- When a child is asked to "try again," the entire bracketed section is counted as one error, regardless of how many substitutions were made within that section.

- A teacher prompt is not counted as an error, but the initial substitution is, regardless of whether or not the child eventually gets the word. Additional attempts at the word are not counted as errors.

ratio of errors to total words read. For example, in the first running record to follow you'll see that Sarah made 12 errors out of 131 words. To find her approximate rate of accuracy, I think to myself: 10 percent of 131 words would be about 13 errors, and Sarah did a little better than that because she made only 12, so her accuracy rate with that text is about 91 percent. I ask one or two key questions either during her reading, if the text is longer or I think she's not understanding it, or after she's done.

I'm comfortable estimating accuracy rates because, realistically, it's the best I can do in a classroom setting. I don't presume to be a Reading Recovery teacher or a trained reading diagnostician. I try to learn as much as I can about my children's reading, and then use that information to inform my teaching. My assessments aren't perfect, but they're definitely better than not learning about my children at all.

While all errors are counted, they're not all treated with equal weight. Those that interfere with meaning or indicate a child no longer understands what he's reading are counted fully. Others are less significant and occur quite naturally even among the most proficient readers.

For example, if a child reads "Danny said" for "said Danny" as Sarah did in the running record which follows, this "counts" as two errors, but neither carries the weight of the more consequential errors she makes, such as reading "dozens" for "dishes" and "but" for "that." (See Sarah's running record of *Liar, Liar, Pants on Fire!* which follows.) I consider the *import* of each error along with the total *number* of errors the child makes when estimating a child's rate of accuracy with a given text. Therefore, an accuracy rate of 93 or 94 percent *might* be acceptable for independent reading if several errors were less significant ones.

Marie Clay categorizes books a child can read with 95 percent to 100 percent accuracy as *easy*, and those that can be read with 90 percent to 94 percent accuracy as *instructional*. When a child's word accuracy rate is below 89 percent, the book is *hard* and best used in situations where there is more support, for example read aloud and shared reading.

In translating Clay's levels of text difficulty into my classroom practice, I've adapted them as described in Figure 5–3.

Books children can read with between 95 percent and 100 percent word accuracy are suitable for independent reading. For guided reading situations, I try to find books that the children can read with 92 percent to 97 percent accuracy. This means that there are some books

FIGURE 5–3 Guidelines for Teaching Based on Text Accuracy

95%—100%	Just right for independent reading
92%—97%	Just right for guided reading
Below 92%	Too difficult for children to read by themselves, but may be just right for read aloud and shared reading

in the 95 percent to 97 percent range that I can use for guided reading as well as recommend for independent reading. To facilitate children's progress, I prefer to err on the side of the book being too easy rather than being too difficult.

When I meet with children for guided reading, I want them to know enough of the words so they can devote most of their attention to effectively using the reading strategies I've noted. If the text is too difficult, children are likely to focus too much on figuring out words they don't know and too little on the strategies I want them to practice. Even when the strategy the children need to work on is "attending to visual cues," they can do this as effectively when they come across fewer, rather than more, unfamiliar words.

Using Oral-Reading Records to Match Children with Books

During the first month of school, I use both my reading and writing conferences to learn about the developmental stages my children are reading at and to match them with books they can read on their own. Running records, along with retellings and reading discussions (discussed in Chapter 4), are the assessment tools I use.

The books best suited for independent reading offer children just the right balance of supports and challenges. They enable children to engage in reading for extended periods of time and use a range of strategies and information sources when they meet new words. They're typically books children can read within a 95 percent to 100 percent rate of word accuracy.

If children read books that are too difficult, it's unlikely they'll be able to sustain their independent reading long enough to practice the skills they need to work on. In addition, once the meaning of the text is lost, as generally happens when a book is too hard, children must resort to sounding out each unfamiliar word they meet. They need to read books that support their use of background knowledge and language structure, as well as letter-sound relationships.

Throughout the year, I continue to confer with children, helping them find new books for their bags. Matching them with "just-right" books allows them to use a variety of information sources and strategies as they read and stay engaged in their reading longer. This gives me the time I need to work with guided reading groups and confer with other readers.

Finding a "Just-Right" Book for Sarah

I usually have a "heavy hand" in helping children, especially emergent and early readers, select books for independent reading. Most new books for their book bags are selected during reading conferences. Occasionally, however, a child will find a book herself and then ask for a conference to see if it's "right" or not. This was the case with Sarah.

During the day's first independent reading time, Sarah found a book that she thought she'd like to try. Although she was making good progress in reading, she was growing impatient with herself. She was eager to get to the "harder books" that many of her classmates had recently begun reading. Sarah asked for a conference so I could hear her read *Liar, Liar, Pants on Fire!* by Miriam Cohen. This would be the first time she read it.

SARAH'S RUNNING RECORD OF *LIAR, LIAR, PANTS ON FIRE!*

Sarah had no trouble reading the title, leading me to assume she had previously heard the chant, "Liar, liar, pants on fire," and had a working knowledge of the story's theme. Consequently, I didn't introduce the book, as I often do, to give her added support.

The extent to which I introduce a text depends on a child's stage in reading and my purpose for taking the running record. If I want to see if it's a good book for a child to read on her own, as was the case with Sarah, I may not introduce the book much at all, but just state the title and a sentence or two about the book, if I happen to know about it. On the other hand, if I want to provide some added support for chil-

dren when they're reading it independently, as well as learn how they handle the text and the strategies they use, then I may discuss it in greater length before they start reading. I'm much likelier to give lengthier introductions to emergent readers, who rely on outside support to help them with the challenges of acquiring this new skill, than to children at the other reading stages.

See Figure 5–4 for Sarah's Running Record of *Liar, Liar, Pants on Fire!*

Counting Sarah's Errors and Estimating Her Rate of Accuracy

Immediately after taking this running record for *Liar, Liar, Pants on Fire!*, I counted Sarah's errors. (Sometimes I record a tick for each error the child makes at the right-hand margin of the line in the notebook where the error was recorded, and then I circle them, e.g. "⟨ / / ⟩" for two errors. More often, I just hold the count in my head.) At this point, I don't spend time analyzing the *types* of miscues/errors the child has made. First, I want to see whether or not the book she's reading is right for her. Most of the time, this is fairly obvious. Consider this brief analysis of her reading:

- On page one, Sarah made three errors. She read "/sh-o-ters/" for "shooters," "so" for "that," and "Bersters" for "Boosters."
- On page two, she made two errors. She read "him" for "them" and "medal" for "model."
- On page three, she made three errors, reading "ak-tin" for "action" and "said Danny" for "Danny said." Although she initially read "track" for "trick," she corrected herself.
- On page four, she made no attempt at the word "Chanukah," so I told her.
- On page five, she made three errors. She omitted the word "a," said "really" for "real" and "pointy" for pony.
- At the end of page five, I interrupted Sarah's reading to ask if she understood what had happened so far in the story. She said, "They're asking all kinds of questions. Sara was telling about her new hamster, and everybody wants to know about it. And Alex asked: 'Is it a really [sic] pony?'" Then I pressed further, asking, "So what's Alex doing all the time?" I'd hoped she'd realized that he'd been lying to his friends (even though this isn't stated explicitly in the text until page seven). And Sarah said, "He's

FIGURE 5–4 Sarah's Running Record of *Liar, Liar, Pants on Fire!*

Text, p. 1	Page 1:	Running Record, p. 1
Danny told Jim what he wanted for Christmas.	Danny told Jim what he wanted for Christmas.	/ / / / / / /
"It's a racer car, with rocket shooters in the back.	It's it's a racer car, with rocket sh-sho-ters in the back [pause] in the back.	↓√ R / / / / / sh–shō–ters / shooters ↓√ / / / ⌐ R
And it goes two thousand miles an hour!"	And it goes two [pause] thousand miles an hour.	/ / / / / / thousand / / /
"How can it go that fast?" Jim asked.	How can it go so fast? Jim asked.	/ / / / so / that / / /
"Boosters," Danny said.	Bersters, Danny said.	Bersters / Boosters / /

Text, p. 2	Page 2:	Running Record, p. 2
The new boy, Alex, heard them. "I've already got	The new boy, Alex, heard him. I've already got	/ / / / / him / them / / /
one of those. But mine is a triple-rocket model.	one of those. But mine is a triple-rocket medal.	/ / / / / / / / / medal / model
It goes two thousand miles an hour."	It goes two thousand miles an hour.	/ / / / / / /

Text, p. 3	Page 3:	Running Record, p. 3
"Has it got trick-action?" Danny wanted to know.	Has it got track trick ak-tin? Danny wanted to know.	/ / / track ⓢⓒ / trick ak–tin / action | T / / / /
"Of course," Alex said.	Of course, Alex said. Of course, Alex said.	↓√ / / / / ⌐ R
"Let's build a fort, Jim," Danny said.	Let's build a fort Jim, said Danny.	/ / / / / said / Danny Danny / said

Text, p. 4	Page 4:	Running Record, p. 4
At lunch, Sara was telling about her new hamster.	At lunch, Sara was telling about her new hamster.	/ / / / / / / / /
"I'm going to call her Chanukah,	I'm going to call her [long pause] [teacher told—Chanukah].	/ / / / / Chanukah | T
because that's when I got her."	because that's when I got her.	/ / / / / /

Text, p. 5	Page 5:	Running Record, p. 5
"I have a pony," Alex said.	I have a phony [pause] pony, Alex said.	phony ⓢⓒ / / / pony / /
"Is it a real pony?" George wanted to know.	Is it really pointy? George wanted to know.	— really pointy / / a real pony / / / /
"Could I see it?"	Could I see it?	/ / / /
"Sometime, but not today. He's sick," said Alex.	Sometime, but not today. He's sick, said Alex.	/ / / / / / / /

always asking questions." She hadn't understood that George and Jim were asking Alex, the new boy, questions about the things he claimed to have. In fact, the part about Sara's new hamster was the only part she seemed to relate to and accurately recall.

Sarah's accuracy rate—12 errors out of 131 words or about 91%—together with her inadequate understanding of the story, indicated that this book was too hard for her to read independently. However, I noted on my clipboard that other books from Miriam Cohen's series about "Jim and his first-grade friends" might be suitable for Sarah in a guided reading group setting.

Then we went to the book pots together and selected some other books for her to try. Noting that *Liar, Liar, Pants on Fire!* had too many characters and too much dialogue to provide the kind of support she needed, I sought out books that were more straightforward. Of the new books we gathered for her book bag, the one she wanted to read first was *The Lad Who Went to the North Wind* by Ann Douglas.

SARAH'S RUNNING RECORD OF *THE LAD WHO WENT TO THE NORTH WIND*

Before Sarah started reading, I gave a brief introduction by reading the title and the following publisher's summary on the back of the book: "The North Wind gives a poor boy magic gifts to make up for blowing away all his flour. But somehow, the gifts always seem to lose their magic." I explained that now she'd read about how this happened.

See Figure 5–5 for Sarah's running record—*The Lad Who Went to the North Wind.*

Counting Sarah's Errors and Estimating Her Rate of Accuracy

After taking this running record, I noted:

- On page three, Sarah made no errors. She had trouble figuring out "piled," but got it

---

FIGURE 5–5 Sarah's Running Record—*The Lad Who Went to the North Wind*

Text, p. 3	Page 3:	Running Record, p. 3
Once there was a lad who lived with his mother, a poor widow.	Once there was a lad who lived with his mother, a poor widow.	✓✓✓✓✓✓✓ ✓✓✓✓✓✓
One day she sent her son out to the storehouse to get some flour to bake bread.	One day she sent her son out to the storehouse to get some flour to bake bread.	✓✓✓✓✓✓✓ ✓✓✓✓✓✓✓ ✓✓✓✓
The lad piled a good bit of flour into the dish and started walking back to the house.	The lad pled pl- pi- piled a good bit of flour into the dish and started walking back to the house.	pled | pl-pī | ✓ / piled // ✓✓ ✓✓✓✓✓✓✓ ✓✓✓✓✓ ✓

Text, p. 4	Page 4:	Running Record, p. 4
But the North Wind came by, puffing and blowing, and blew all the flour away.	But the North wind Wind came by, puffing and blowing, and blew all the flour away.	✓✓✓ wind (SC)/Wind ✓ ✓✓✓✓✓ ✓✓✓✓✓
So the lad went back to get some more flour, but this blew away too.	So the land [pause] lad went back went back to get some more flour, but is this blew away too blew away too.	// land (SC)/lad ✓✓/R ✓✓✓ // is (SC)/this ✓✓✓✓/R
The third time the lad tried, the North Wind blew it all away again.	The bird [pause] third time the lad turned, the North Wind blew it all again.	/ bird (SC)/third ✓✓✓ turned/tried / ✓✓✓ —/away /

(continues)

FIGURE 5–5 (*Continued*)

Text, p. 5	*Page 5:*	*Running Record*, p. 5
The lad was angry.	The lad was angry.	////
He thought he would go to the North Wind and ask for the flour back.	He thought he would go to the North Wind and ask for the flour back.	////// ////// //
He walked and walked and at last he came to the North Wind's house.	He walked and walked and at last he came to the North Wind's house.	////// ////// //

Text, p. 6	*Page 6:*	*Running Record*, p. 6
"Good day!" said the lad. "Thank you for visiting us yesterday."	Good day! said the lad. Thank you for visiting us yesterday.	///// ///// /
"WHAT DO YOU WANT?" boomed the great voice of the North Wind.	What do you want? b-um-ed, boo-med [teacher told—"boomed"] the great voice of the North Wind.	//// $\frac{b\text{-}um\text{-}ed \mid b\bar{o}\text{-}med}{boomed \qquad \mid T}$ // /////
"Would you please give me back all the flour you blew away?"	Would you please give me back all the flour you blew away?	///// ////// /
"We are poor folk, and we can't afford to lose it."	We are poor folk and we need [pause] can't [pause] afford to lose it.	///// $\frac{need \;\text{ⓢⓒ}}{cant} \quad \frac{/}{afford}$ ///

Text, p. 7	*Page 7:*	*Running Record*, p. 7
"I haven't got your flour," said the North Wind more gently.	I haven't got your flour, said the North Wind more g-ent-ly [pause] glently [pause] gently.	////// //// $\frac{j\text{-}ent\text{-}ly \mid glently \mid /}{gently}$
"But I can give you a magic cloth which will set itself with dishes of food when you say, 'Cloth, cloth, spread yourself.'"	But I can give you a magic cloth which will set itself with dozens of food when you say, cloth, cloth, spread yourself.	/////// ////// $\frac{dozens}{dishes}$ ///// ////

Text, p. 8	*Page 8:*	*Running Record*, p. 8
The lad thanked him, and began to walk home.	The lad thanked him and began to walk home.	///// ////
But the way was so long that he stopped at an inn to spend the night.	But the way was so long the way was so long but he stopped at an [pause] ine [teacher told—"inn"] to spend the night.	$\sqrt{} ////// \quad \frac{but}{that} /$ /// $\frac{ine}{inn \mid T}$ ////

after several attempts at sounding out the word.

- On page four, she made two errors. She also self-corrected four other substitutions, demonstrating her ability to monitor her reading of this text for meaning, structure, and letter-sound relationships.

I interrupted Sarah's reading at the end of page four to ask if she understood what was happening. She said: "The third time he (the boy) tried, the Wind blew all the flour away." This wasn't exactly what had happened, since the Wind blew the flour away from the boy *all* three times. But I was encouraged by her self-corrections and her comments about the story (to follow later in this section), so I let her continue reading.

- On page five, she made no errors.
- On page six, she made one error. I told her the word "boomed." Although she read "need" for "can't," she self-corrected.
- On page seven, she made one error, reading "dozens" for "dishes." After several attempts, she got the word "gently."
- On page eight, she made two errors. She read "but" for "that." And after she said "īne" for "inn," I told her the word.

  Throughout the reading, Sarah's comments and her ability to use her background knowledge, demonstrated that she understood the story:
- As she looked at the first page, she noticed the picture of the windmill, and said: "They must be grinding the wheat into flour." She inferred this from our class study of New Amsterdam where the early colonists used windmills for this purpose.
- After reading page three, she paused to ask: "Can I get those fairy tale books that I used to like?" She was referring to the *Once Upon a Time 9–14* series that we have in our leveled book pots. This folktale must have reminded her of them.
- After reading page four she said: "The boy looks like he's Dutch from the way his clothes look." Both this comment and her earlier one about the windmill show she was trying to use background knowledge to understand what she was reading.
- After she read the word "afford" on page six, she commented: "At first I said 'af-id,' in my mind, and then I asked myself, 'Does that

make sense?' It didn't, so I changed it to 'af-ford'."
- When she read that the lad would spend the night at the inn, she asked, "What about his mommy? If he's spending the night, won't she be worried?"

I interrupted Sarah's reading at the end of page eight to ask what was happening. She said, "The North Wind gave him food and said you have to say, 'Cloth, spread yourself' and then you'll have a feast."

Then I asked if she knew what might happen next. She looked through a few more pages of the book and said, "He'll come home and bring it to his mommy, and it didn't work." She kept looking through the book, and revised her thinking. "Now I'm looking at the pictures. The man stole the real cloth and gave the boy a fake one."

- Sarah asked again if she could take several of the fairy tale books that she mentioned earlier to put in her book bag. She said, "Even though I read them before, I want to read them again. I enjoy them." Of course I said she could.

At this point in the reading, I had enough information to make a decision about the appropriateness of this text (and others like it) for independent reading. Since Sarah made only 6 errors out of 252 words, her accuracy rate was about 97 or 98 percent. In addition, her comments and interaction with the text indicated this text was just fine for her to read alone.

Note that in this running record, Sarah made 5 self-corrections out of 11 miscues (the times she read something different than what the text said, before her self-corrections), as compared with her reading of *Liar, Liar, Pants on Fire!* where she only corrected 2 of her 12 original miscues. This illustrates that when books are at children's independent reading levels (between a 95 percent and 100 percent rate of accuracy), they're better able to combine their use of semantic, syntactic, and graphophonic cues, helping them read more effectively. They can't do this when a book is too hard.

It's also important to note that when children understand what they're reading, they often comment on the story as they go. Many times they don't wait to be asked what the story is about, but may react to the story as they read.

So what started with, "Sharon I need a conference because I want you to hear me read," ended with me helping Sarah identify books more suited to her abilities as a reader, her asking to read more of the fairy tale books we have in class, and me noting that other books by Miriam Cohen about "Jim and his first-grade friends" might be good choices for a guided-reading group.

In a way, Sarah knew her conference would be "bigger" than her just reading to me. It always is! Each time I confer with children, I try to relate what I already know about their reading to what I learn during the conference, and then use that information to direct my teaching. Each thing we do in our classroom is related to everything else. Making these connections is part of what it means to teach. It's also what it means to learn.

Using Oral-Reading Records to Learn About the Cueing Systems Children Use

While it's essential to help children find appropriate books by counting the errors in their running records and estimating their rate of accuracy, it's equally important to use running records to access children's "thinking." Miscues have a logic of their own, conveying children's understanding of what it means to read.

When children read, they need to consider what makes sense (semantic or meaning cues), whether their reading sounds like the form of English most of us accept as standard (syntactic or structural cues), and whether what they read matches the sounds the letters in words represent (visual or graphophonic cues). By looking closely at the substitutions they've made and the cues they've used to self-correct, I can learn which cueing systems children use most effectively and which they still need to adopt.

Assessing Sarah's Substitutions and Self-Corrections

Once I'm confident children are reading books that appropriately support and challenge them, as I was after Sarah read *The Lad Who Went to the North Wind*, I can look more closely at their use of the three cueing systems. While I don't have time during the reading conference

to scrutinize each running record, I do assess children's substitutions and self-corrections to get a better sense of what they've done. The insights I gain allow me to help them integrate additional cueing systems and strategies into their repertoire.

With this in mind, let's look at the substitutions and self-corrections Sarah made while reading *The Lad Who Went to the North Wind*. I need to restate, however, that while it is informative to assess children's substitutions and self-corrections on any given running record, it's even more enlightening to consider their pattern of miscues gathered from several *successive* running records, as this collective record is more indicative of their typical reading behaviors. Throughout the following discussion, I refer specifically to Sarah's miscues—which are her errors—and to her self-corrections.

- *On page four*, Sarah made six miscues (four of which she self-corrected).
- *Line one*: In the phrase "But the North Wind came by," Sarah read /wĭnd/ for "Wind," and then self-corrected at the point of the miscue. When she miscued, she appeared to be using visual cues (V) as she was trying to use a spelling pattern she knew, "-ind" (as in find), to figure out "Wind." However, she wasn't using meaning (M) or syntax (S), as /wĭnd/ didn't make sense or sound right in the context of this story. When Sarah realized this, she combined meaning, syntax, and graphophonics to self-correct. (In this and all further "analysis" of Sarah's substitutions and self-corrections, I infer which cueing systems she used based on her behaviors. There's no way to get "inside" her head to know for sure what she was thinking.) Note that after each analysis, I've circled the cueing system/s she used for each substitution—"M" for meaning, "S" for syntax and structure, and/or "V" for visual.

Substitution: M S Ⓥ Self-Correction: ⓂⓈⓋ

- *Line three*: Instead of reading, "So the *lad* went back to . . . , Sarah read, "So the *land* . . ." She paused a little after reading "land" which leads me to believe that she was reading on a bit in her mind, even though she didn't actually say the words. Then she self-corrected, changing *land* to *lad*. Here she used visual and structural cues for her substitution (up to that point "land" is the right kind of word for its place in the sentence), and added meaning to self-correct.

Substitution: M Ⓢ Ⓥ Self-Correction: ⓂⓈⓋ

• *Line four*: Instead of reading, "So the lad went back to get some more flour, but *this* blew away too," she read, "So the lad went back to get some more flour, but *is* blew away too. It appears that she initially relied only on visual cues, but used meaning and syntax to self-correct. (Sarah may have confused "is" and "his." If this was the case, the substitution "is" would make more sense than the way I've interpreted it.)

Substitution: M S Ⓥ Self-Correction: ⓂⓈⓋ

• *Line five, miscue one*: Instead of reading, "The *third* time he . . . ," Sarah read, "The *bird* . . . ," using the "ird" spelling pattern in "third" and structural cues first. Then she immediately self-corrected for meaning. Her initial focus on the "ird" spelling pattern is similar to what happened on page 4 when she read /wīnd/ for "Wind." We'd been learning how to use known spelling patterns to figure out new words so Sarah may have been overattending to this strategy.

Substitution: M ⓈⓋ Self-Correction: ⓂⓈⓋ

• *Line five, miscue two*: Instead of reading, "The third time the lad *tried*," she said, "The third time the lad *turned*." She used visual and structural cues, but not meaning. Although "turned" didn't make sense in this story, she didn't self-correct.

Substitution: M ⓈⓋ Self-Correction: M S V

• *Line six*: Instead of reading, ". . . blew it all *away* again," Sarah read, ". . . blew it all again." She omitted the word "away," but didn't self-correct. She used meaning and syntax, but not visual cues (since she omitted the word altogether).

Substitution: ⓂⓈ V Self-Correction: M S V

• *On page six*, Sarah made two miscues and self-corrected once.

• *Line three*: Sarah tried to sound out the word "*boomed*," but couldn't. After several attempts, I told her the word.

Substitution: M S Ⓥ Self-Correction: M S V

• *Line seven*: Instead of reading, "We are poor folk, and we *can't* . . . ," Sarah read, "We are poor folk, and we *need* . . . ." Then she self-corrected. She used meaning and syntax for her substitution, and then added visual cues to self-correct.

Substitution: ⓂⓈ V Self-Correction: ⓂⓈⓋ

• *On page seven*, Sarah made one miscue.

• *Line four*: Instead of reading "*dishes* of food," she read, "*dozens* of food." She didn't self-correct. She used meaning to a limited extent and visual cues even less—only attending to the "d" at the beginning of the word and the "s" at the end.

Substitution: Ⓜ S Ⓥ Self-Correction: M S V

• *On page eight*, Sarah made two miscues.

• *Line two*: Instead of "But the way was so long *that* . . . ," she read, "But the way was so long *but* . . . ." Here she actually used all three cueing systems. Visual: she attended to the final "t" in both words. Structure: since she repeated "the way was so long" and then said "but," she was grammatically correct. Meaning: "but" makes sense.

Substitution: ⓂⓈⓋ Self-Correction: M S V

• *Line three*: Instead of reading, ". . . he stopped at an *inn* to spend the night," she read, ". . . he stopped at an "*ine*" (/īne/) . . . ," using visual cues. After making this substitution, she stopped because she knew "ine" was wrong, but didn't know how to fix it. She appeared to have never heard of an "inn." I told her the word and what it meant so that she could continue with her reading.

Substitution: M S Ⓥ Self-Correction: M S V

DRAWING CONCLUSIONS FROM SARAH'S READING

As we review Sarah's substitutions and self-corrections, we can't help but notice her tendency to use visual cues (and structure to a lesser extent) as she reads, and then add meaning to self-correct. However, we need to be careful not to overgeneralize from such limited information. We need to look at additional running records to see if this pattern persists. Remember it's the child's *pattern of miscues* over time that gives validity to the information we gather and the conclusions we draw.

Since I keep all my running records of children's reading in their assessment notebooks, I can easily look back to see which cueing systems they've used most consistently. The running record I took before *The Lad Who Went to the North Wind* was for *Nate the Great and the Missing Key*, a book Sarah had read once or twice before, according to my notes. Of the 234 words she read from the "Nate the Great" book, she made eight substitutions and two self-corrections. Of the eight substitutions, she used visual or graphophonic cues—but not meaning—for five of them. She added meaning on both self-corrections.

So from just these two running records, there appears to be a pattern developing. One that I certainly want to consider when working with Sarah during reading conferences and throughout the reading workshop. I want to:

- affirm what she's doing well, namely, using visual and sometimes structural cues initially, and then adding meaning to self-correct
- help her integrate the use of meaning with visual and structural cues in her *initial* attempts at words, while continuing to self-correct as needed

I didn't analyze Sarah's miscues on *Liar, Liar, Pants on Fire!* because it wouldn't have given me the information I needed on her use of the cueing systems. The book was too hard for her. I would *expect* her (as I would any child reading books that are too hard) to rely heavily on visual cues when what she's reading doesn't make sense or sound right. Instead, I want to learn which cueing systems she uses while reading books that are "just right" or at least close to her independent reading level.

Two Common Patterns in Children's Reading

The following patterns are ones I've noticed most frequently in children's reading. When I consider which cueing systems children use when they read, I look for their areas of strength—which cueing systems they use well—and then which sources of information they need to use more consistently. Sometimes I write "M S V" alongside the substitution in the child's notebook and then circle the one/s I observe her using. At other times, I just look through the substitutions to get a sense of what the child's doing. Once again, I adapt to the classroom circumstances at any particular time.

CHILDREN WHO USE VISUAL AND STRUCTURAL CUES, BUT NOT MEANING

Readers who use visual/graphophonic and structural cues, but not meaning, need to add semantic cues to their repertoires. I'm not saying these children use visual/graphophonic and structural cues exclusively and never use meaning as they read, but that they need to use meaning more consistently.

In addition, these children are often less consistent in their use of structural cues than visual ones. The extent to which they use structural cues depends on how well they understand that what they read needs to sound right and how capable they are of cueing in to English syntax. In the previous example, Sarah used structural cues well, while Hiro and Chad (below) didn't.

- Sarah understands that many of the words she is trying to read can be "decoded"—that is, she knows there's a somewhat dependable relationship between many letter patterns and the sounds they represent—and so she uses visual cues as her primary source of information. In addition, she obviously has a strong sense of how the English language sounds, as this comes into play in her initial attempts at words. Then, when she miscues, she often self-corrects by adding meaning. (See examples from her running record and my analysis of her substitutions.)
- Hiro speaks Japanese at home. When he reads English, he generally lacks a solid enough understanding of its complexities to be able to use meaning and structure effectively. Some examples of the substitutions he makes are /cas/ for "case," /clenned/ for "cleaned," /penles/ for "pencils," and /herslef/ for "herself." Constance Foland, his English-language teacher, tries, along with me, to help Hiro consider meaning and structure when he reads. We want him to understand that he can't say words that don't make sense and keep right on reading.

Since Constance comes into the classroom to work with Hiro instead of "pulling him out," she writes notes about his reading and what they've worked on in his assessment notebook. I can read what she's working on and she can see what I'm doing. We both want to help Hiro become more aware of times when his reading doesn't make sense, and self-correct when he can.

- When Chad entered my class midyear, he could barely read. When I took running records of his reading, I noticed he relied almost exclusively on visual cues without taking meaning into account. After talking with his parents, I learned that in his former school, he had been instructed to "sound words out." And so this was what he was doing. In fact, this was all he was doing.

When he came to words he didn't know, he "huffed and puffed" out the sounds, and rarely used either meaning or syntax. He seldom self-corrected because he hadn't been taught to consider the three cueing systems together.

CHILDREN WHO USE MEANING AND STRUCTURE, BUT NOT VISUAL/GRAPHOPHONIC CUES

Readers who rely primarily on meaning and structure need to add visual/graphophonic cues to their repertoire. They need to understand the importance of accurately reconstructing the author's message. They shouldn't be making up their own story as they read; the time for that is when they write.

- Amelia relied heavily on meaning and syntax right from the start of the year. When she entered first grade she was just beginning to read. At that time, she only read three of the twenty high-frequency words on the Ohio Word Test accurately. (See Appendix K for the Ohio Word Test.)

The first book she brought to our reading conference was *The Big Egg* by Molly Coxe. When she came to a word she didn't know, she often substituted a word that made sense and began with the same initial sound as the text word she was trying to figure out. But she didn't attend closely enough to the sounds represented by the middle and ending letters. For example, she read the sentence: "'This is not my egg!' says Hen," as "There is one. My egg. See Hen." This early in the year, Amelia didn't know enough sight words or have a broad enough knowledge of letter-sound relationships to help her figure out unknown words. So she relied mainly on meaning and structure.

In addition, she frequently didn't attend closely enough to other visual cues on the page. Either she didn't "notice" periods, exclamation marks, quotation marks, or capital letters, or didn't understand their function. So she constructed her own version of the text as she read.

Even when we found books that were better suited to her stage in reading, Amelia continued to rely heavily on semantic and syntactic cues. Several weeks later, her running record of *Animals at the Zoo* by Rose Greydanus showed that instead of reading, "At the zoo, you can see big animals. You can see <u>little</u> animals," she said, "At the zoo, you can see big animals. You can see <u>small</u> animals." She seemed not to have considered that "small" begins with an "s" and has a /s/ sound, and "little" begins with an "l" and has a /l/ sound.

Although Amelia's reliance on meaning was partially due to the fact that she hadn't yet learned enough about letter sounds, she at least needed to become aware that this is a goal to strive toward. But, in addition, helping children *use* the skills they do have is often a challenge in and of itself. For example, although Amelia "knew" that "s" represents a /s/ sound, she didn't apply this when she read the word "small" for "little." Her attention needs to be directed to the fact that, in addition to making sense and sounding right, what she reads must also match the sounds of the letters in words she's trying to read.

This is where advocates of "decodable" texts (texts that are written to match the sequence of letter-sound relationships that have been "taught") might argue that their method ensures that children have the phonetic skills to handle every text they read. But I find that this lock-step method is too controlled and unnatural for most children and teachers, and that it encourages a narrow range of strategies when children come to words they don't know.

I prefer helping children find texts that support their strengths and needs, and encouraging them to try a broad repertoire of skills and strategies when they meet unfamiliar words. I know how to help Amelia. And when she's finally integrating all three cueing systems, she'll be better equipped to handle the range of text she's likely to read, and more flexible in her use of strategies.

Noting Progress over Time

By taking running records on children's reading throughout the year, I get to review the progress they've made from the beginning of the year to the end. One of my favorite end-of-the-year activities is to go through children's assessment notebooks with them and note the changes in their reading. Most often, they can't believe the progress they've made.

If I only reflected on children's growth at the end of the year, however, I would miss out on a lot of information about the child's reading that could have informed my teaching. So I build time into my reading conferences to regularly consider the progress children are making.

I've selected four excerpts of running records from Jasmin's assessment notebook that illustrate changes in his reading over the year. (Jasmin is a boy, by the way, whose name is pronounced "Yaz-meen.") His September running record of *A Zoo* by Andrea Butler shows that he is at the beginning of the emergent stage. In December and February, excerpts from his running records of Harriet Ziefert's *A Dozen Dogs* and Sid Hoff's *Sammy the Seal* document his movement from the beginning to the end of the early stage. In May, he was a transitional reader, just starting the "M & M" series with Pat Ross's *M & M and the Bad News Babies*. See Figures 5–6, 5–7, 5–8, and 5–9 for Jasmin's reading on September 11, December 15, February 2, and May 8.

As I typically can't record my observations as extensively as those that follow, these reflections are reconstructions of my thoughts at the time I conferred with Jasmin. But the key point I want to demonstrate is that my thinking about children's attitudes, understandings, and behaviors leads me to consider what I need to do to help them improve.

FIGURE 5-6 September 11—Jasmin's Reading of *A Zoo* by Andrea Butler

9/11 Jasmin brought
A Zoo to read

After he read, I read the book to him, pointing to and emphasizing each word — show how he had left "a" off. He reread book again.

Jasmin's at beginning of emergent stage. — 1/26 on Ohio Word Test.

Text:	Jasmin's Reading:
A lion,	lion,
a tiger,	tiger,
a monkey,	monkey,
a zebra,	zebra,
a giraffe,	giraffe,
a bear . . .	bear . . .
A zoo.	zoo.

September 11—Some Reflections

1. Jasmin is eager to read this book, which he selected from the table book pots, and seems enthusiastic about reading in general. I need to help him find his first set of "just-right" books for his bag.
2. Jasmin is at the beginning of the emergent stage. He only read one word, "the," correctly on the Ohio Word Test I gave him on September 8. As he read, he looked at the picture of each animal before he "read" the page.
3. He didn't attend much to the words and never attempted to sound them out. In fact, as he read, he omitted the article, "a," before the name of each zoo animal and before the word "zoo" itself.
4. I wonder about Jasmin's concepts about print. When he reads a line of text, instead of one word, will he know to move from left to right? Will he make a one-to-one match between words he says and words on the page? Jasmin and I have a lot of work ahead of us.

FIGURE 5–7 December 15—Jasmin's Reading of *A Dozen Dogs* by Harriet Ziefert

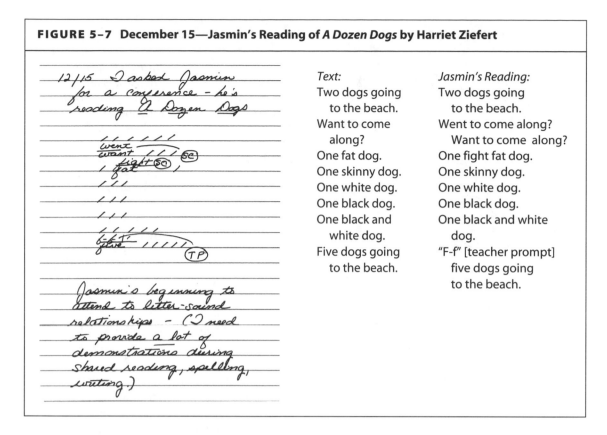

Text:
Two dogs going
   to the beach.
Want to come
   along?
One fat dog.
One skinny dog.
One white dog.
One black dog.
One black and
   white dog.
Five dogs going
   to the beach.

Jasmin's Reading:
Two dogs going
   to the beach.
Went to come along?
   Want to come along?
One fight fat dog.
One skinny dog.
One white dog.
One black dog.
One black and white
   dog.
"F-f" [teacher prompt]
   five dogs going
   to the beach.

December 15— Some Reflections

1. Jasmin selected *A Dozen Dogs* from his book bag to read. I've noticed he enjoys rereading books. He's quite happy reading them again and again until he "gets them right."

2. He's tracking print and has learned some high-frequency words. This is showing up in his writing as well. In September, he only wanted to copy text from books, now he knows how to write a few words from memory and "invents" the spelling of the rest. Our work in spelling and writing is definitely supporting Jasmin's reading development— and the support is in both directions.

3. Of the three miscues he made, he self-corrected two of them. He's beginning to understand that it's his responsibility as a reader to get the author's message right.

4. Although he still uses the illustrations as he reads, he now uses them more to confirm what he's read, rather than predict.

5. He's beginning to sound out unfamiliar words and look closely at the sequence of letters in the words. Where before, he was hardly attending to the words at all, now, he's looking closely at the beginning and ending letters and trying to match the sounds. (I need to keep teaching letter-sound relationships during shared reading sessions and word study groups, and encourage Jasmin and others to make sure what they read matches the letters. I've also got to get my spelling pattern word wall in full swing. The "at" spelling pattern in "fat" is one Jasmin should have recognized.)

6. I'm surprised Jasmin didn't know the word "five." (I'll check to be sure the number words are on the high-frequency word wall and call the children's attention to them so they can use them when they read and write.)

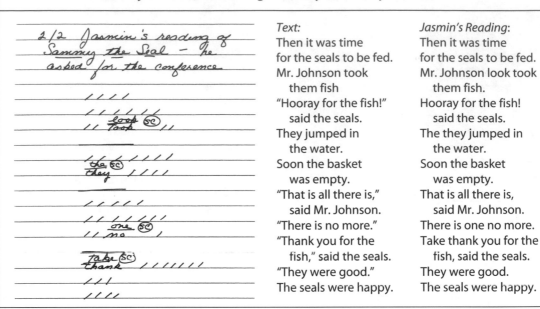

FIGURE 5–8 February 2—Jasmin's Reading of *Sammy the Seal* by Sid Hoff

Text:	Jasmin's Reading:
Then it was time	Then it was time
for the seals to be fed.	for the seals to be fed.
Mr. Johnson took	Mr. Johnson look took
them fish.	them fish.
"Hooray for the fish!"	Hooray for the fish!
said the seals.	said the seals.
They jumped in	The they jumped in
the water.	the water.
Soon the basket	Soon the basket
was empty.	was empty.
"That is all there is,"	That is all there is,
said Mr. Johnson.	said Mr. Johnson.
"There is no more."	There is one no more.
"Thank you for the	Take thank you for the
fish," said the seals.	fish, said the seals.
"They were good."	They were good.
The seals were happy.	The seals were happy.

February 2— Some Reflections

1. Jasmin is pleased with the progress he's making, and so am I.
2. He still rereads a lot and is very serious about his reading. He refers to the books in his bag as the one's he's "working on."
3. Jasmin self-corrects a lot. He corrected all four of his miscues. He read this sample with 100 percent accuracy. He had read it several times before, though, getting better each time.
4. Jasmin has acquired a large bank of high-frequency words. On his second Ohio Word Test (List C) readministered in January, Jasmin read eighteen of the twenty words accurately. Because he's developing a mastery of high-frequency words, he now has the "mental space" to figure out words he doesn't automatically know. And each time he rereads a text, more and more of the words are given to memory. It's having a big impact on his reading.
5. Jasmin is beginning to read longer books. His first book of the year had eight pages, and now this one has sixty-four.

FIGURE 5–9 May 8—Jasmin's Reading of *M & M and the Bad News Babies* by Pat Ross

Text:	Jasmin's Reading:
Mandy put a pink sea	Mandy put a pink sea
castle	castle
into the fish tank.	into the fish tank,
Mimi added six	Mimi added six yellow
yellow stones	ston-is stones
that glowed in the dark.	that glowed in the dark.
The friends M and M	The friends M and M
had been fixing up the old	had been fixing up the old
fish tank	fish tank
all week.	all week.
"Now all we need are	Now all we need are
the fish,"	the fish,
said Mimi.	said Mimi.
"But fish cost money,"	But fish cast coast castle
said Mandy.	[skipped] money
	said Mandy. [returned]
	Cost money said Mandy.

May 8—Some Reflections

1. Jasmin is becoming so confident in his reading skills. When I complimented him on his reading of *Henry and Mudge and the Wild Wind*, the book he read before trying *M & M and the Bad News Babies*, he said: "You told me, 'Jasmin, you need to practice more' and I did. I read and read and read and read and finally I got all the words right."
2. He asked if he could try *M & M and the Bad News Babies*. This is the first chapter book he's tried and his first attempt at a book from this series. I was interested in what his rate of accuracy would be. If it's high, it will mean he's moving into the transitional stage. On this first page he only made one miscue in fifty words. So far so good!
3. Jasmin is comfortable reading this book. He interacted a lot with me and made comments about the book as he read. Congratulations, Jasmin!!

Conclusion

Some educators propose limiting the type of text available to young children when they're learning to read to control the words and concepts they encounter. This is based on the premise that children will read more successfully if teachers first present letter-sound relationships found in the text before the children attempt to read it. This logic oversimplifies and devalues a complex and exciting process.

We need to match children with books that are appropriate for their stage in reading. I do this repeatedly when I confer with children. Instead of trying to *control* children's reading, we need to *support* it.

Support is essential, but excessive control is restrictive, giving the child a skewed view of reading. Reading involves problem solving and meaning making. If we teach a child to rely only on graphophonics (the visual cues), and not meaning and structure, then it's like asking him to read with "one hand tied behind his back."

Programs that rigidly dictate and monitor (through the "unit" tests that follow presentations of specific skills) a decontextualized sequence of letters and sounds, and then provide stories that contain those phonetic elements, are wrongheaded. (Remember Billy's experience in Chapter 1?) We can't assume that just because letters, sounds, and patterns have been "taught," that children have effectively learned to *use* them. Children actually learn best when they understand how the pieces of the whole fit together and have lots of opportunities to practice all the pieces in the context of the whole.

Children need to:

- read books that are matched to their stage in reading
- learn to use a range of cueing systems and strategies flexibly
- see how all of what they're doing fits together and makes sense

Each of these objectives are furthered by taking running records of children's reading, analyzing them to learn what the children do well and how they might improve their reading, and then using that information to teach. Perhaps Jasmin expressed it best when he said: "I read and read and read and read and finally I got all the words." I like to think it's with my help, of course, and with the help of running records.

CHAPTER 6

Retellings and Reading Discussions

ONE MORNING IN MAY, I ASKED JASMIN TO meet with me for a conference. I wanted to see how well he understood the "harder" books we'd added to his book bag the last time we met. He told me all about *Deputy Dan and the Bank Robbers* by Joseph Rosenbloom. He loved the funny parts, giggling at how Deputy Dan talked to the door when Sheriff Digbee told him to "answer" it, and gave the robbers a bath because Sheriff Digbee called them "dirty crooks."

Once I was sure he understood the story, I asked if he'd ever read any *Amelia Bedelia* books. She, like Deputy Dan, does *exactly* what people tell her to do, and ends up doing silly things. Jasmin hadn't, but said he'd like to try one.

After we'd found a couple, Jasmin looked up at me and said: "This was like a conference, but not really." At first his statement surprised me. While there was no doubt in my mind that his retelling of *Deputy Dan and the Bank Robbers* and our brief discussion afterward about the kinds of books he enjoys was indeed a reading conference, Jasmin perceived a difference. He said: "Mostly you just listen to me read the book, and this time you didn't. We just talked."

Yet, during our other conferences—when I took running records of Jasmin's reading, matched him with books, and learned which cueing systems and strategies he used so I could help him add others—I was doing more than "just listening to him read." And likewise, during this last conference when I combined two assessment tools—a retelling and a reading discussion—we were doing far more than "just talking."

In this chapter, I'll describe how retellings and reading discussions help me assess comprehension and direct children to books that will engage and interest them. As with running records, these assessments drive my teaching.

Retelling as a Tool to Assess Children's Comprehension

In my early teaching years, I regularly asked children to write responses or answer comprehension questions to see how well they understood their books. Looking back, I realize that this approach stemmed from my skepticism—I didn't fully appreciate the intrinsic joy they get from learning, and thought I had to check up on them every step of the way. Wanting to hold the children and myself accountable, I thought there was no other way of knowing whether they understood what they read, or whether they read at all.

In addition, writing kept them busy while I worked with other children. How else, I thought, could I manage the class while holding three to four separate guided reading groups each morning? (For a description of what I do now with other readers while I conduct *two*, not four, guided reading groups, see Chapter 8.) But this seemingly productive routine had unanticipated, harmful effects. It may actually have discouraged children from reading. Who would want to read more, if it meant always having to write about it?

It also had a more proverbial, and more problematic, consequence. As described in Keith Stanovich's landmark study of the "Matthew Effect," "the rich got richer and the poor got poorer." The "rich" in my class—the children who were better readers—were also the ones who wrote better. They could write their responses more easily and get back to their reading, which would make them even better readers. Meanwhile the "poor"—those who were at the earlier stages of reading and writing—might spend the entire reading period writing. The very children who most needed practice to improve their reading skills were getting less time to actually read.

What Does Retelling Involve?

Now instead, I ask children to tell about what they've read so I can see how well they understand it. Children who are new to retelling often attempt to relate the entire narrative or factual text. When I asked Jessica to tell me about *Nate the Great* by M. W. Sharmat, she started off recounting each event as she turned the pages to remind herself of what had happened:

> It's about when Annie lost the picture of her dog. Then this girl, Rosamond, lost the kitty and when Nate the Great sat down he went, "Meow," and found the kitty. Then Rosamond said: "You found him." Then Annie and Nate the Great say goodbye . . .

I interrupted her and explained that she needn't tell the whole story, just the main things that happened.

Her second attempt was right on:

> Annie tried to find a picture of a puppy, but her brother hid it underneath another painting. The two heads were the ears and the last head was the tail. He figured it out 'cause it had four legs and mostly no monsters have four legs. And then 'cause all the other paintings were red. This one was orange. Then he figured out that yellow and red make orange. And then he said the picture he lost was a yellow picture.

All Jessica needed was a clearer explanation of expectations.

However, sometimes less secure readers "can't see the forest for the trees." They recount what happened page by page because they've never really put it all together in their minds. The book may be too hard; it may have taken too many days to complete. They may need to learn more comprehension strategies to handle longer text. Or a little of each.

But in general, I trust that if a child talks confidently and accurately about what she's read, she probably has a *reasonable* understanding and can go on, either with her current book or with other books of comparable difficulty. I can never be sure a child understands each and every element of a story, and I don't feel I need to. My children enjoy reading and are getting better at solving problems that arise. And they read a lot.

Reading Growth Requires a Change in Assessment Practices

When Jasmin started school in September, he was just beginning to match spoken words to print and learn letter-sound relationships. In fact, when I gave him the Ohio Word Test, "the" was the only word on the list he could read.

Jasmin worked hard throughout the year, and by the end could figure out most new words he met. He learned to monitor his reading and self-correct when things didn't make sense, sound right, or look right. Equally important, his responses to my queries and our discussions showed he genuinely understood the longer texts he had started to read.

And as Jasmin improved, the types of books he read also changed. His passage from the early stage of reading into the transitional stage was marked by his growing ability to read longer, more complex texts. Many took several days to complete. In addition, the role of the characters were changing. Whereas in emergent and early texts, the characters lacked depth and complexity and were used mainly as props to move the action along, in transitional and fluent texts, their behaviors and personalities drove the story.

The new feature in both *Deputy Dan and the Bank Robbers* and the *Amelia Bedelia* books was each character's too literal rendering of what others said to them. Jasmin could laugh out loud because he's smarter than the characters. He understood what they didn't. Where earlier Jasmin relied on a clear and straightforward delivery of the plot and centered most of his attention on figuring out new words, now he did more interpretation. And it often took more than one day to read a book.

With these changes came a change in assessment tools. The running record, the tool I'd been using to learn what strategies Jasmin used to figure out words, and the one or two questions I asked throughout to check his overall understanding, no longer gave me the information I needed. While I would still use running records occasionally to assess how accurately he could read new books he wanted to try, I now needed to learn how well he understood these longer, more involved texts. To accomplish this, I asked Jasmin to retell what he'd read.

How Jasmin's Retelling Shows He Understands the Story

I've included the entire transcript of Jasmin's retelling of *Deputy Dan and the Bank Robbers* in Figure 6–1, so we can examine it in detail.

However, it's important to note that when I ask children to retell texts they've read, I

FIGURE 6–1 Transcript of Jasmin's retelling of *Deputy Dan and the Bank Robbers*

Teacher: Jasmin, tell me about the book you're reading.

Jasmin: It's so funny. Cause um . . . first in the beginning, it's peaceful. There's no job. But then Elmer Stubbs comes in, and . . . it's so funny.

He's so tired and out of breath cause it's a hot day, and then he tells Sheriff Digbee and Deputy Dan about the bank robbers. The first plan they try was to trick the robbers into stealing the bank money again—but this time they'll catch them. But the robbers really steal the money again, and Deputy Dan and the sheriff don't get them.

Then the boss, Sheriff Digbee, he tells Deputy Dan to "pick up his horse," and he picks it up with a machine. Then he says, "No, I did not mean *pick up* your horse. I meant *bring* your horse and catch the robbers." And then Deputy Dan says, "You said, 'Pick up my horse," and he said, "I did not mean it."

And it was funny when he said, "Go get the door," and then Deputy Dan was talking to the door. He said, "I did not mean talk to the door. I meant open the door." And that's the part when Elmer comes in, and Elmer tells him the bank robbers were dirty crooks. And masked men.

And then he tells Deputy Dan to check the bank for cues. So Deputy Dan takes a crayon and makes a check mark on the wall, the ceilings, the furniture. He even checks Elmer. Then Elmer said, "It tickles." (He laughs.)

Teacher: It what?

Jasmin: Elmer said, "It tickles." I want to show you the page. (He opens the book to look for the page.) That's Elmer. That's why he looks so surprised. I want to show you. See. He's checking him. Then Deputy Dan says, "I do not find a single thing. I even checked Elmer Stubbs. He says it tickles."

Teacher: Does Deputy Dan ever find the bank robbers?

Jasmin: Yeah. He got them by staring at them. And staring at them longer and harder. Then they got scared and shaked, and they say, "Alright, you win." And then he catched them.

And then Elmer said, "Did you catch those dirty crooks?" Deputy Dan said, "The crooks are not dirty anymore." He said, "How come?"

I start out with a generic prompt to see where Jasmin takes it.

Jasmin starts retelling the story from the beginning, trying to relate the events in the order they happened. (Readers who are able to summarize more effectively frequently start with a general statement of what the text is about. Jasmin doesn't. He starts out with the first page, and then summarizes later and partially because of my prompting.)

Jasmin could hardly wait to tell about the funny parts—how Deputy Dan misinterprets what Sheriff Digbee tells him to do! He gives three examples, complete with his version of the dialogue.

I wasn't familiar with the book so I needed to ask him what he meant.

This is the first time Jasmin refers to the actual book, looking through it to find the page that supports his statement. (Some less confident readers over-rely on the text and illustrations as they retell the story. Jasmin's reference to the text shows a better understanding of the story.)

I ask this question to redirect Jasmin from the funny parts back to the plot.

And as soon as he answers my question, he directs me back to the funny parts!

Jasmin uses the text again to make his point.

(continues)

FIGURE 6–1 *(Continued)*

Then he says, Deputy Dan says, "I gave them . . . I told them to take a bath." It's at the end. I want to show you the page. It's somewhere in the back. (Jasmin finds the page he's looking for.)

Teacher: Oh yes, there they are on page forty-two.

Jasmin: Yeah, and he found out what . . . Deputy Dan, he found out what . . . I'll tell you. It's somewhere at the beginning. It's at the end too. (Jasmin looks through the book to find the clue that the robbers wrote on the notes they left.) They signed their names . . . (he points to the symbol "SGEG")—it means "EGGS"—see "EGGS"—like the eggs are all scrambled.

Teacher: Oh, so it's like a clue.

Jasmin: Yeah, scrambled eggs—cause they eat scrambled eggs. And the clue has the same letters in it, only scrambled. (Jasmin finds the page again.)

Teacher: Is that how he caught them?

Jasmin: Yeah. When they were eating scrambled eggs. Look. This is him, staring. (He points to Deputy Dan.) See . . . (Jasmin reads from the book.) "I stare at the men. I stare at them long and hard. Soon they begin to shake with fright. Finally they say, 'Okay, you win!' They tell me everything. They even show me where they hid the stolen money. The scrambled egg gang goes to jail." See . . .

Teacher: Oh, that's great. Did you read the whole book today?

Jasmin: Yeah, I read it two times.

Jasmin tried to explain the clue that Deputy Dan used to catch the robbers. When he has difficulty doing this, he tried to find it in the book. Once again, he's using the book to support his explanation.

He finds the clue.

It's obvious that Jasmin understands what he's read. He's able to talk about it confidently and accurately. And he even reads from the text to support what he's saying.

Hooray Jasmin! It's nice to learn that he's working so hard during reading time, and that he understands the value of rereading.

---

typically record only *portions* of what they say (see Figure 6–2).

It was obvious from early on in Jasmin's retelling of *Deputy Dan and the Bank Robbers* that he understood it well. He appreciated the humor and talked confidently about what had happened and the parts he enjoyed most. He used the text to support what he wanted to say, not to recall it.

Because it's impossible to know each and every book my children read, I need ways to help me assess their understanding. If I don't know the book, I look through it quickly before the child starts to retell it. If there's a summary on the back cover, I read it. I might also scan the table of contents and glance at the pictures,

if there are any, to get an overview. In many ways, I use some of the same strategies I ask children to use when they're starting a new book and want to get an idea of what it's about.

While the following statements refer to Jasmin's retelling, they exemplify some general qualities of effective retellings.

Jasmin Provides Both General and Specific Information

Jasmin's understanding of the story elements—setting, characters, main events, problem, and resolution—is revealed in his attempts to retell the story (at first quite literally and then more summarily), in his responses to my questions

FIGURE 6–2

Dari's Retelling of
The Snowball War
by B. Chardiet and
Grace Maccarone

```
12/13  I asked Dari to retell
The Snowball War

Bunny went back to
school - hurt back - BAT
shot snowballs at her -
when came home - did it
again - Brenda told
secret to Bunny - Cynthia
sad - they hide - Cynthia
crying - Martin and
Sammy on BAT's team
- throwing snowballs ...
(he understands)
```

Jasmin Refers to the Text Appropriately for Support

When Jasmin wanted to make a point or when he had difficulty explaining something that happened, as he did when he tried to describe the clue left by the robbers, he went to the text for help.

Sometimes children who are less sure of what they've read use the book and its pictures as props during the retelling. They page through the book to recall or even understand (for the first time) what happened. Jasmin didn't do this. He knew very well what happened, and used the text to help him communicate. He even read from the book to show me what he meant.

Jasmin Connected Emotionally to the Story

Jasmin loved this book because it was funny. In fact, "It's so funny" were the very first words out of his mouth. More than anything, he wanted to relate all the silly things Deputy Dan did. And when I tried to get him to talk about the sequence of events in the story, he obliged momentarily, but went right back to the funny parts and actually laughed out loud as he retold it. He had connected to the story and was moved by it. And what better motivation is there to read?

Jasmin Read the Text More Than Once

Jasmin read the book two times and, as you'll see in the second part of this chapter as his retelling changes into a reading discussion, he did this because he enjoyed the book, not because he didn't understand it. Although rereading is certainly a strategy I encourage when children are having difficulty understanding what they've read, in this instance, Jasmin's rereading was motivated by his desire to reexperience the story. Just the same, as he reread the text, his understanding of what happened grew even stronger.

about how the story turned out, and in the examples he offers to support his statements. Although he's unable to summarize the story and the character's quirkiness as precisely and independently as a more experienced reader might, he accurately recounts what happened.

Jasmin volunteered some of this information on his own, and some he gave with the help of my prompts. I only intervened with the question, "Does Deputy Dan ever find the bank robbers?" when I thought his preoccupation with the "funny" parts would keep him from getting to what happened, and two other times—once, to clarify a statement he'd made about how Deputy Dan caught the robbers, and again to ask if he read the entire book that day. His ability to confidently and accurately respond to my questions and then get back on track demonstrated a sound understanding of the story.

Jasmin's retelling was full of details. Not only did he relate instances where Deputy Dan misinterpreted what Sheriff Digbee asked him to do, he also recalled specific dialogue between the characters and knew where to look in the book to find the parts he wanted to share. When he wanted to show me how Deputy Dan gave the "dirty crooks" a bath to clean them up, he says: "It's at the end. I want to show you the page. It's somewhere in the back."

Although I was unfamiliar with this story before Jasmin retold it, what Jasmin said and how he said it sounded right. In addition, the title of the story, *Deputy Dan and the Bank Robbers*, cued me in to the plot, and at the very beginning, Jasmin told me it was funny.

And of course, I'm always asking myself whether what the child is saying is making sense. If the retelling sounds inaccurate or incomplete, I question the child further.

Procedures for Asking a Child to Retell Texts

When I want to know how well a child understands what he's read:

1. I EXPLAIN MY PURPOSE AT THE START OF THE CONFERENCE.

I explain that I'm trying to see how well he understands what he's reading. Then I ask him to "tell me about" the story or text. It doesn't matter whether the child has finished reading the text or is still reading it. He only needs to retell what he's read so far. If a child has just started a book, it would be wiser to wait until he's read a couple chapters before asking him to tell about it.

I leave it open for the child to begin retelling any way he chooses. Then I can see if he's able to summarize the story without my help or whether he needs me to prompt him. My explanation beforehand also conveys the expectation that comprehension is a requirement of reading.

2. I RECORD ONLY ENOUGH TO ASSESS HIS COMPREHENSION.

For Jasmin's retelling of *Deputy Dan and the Bank Robbers*, I tape-recorded and later transcribed his exact words to show readers of this book what they revealed about his understanding of the story. But in my day-to-day conferences, I don't do this.

I enter the date and the title of the book a child's retelling in his assessment notebook. As he retells the text, I record the gist of what he is saying in phrases, not whole sentences. (See Figure 6–2.)

After I've heard enough to decide whether the child understands the text, I make an ellipsis (. . .) to show the child had more to say but that I've stopped recording.

3. I DETERMINE HOW WELL THE CHILD UNDERSTANDS THE TEXT.

Sometimes children respond to the prompt: "Tell me about the story," by summarizing what they've read. This generally happens with more experienced readers.

Consider the following transcript of Elisa's retelling of *The Turkeys' Side of It: Adam Joshua's Thanksgiving* by Janice Lee Smith. Elisa asked for a conference because she wanted to know if she could start reading some of the "green" books (the fluent-level books). She'd borrowed a book from her sister over the weekend, and wanted to continue it in class. When I asked her to tell me about the story, this is what she said:

Elisa: It's when Adam Joshua's class is putting on a play of Thanksgiving and Adam Joshua and Nelson didn't get the parts they wanted. And Miss Cutwell was yelling a lot that they're not doing the right stuff. And it's going to be soon—the night before Thanksgiving vacation and the turkey costumes that Adam Joshua and Nelson have to wear look very silly.

Teacher: And so the story's almost over. Do you think anything exciting is going to happen at the end?

Elisa: The play's going to be okay. They're not going to look too silly.

Teacher: Who looks silly? (I really didn't remember who she's referring to.)

Elisa: Adam Joshua and Nelson. (Elisa laughs as she shows me the picture of Adam Joshua and Nelson in turkey costumes.)

Teacher: They're both turkeys.

Elisa: Yeah (and laughs).

Teacher: Oh, for heaven's sake. That is silly.

Elisa began her retelling by summarizing the part of the story she'd read without any further prompting from me. In one burst of enthusiasm, she included the names of characters, the exact day the play was to take place, and the problem the characters were dealing with. Throughout the retelling, she referred to the book only once—when she found the picture of Adam Joshua and Nelson in turkey costumes—to illustrate her point in response to my question. Elisa's precise summary and her confident and efficient delivery demonstrated that she understood the book.

After Elisa's retelling, I felt confident in her ability to read and understand many of the other books in the "green" pots and certainly more books in the Adam Joshua series. So for a while at least, I could meet with her less frequently. And Elisa certainly didn't need to respond in writing to each book she read.

I knew she was reading and getting better at it. I observed her during the workshop sitting off by herself, working very hard. I checked her Weekly Reading Logs to see that she was reading a variety of genres. I could see through our discussions and by her occasional written responses how efficiently she was relating books she'd read to one another and to her own life. Finally, by looking through her assessment notebook, I could evaluate her current reading in light of what she'd done earlier in the year.

Elisa was a self-improving reader. She would continue to improve by applying all she knew about reading to the different genres she tried. I would continue to include her in guided reading groups to help her become as confident reading factual texts and poetry as she was reading fictional text, and in book discussion groups to help her respond in her own unique ways. But for now, Elisa *could* and *would* get better at reading by reading.

I emphasize both "could" and "would" because years ago I thought this happened automatically. But now I know *my* very important role in making it happen. And because Elisa was set for a while, I could concentrate on the children who need a different kind of help from me—the children who don't understand what they're reading as well as Elisa does.

Many retellings are much more ambiguous. It's not always as clear as it was with Elisa whether they've understood what they read. I often need to take additional cues from their behaviors. The chart in Figure 6–3 contains guidelines for determining a child's understanding of the text he's retelling.

4. I NOTE WHETHER THE CHILD UNDERSTANDS WHAT HE'S READ.

When I've determined that the child understands what he's read, I note it by writing "He understands" alongside my record of his retelling. If he doesn't, I note that also.

5. I FIND OUT WHY A CHILD'S COMPREHENSION IS QUESTIONABLE.

When I think a child may not understand what he's read, I need to figure out why. The difficulty may lie at the *word level* or at the *text level*.

If his accuracy rate with a text he's reading independently is below 95 percent, it's reasonable to assume that his difficulty lies at the word level. There are too many words he doesn't know, and therefore, he has to focus most of his attention on figuring them out. He has little left over to direct toward the meaning of what he's reading. And if his accuracy rate is very low, it's likely that the text holds little meaning for him as well.

If his accuracy rate is 95 percent or higher, and yet he still doesn't understand what he's read, it may be that his difficulty lies at the text level. While he can articulate the words, he can't integrate the parts of the story into a meaningful whole. He may be used to reading shorter books that he could finish in one sitting, and now the stories he reads may take several days. These longer stories have more complex plots, with more characters, settings, problems, and events. A child in this situation may not be able to read with the fluency that good comprehension requires. Sometimes children with a nominally appropriate accuracy rate have had to read so slowly and work so hard at the words, that although they finally get them, their reading was too labored for them to hold on to what the author was saying.

This aspect of reading confuses many parents. They think that because their child can ar-

---

FIGURE 6–3 Guidelines to Assess a Child's Comprehension

When a child understands what he's read, he may:	When a child doesn't understand what he's read, he may:
begin by summarizing what happened	begin with a lot of details—getting very specific about what happened in the first couple pages. He may have only understood that part, or think this is what he's supposed to do.
use the illustrations to *support* what he's saying	over-rely on the illustrations to *tell what happened*
refer to the text to back up what he's saying	refer to the text too much *or* not at all
give examples	give no examples
appear confident and at ease	appear uncomfortable—sort of trapped. He may hesitate a lot, with many "ums."
spontaneously give information about the story or text	rely on the teacher's prompts to get through the retelling
respond emotionally to the text. He may love it or hate it. He may laugh or express how sad it made him feel.	not respond emotionally
make connections between this book and others he's read, or relate the book to experiences he's had	make no connection between this and other books, or between the book and his experiences

ticulate words, that they are reading. They fail to distinguish between reading with comprehension and "word calling" without a clear understanding of the meaning the words convey. And so these parents too often encourage the child to read harder texts than he is actually capable of reading, leaving him with little "mental space" to attend to comprehension.

This situation has a way of compounding itself. A child may be able to read one or two pages like this and know what's happening. But as he reads more pages, and reads over several days, what was manageable at first becomes increasingly problematic, causing him to work so hard that he no longer understands what he's reading. This scenario is all too common with children who are moving from the early into the transitional stage of reading. While they appear to be able to read the words, they're often unable to comprehend the story.

English-language learners have the added disadvantage of not bringing a rich oral English vocabulary to the texts they read. While they may be able to sound out the words accurately, they may not know what the words mean. It takes extra time and intervention from me and the English-language teacher to help them bridge the gap between words they can sound out and words and whole text they can understand.

Combining a Retelling and a Running Record to Learn Why a Child Doesn't Understand the Text

When I met with Christine, I asked her to retell M. W. Sharmat's *Nate the Great and the Snowy Trail*, the book she'd just finished reading. I wanted to see how well she could handle "longer" texts, since greater length is one of the challenges readers entering the transitional stage face.

Christine's retelling indicates that she didn't understand a lot of the story's key parts. (See Figure 6–4 for Christine's retelling of *Nate the Great and the Snowy Trail* and the running record I took afterward.)

I needed to find out whether this was because she'd read too many words incorrectly (in which case I'd help her select easier texts) or because she wasn't yet thinking about the story at the whole-text level (in which case I'd help her acquire comprehension strategies to understand these longer texts). The best way to determine this was to take a running record of her reading the text, and then, based on my

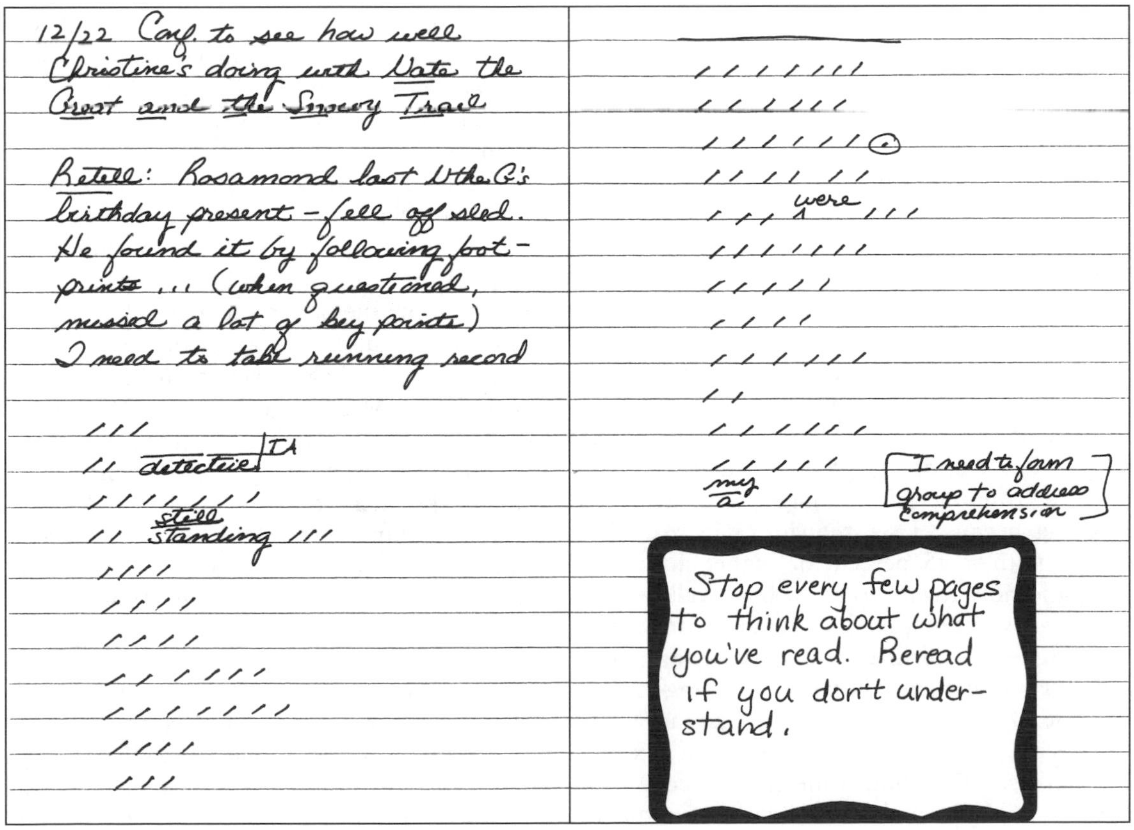

FIGURE 6–4

Pages from Christine's Assessment Notebook

analysis of her miscues, consider what to do next.

I analyzed her miscues to see how many times she substituted her own word for the text word, and whether they were the type of substitutions that would interfere with her understanding of the story. I found that of the 121 words she read, she made four errors. She needed my help with "detective" in the first sentence (this puzzled me because that word is central to each "Nate the Great" book).

Christine's first substitution, "I was *still* in the snow with my dog Sludge . . ." for "I was *standing* in the snow with my dog Sludge . . ." made sense. Her second one was reading, "She was pulling her four cats, Super Hex, Big Hex, Little Hex, and Plain Hex, on a sled" as two sentences. She read, "She was pulling her four cats. Super Hex, Big Hex, Little Hex, and Plain Hex *were* on a sled." She added "were" so it would make sense. And her last substitution *my* for *a* didn't change the meaning of the story at all.

Her reading of these two pages convinced me that her main difficulty with this text probably lay in her ability to integrate all the parts together into a meaningful whole, not in identifying individual words. This certainly changed how I would intervene.

If she had been having difficulty reading the *words*, I might have decided to give her an easier book. But since this didn't appear to be the case, at least based on the two-page sample of her reading. So instead, I noted in Christine's assessment notebook and on my Guided Reading Planning Sheet that she needed to be in a guided reading group where "Stopping to Think" was the focus strategy, and left a reminder note for her to reread parts of the story that don't make sense.

Many times at the start of a conference, I set out to implement one type of assessment—either a running record or a retelling—and find I need to switch to the other to get more information or check on the accuracy of what I've found. For example, a conference that starts with a running record might end with a retelling because I see the child can read the words with a 95 percent or higher accuracy rate, and now I want to know how well he *understands* what he's read. Or it may start with a retelling, as it did in Christine's case, and end with a running record because I'm trying to figure out *why* the child doesn't understand what she's read. Just as I want children to be flexible in their use of reading strategies, I need to remain flexible in my use of assessment tools,

moving from one to the other as the situation dictates.

Reading Discussions as a Tool to Assess Attitudes and Reading Preferences

Reading discussions help me understand children's attitudes about reading and the kinds of books they enjoy most. Sometimes they arise spontaneously in response to comments children make as they read orally or retell a text. At other times, the discussion is "planned," preceding or following a running record or a retelling.

"Impromptu" Reading Discussions

I try to create a relaxed atmosphere as I confer with children so that they can express their feelings about reading or comment on the kinds of books they enjoy. Their statements often prompt me to probe further.

For example, when taking a running record of Chelsea reading *Lulu Goes to Witch School* by Jane O'Connor, she looked up at me and said: "I don't want any chapter books." Since we were in the middle of a running record, I didn't stop right then to ask her what she meant, but I was surprised by her remark, especially since she wasn't reading a chapter book. After she finished we talked about what she meant by her comment: Had she ever tried reading chapter books? Were they too hard? Did she feel she had to read them? It turned out she was just letting me know that she didn't feel ready for them just yet, and that she was quite happy reading the books she had in her bag.

In another instance, when discussing how Amelia Bedelia always tries to follow the instructions in Mrs. Roger's notes, Jasmin recalled that one note said to "dust the furniture" and Amelia Bedelia thought this meant to put "dusting powder" on the furniture. He said: "That's the kind of books I like. Then I read them like a hundred . . . a lot of times. Cause it's so funny. Cause when they tell you to 'dust the furniture,' it means clean the dust off, not put the dust on."

This exchange with Jasmin wasn't planned, but as a result of it, I learned more about his interest in funny books. While his retelling in Figure 6–1 clearly showed he enjoyed the humor in *Deputy Dan and the Bank Robbers*, his impromptu comment indicated that this is the *kind* of book he likes to read.

This was valuable information because as Jasmin moved into the transitional stage of reading, it would become increasingly important that he select books with strong personal appeal. The books he would read from here on would be longer, requiring more of a commitment, and Jasmin would be more likely to commit to books he enjoyed.

Chelsea's and Jasmin's statements are good examples of the types children sometimes make in the midst of a running record, retelling, or while we're at the book pots looking for books. These comments often reveal useful insights about their reading, information I didn't set out to learn, but no less helpful for their serendipity. While I often learn about children's attitudes and preferences through these impromptu conversations, there are times I deliberately set out to learn more.

Planned Reading Discussions

There are two types of "planned" reading discussions. One is to gather *basic* information about a child's attitudes toward reading and the books he likes to read. These discussions usually take place during the first few reading conferences at the start of the year when I'm trying to help the child find a set of just-right books for his book bag.

The second type helps me gather more *specific* information about the child's attitudes and preferences so I can support his reading and direct him to books of a particular genre or ones that relate to a specific interest. These discussions take place as the need arises throughout the rest of the year.

GATHERING BASIC INFORMATION AT THE START OF THE YEAR

At the start of the year, when I'm helping a child select books for his book bag (it takes two or three conferences before we get it right), I need to help him find books he can read independently, and also enjoys. Instead of asking: "What kind of books do you like to read?" I state my inquiry as a prompt: "Tell me about the kinds of books you like to read." Prompts often elicit more productive responses than questions, giving the child less of an opportunity to say: "I don't know."

I'm particularly curious about the child's literate life outside of school. Does he enjoy reading? Does he read at home when he might be doing other things? Is there someone at home who reads to him? In each of my reading discussions with Sophia, Georgie, and Tiffany that follow, this one prompt—"Tell me about the kinds of books you like to read"—opens these and other topics up for discussion.

Figure 6–5 contains a transcript of Sophia's reading discussion during her second reading conference of the year.

During her first conference, she scored 20/20 on the Ohio Word Test, and I helped her select a few books from the leveled book pots for her book bag. I also took a running record of her reading one of them—*Nate the Great and the Halloween Hunt*. But at that time, I still wasn't sure how well she understood what she read, as I hadn't yet asked her to retell it.

By the time we conferred again, my observations of her during read aloud and shared reading discussions told me that Sophia was quite a capable reader and that the first books we'd selected for her book bag were, as I suspected, too easy. I hoped our reading discussion would enlighten me so that by the end of this or the third conference we'd find books that better matched her needs and interests.

I prefer to give a single prompt: "Tell me about the kinds of books you like to read" and see where it leads, rather than asking many questions. Young children can't respond in writing to a written survey as older children can, and I certainly don't have the time to record their responses to a lot of questions. More importantly, I find that I can uncover more interesting information by opening the discussion with this prompt and then asking supportive, clarifying, or extending follow-up questions.

Through my reading discussion with Sophia, I learned that she's a confident and probably proficient reader with specific tastes. (I didn't take a running record of Sophia reading *M & M and the Bad News Babies* by Pat Ross, but I "knew" from the running record I took of her reading *Nate the Great and the Halloween Hunt* that this book would be more appropriate.) At the time of this conference I didn't yet know how well she understood the "M & M" book she was reading, but she seemed to enjoy reading and said she read a lot at home. She has favorites from "The Young Collector's Illustrated Classics," such as *Heidi* by Johanna Spyri and *The Secret Garden* by Frances Hodgson Burnett, and she likes to read "thick" books but doesn't like to reread them. This conversation revealed information I could use to help Sophia select books and decide what she needs next.

FIGURE 6–5 Transcript of Reading Discussion with Sophia

Teacher: Sophia, tell me about the kinds of books you like to read.

Sophia: I like to read . . . I like to read the classics. And I like to read "Amelia Bedelia" and "Nate the Great."

Teacher: What do you mean " the classics?"

Sophia: Well. They're kinds of books. They're all the same, but they have different stories.

Teacher: They're all the same but they have different stories?

Sophia: They're books, but they're all "illustrated classics." Like *Peter Pan* and *Heidi*.

Teacher: I see. Do you have any favorites?

Sophia: *Heidi* and *The Secret Garden*.

Teacher: Why do you like those?

Sophia: Because I think they're good, and I like the stories.

Teacher: When you go to a bookstore or library, what books do you ask mom to get for you?

Sophia: I like illustrated classics and chapter books.

Teacher: What kind of chapter books? You mean like *Nate the Great*?

Sophia: Thick ones. I like thick ones.

Teacher: Why thick ones?

Sophia: Because I like to read a lot of them. Because most of the time when I have big books and I finish them, I don't read them again. It's kind of boring. When I try to read them again, I read a little bit but then I stop.

Sharon: Are there any books in the classroom that you think you'd like to try? (Sophia hesitates.) Why don't you go over to the pots that have the series books and the "red" pots (I suggest the transitional books instead of the fluent ones because I don't know yet whether she reads as well as she appears to) and find a couple you'd like to try.

(Sophia goes to the pots, and returns in a few minutes with three books.)

What did you find?

Sophia: I got *All About Stacy, M & M and the Mummy Mess*, and *M & M and the Bad News Babies*.

Teacher: Have you read "M & M" books before? (I started here because she'd selected two from this series.)

Sophia: No.

Teacher: They're good books. They're about two friends. (I point to Mandy and Mimi on the cover of *M & M and the Bad News Babies*.) The two friends look like they're twins, but they're not. They're friends who live in the same apartment house.

Sophia: And then two babies get born. (She's looking at the cover of the book and predicting what she thinks has happened.) And then they look the same.

Teacher: (I start again to explain the characters.) Here's Mandy and Mimi. They're babysitting for babies that are twins. And the twins are called "the bad news babies."

Sophia: Because they always give bad news.

Teacher: Oh, so you think they're called "bad news babies" because they give bad news?

Sophia: They always *make* bad news.

Teacher: What does that mean?

Sophia: They always do stuff that makes bad news. You know, like if someone was talking about it in a newspaper. See (referring to the cover illustration). They're pulling out the plant.

Teacher: So you'll be okay with those.

Sophia: Yes.

As children talk about their reading, I make notes in their assessment notebook about some of the main points they're making. Later, I accent these notes with a highlighter so they stand out from their running records and retellings.

A reading discussion with Georgie accessed information of a different kind. After I took a running record of Georgie reading *Jim Meets the Thing*, we selected more books by Miriam Cohen, the author of the series about "Jim and his first-grade friends," for his book bag. I asked Georgie about the kinds of books he likes to read. See Figure 6–6.

I learned that Georgie likes funny books and that his aunt reads to him on a regular basis. Georgie's aunt seems pretty well attuned to his interests and to the type of books that are good to read aloud. She reads him funny books from

---

FIGURE 6–6   Transcript of Reading Discussion with Georgie

Teacher: Tell me about the kinds of books you like to read.

Georgie: I like to read "dog" books, like *Henry and Mudge*. I like them 'cause they're funny and stuff. (Georgie notices a book in the table book pot by Melvin Berger.) I've read a book by him (and he shows me his Weekly Reading Log where he has recorded the title of another book by Melvin Berger that he'd read that week).

Teacher: (I rephrased my original prompt to get him to talk more.) So, when you go to a library or bookstore, you look for "dog" books?

Georgie: Yes.

Teacher: What else?

Georgie: Sometimes we get books to read for bed. My Aunt Molly reads to us. She reads "Junie B. Jones" books. I like that. They're funny.

Teacher: Did you ever read one by yourself?

Georgie: No. And she reads us *George's Marvelous Medicine*.

Teacher: And now you've got a few books in your bag that you can read yourself. Let's see what you've got. Oh . . . (I look in Georgie's book bag.) *Jim Meets the Thing*, *The World of Ants*, and *Nate the Great and the Missing Key*. Which one would you like to try now?

Georgie: *Jim Meets the Thing*.

---

the "Junie B. Jones" series and *George's Marvelous Medicine*. Georgie is not yet able to read these on his own—but soon will—and these experiences of being "read to" are preparing him to be successful when he does attempt books of that kind. He's got a realistic, yet confident approach to reading, and it's no wonder. He receives a lot of support at home, and I can build on that in school.

During her conference, Tiffany said she liked "The Three Little Piggies." See Figure 6–7 for Tiffany's reading discussion. She also liked bear stories, *Green Eggs and Ham*, and *One fish two fish red fish blue fish*. Although she said no one reads to her at home, it's more likely that she just didn't want to admit she couldn't read the books on her own yet. (For I know in fact that her mother is very

---

FIGURE 6–7   Transcript of Reading Discussion with Tiffany

Teacher: Tiffany, tell me what kinds of books you like to read.

Tiffany: (She looked around the table and noticed a book about a turtle on a stack of books I had sitting on the table.) I like to read "turtle" books. And I like to read "The Three Little Piggies." And I like to read the ones with some bear stories.

Teacher: Why do you like those stories?

Tiffany: 'Cause I read them a lot at home.

Teacher: Does someone read to you at home?

Tiffany: No. (I know that's not the case, and I suspect she didn't want me to know that she wasn't yet able to read the books on her own.)

Teacher: Do you read a lot at home?

Tiffany: Yes. I have lots of books. I've got lots of shelves for my books.

Teacher: When Mom takes you to the library, what kinds of books to you like to get?

Tiffany: *One fish two fish*, *Green Eggs and Ham*. And I like the ones that have the fox.

Teacher: The fox?

Tiffany: It's the one they have in the library and I forget who . . . (she doesn't continue with the rest of the sentence).

Teacher: So, you like "Dr. Seuss" books? (Tiffany looked puzzled. She didn't appear to understand that I was referring to the author, so I restated my question.) You like books like *Green Eggs and Ham*?

Tiffany: Yeah.

Teacher: Would you like me to help you find some books?

Tiffany: Yes. (We found *The Foot Book* and it was too hard for her to read alone so I read some of it with her. After I read with her, she said: "This book is so easy I can read it.")

supportive of her reading and reads to her a lot.)

In each of these reading discussions with Sophia, Georgie, and Tiffany, I learned very different, but equally helpful, information about their general feelings about reading, their confidence, the kinds of books they enjoy reading, and their skills as readers.

Sophia, who was the most proficient reader of the three, had very definite tastes in books. She liked "Illustrated Classics," and when she went to the leveled book pots alone, she had no difficulty selecting three books to try. As the year went on, I would learn more about her preferences and be able to lead her to specific authors she liked. But for now, Sophia was content "experimenting" with the new titles she'd found in class.

Georgie was at the early stage of reading, approaching the transitional stage. He had a realistic sense about himself as a reader and was effectively supported at home. He was the only one of the three that chose factual texts. (He read some earlier that week and recorded the titles on his Weekly Reading Log). I would certainly try to help all three children read more factual texts and poetry throughout the year. For now, Georgie was happy reading more books from the "Miriam Cohen" series about "Jim and his first-grade friends." Georgie had the year ahead to refine his abilities and his tastes as a reader. And as he did, I'd direct him to additional books, authors, and topics that appealed to him.

Tiffany was at the beginning of the emergent stage in reading. She didn't yet have the command of authors and types of books that Sophia and George had. She didn't recognize Dr. Seuss as the author of her two favorite books when I mentioned him. She claimed to like reading about turtles because she saw the book about turtles on the table. She also liked reading "bear" books and "the one about the fox," which were more akin to fairy tales or folk tales. But Tiffany liked reading, and that's a good place to start.

Using what I learned from these reading discussions, my responses and interventions are tailored to each child's particular needs.

GATHERING INFORMATION AS THE YEAR PROGRESSES

It's important that each child enjoys what he reads, and there's a wide range of materials available to match their preferences. Later in the year, after our routines are established and I feel confident the reading workshop is running smoothly, I devote more time and attention to the children's specific reading interests and attitudes. I ask questions or prompt discussions to gather information about their reading preferences or probe the meaning of earlier responses I found puzzling.

I ask children a question from a list that I keep in their reading folder (see Figure 6–8 and Appendix M), and let their responses lead to further discussion about the topic.

As they answer these questions, I record important parts of their response in their assessment notebook. I select only one question at a time—the one that is most likely to get at the most helpful information. I write the date alongside the question so that I know I've asked it and where to look for the response. I also highlight his response with a colored marker so that it stands out in the child's assessment notebook.

Conclusion

Although I've discussed running records, retellings, and reading discussions separately, in practice I may employ more than one type in a single conference. It might start out with a running record of a child who's on the borderline between early and transitional reading. If the running record shows he can read the text with the desired accuracy, then I might go to a retelling to see how well he understood it.

Alternatively, I might start with a retelling and then use a running record to see whether the child's retelling reflects a genuine lack of understanding or whether his limited comprehension results from substituting too many of the text words with his own. Or just as likely, I'll start by talking with the child about his reading, and then move into a running record or retelling. In sum, these are not different types of conferences so much as different types of assessment tools, which I generally use in combination.

FIGURE 6–8 Questions to Ask Children as the Year Goes On

---

1. *To find out the kinds of books children like to read*:

1. a. _____ How would you feel if you got books as a gift?

1. b. _____ Are there other books besides the ones we have that you'd like to see in our classroom? What are they?

1. c. _____ If you were going on vacation and wanted to take some books along, which would you select?

1. d. _____ If you were going to sleep over your grandma's for the weekend, what book would you bring?

1. e. _____ If you were the teacher, what book would you read aloud to the class?

1. f. _____ What book do you ask mom or dad to read to you?

2. *To learn about children's attitudes toward reading*:

2. a. _____ Do you like to read? Would you rather read than play outside? Go to the movies? Watch television? Play with a friend?

2. b. _____ What are the times in school when you are really happy? Is reading one of them?

2. c. _____ What are the times of day when you feel most confident? Is reading one of them?

2. d. _____ Do you notice other kids in the classroom getting absorbed in their reading? Does that ever happen to you?

2. e. _____ Are there ever times when you're "lost in a book" and don't know what's happening around you? Tell me about them.

3. *To find out how children select books to read*:

3. a. _____ How do you select a book? Do you look at the title? Read a few pages? Get recommendations from friends?

3. b. _____ If you were buying a book for a friend, how would you go about choosing it? What would you do?

4. *To learn about a child's reading habits*:

4. a. _____ When is your favorite time of day to read? In class? In the morning before coming to school? Before dinner? At bedtime?

4. b. _____ Do you like to read in a room by yourself? Do you like to read where others are gathered?

4. c. _____ How many books do you read a week?

4. d. _____ Do you like to read one book at a time (finish a book before starting a new one) or do like to read a couple at once?

Photo Credit: Herb Shapiro

PART THREE

Demonstrating Strategies: Whole Class, Small Group, One-on-One

CHAPTER 7

Read Aloud and Shared Reading: Demonstrating Strategies in Whole-Class Settings

With this chapter we move from assessments of children's reading to demonstrations of the reading strategies they need to learn. The whole purpose of assessments is to find out what children do well and what we need to teach them. Demonstrating reading strategies during read aloud and shared reading is one way to scaffold children's learning in response to their needs.

The Importance of Being "Systematic"

When Mikey read a book to me during a conference, he didn't know some common words like "from" and "fun." Yet when we read *Tarantulas Are Spiders* together later in the conference, and came to the phrase "in the world," he read it correctly on his own. I complimented him on knowing a hard word like "world," and noted in my assessment notebook how he'd used meaning, structure, and graphophonics to figure it out. Then Mikey said: "You know how I knew the word. I was writing it in my story yesterday."

And he was! The day before Mikey had written about "the bigst bal in the wald," and although he spelled "world" "w-a-l-d," the experience of using the phrase in his story and sounding the word out to write it helped him transfer the syntax and spelling from his writing to his reading.

Occurrences like this one happen a lot in my classroom. A child expresses a connection between something he's done earlier and something he's doing now, between something he already knows and something he's at the point of learning.

I support connections like these by being systematic in my teaching. For example, my whole-group demonstrations during read aloud and shared reading allow the children to first experience how a particular strategy "works" without having to implement it on their own. Later, when we "revisit" the strategy in small groups or during reading conferences, the children are already familiar with it. They can see the connections between what they've done and what they're doing now. (See Chapter 8 on guided reading and Chapter 9 on demonstrating strategies to children one-on-one.)

How Read Aloud and Shared Reading Support My Goals

This chapter discusses how read aloud and shared reading support my demonstrations of reading strategies and ultimately help me achieve my first goal of helping children become strategic readers. (See Figure 7–1 for a definition of read aloud and shared reading.) Before laying this out, I want to briefly describe how read aloud and shared reading advance my other three, equally important goals. (Please refer to Chapter 2 for a fuller description of my reading goals for children.)

I Want Children to Read a Variety of Genres

Read aloud and shared reading provide opportunities for me to share different genres with children and familiarize them with some of their features.

I select fiction, factual texts, and poetry that children may not be able to read on their own.

FIGURE 7–1 Definition of Read Aloud and Shared Reading

During *read aloud,* the teacher reads a book *to* the children that is beyond what they can read on their own. Since the children aren't reading the text themselves, she only shows children the actual text when there are illustrations to share. It's always preferable to have the children sitting up close to give them a feeling of community as they listen and respond orally.

During *shared reading,* the teacher reads a Big Book or enlarged text *with* the children, who are sitting up close so they can see it and read along. The texts are ones the children may not be able to read independently, but can read successfully in unison with the teacher and their classmates.

Shared reading was developed by New Zealand educator Don Holdaway who wanted to simulate for children in school the "lap reading" experience that many are fortunate enough to also have at home as they hear, read, and discuss stories with adults in emotionally comfortable, risk-free settings.

FIGURE 7–2 Extending Vocabulary During Read Aloud and Shared Reading

Although vocabulary is not studied formally until third grade, "new words" come up during read aloud and shared reading. Sometimes as I'm reading, I explain the meaning of a word as an aside, or when a child asks what a word means.

Most of the time, not wanting to interrupt the flow of the story, I explain what the word means as unobtrusively as possible and go on. But other times, we record the word, and then later examine ways we might have figured it out. I encourage children to use contextual or orthographic cues whenever possible, because stopping to look in a dictionary, while a good way to explore the meaning of words, is impractical while the children are reading. The children learn they can:

- Use the sentence or paragraph in which the word appears—what comes before and after—for clues to its meaning.
- Read a couple sentences past the word. The meaning is often explained in the text that follows the unfamiliar word.
- Look closely at the word for orthographic cues, like prefixes, suffixes, root words, and derivatives.

Young readers not yet able to read on their own the wonderfully evocative *Like Butter on Pancakes* by Jonathan London can appreciate its imagery and relate to it as they hear it read aloud and respond to it afterward. They may hear words they've never before heard and familiar words used in new ways. (See Figure 7–2 for strategies I use to extend children's vocabulary during read aloud and shared reading.) Poetry anthologies, such as *Secret Places,* edited by Charlotte Huck, demonstrate how the central theme of a collection connects its poems and often motivates children to collect poems for their own anthologies.

Poetry anthologies, like many factual texts, help readers see how it's okay to read a *portion* of the whole text because it's particularly appealing or because it answers a question they have. They don't have to read the book from cover to cover since, unlike fiction, there's no story line to follow.

When choosing factual texts, I generally select books on topics we're studying in social studies and science, or subjects in which the children have expressed an interest. I use read aloud and shared reading sessions to demonstrate how features of factual texts such as glossaries, indices, captions, side bars, and pronunciation keys can help them understand what they're reading.

In addition, sharing a variety of genres with children helps them distinguish among them. When I read *The Story of the Statue of Liberty* by Lucille Recht Penner and then later read *Lily and Miss Liberty* by Carla Stevens, the children begin to understand how the first "story" recounts actual events, while the second story "could have happened, but didn't."

I Want Children to Use Writing to Deepen Their Understanding of What They Read

Read aloud and shared reading offer opportunities for children to respond orally to texts and familiarizes them with the types of responses they'll later be asked to write.

Sometimes children respond spontaneously to what I read aloud with comments and questions. Other times I ask them what they think about the book or the part I've read so far. As with retellings, this type of open-ended question or prompt gives children the flexibility to respond genuinely and reflects their thinking. Then I guide them to tell more about the parts they liked, how a book reminds them of others they've read or events in their lives.

Children's oral responses lead the way for their written ones, helping them feel more confident about what they have to say and making it easier to put their ideas in writing later on.

I Want Children to Love to Read

Read aloud and shared reading promote children's love of reading.

NBC's "Today Show" ran a spot on teaching reading. Matt Lauer interviewed Dr. Annemarie Sullivan Palinscar from the University of Michigan School of Education and asked, "Just how important is it that children enjoy reading?" Dr. Palinscar responded, as you would expect, that enjoyment of reading is critical: "If children aren't motivated to read, it would be very difficult for them to sustain their attention and interest in reading."

I sense the power of stories to engage young readers when I read stories like *Chocolatina* by Erik Kraft and see the look of foreboding on the children's faces as Tina, while biting off the ear of a chocolate bunny, defiantly stands up in Health Class saying she wishes Mrs. Ferdman's warning that—"You are what you eat"—were true. Or when reading *Tops & Bottoms* by Janet Stevens, I see the flash of recognition as the children realize the craftiness behind Hare's plan to give Bear a choice of either the tops or the bottoms of plants before planting the crop so he can trick him out of the part that's edible.

When selecting books for read aloud and shared reading, I always try to be aware of the distinction between books I love and those that appeal to children. Of course, there are universal favorites, like *Noisy Nora* by Rosemary Wells and *Charlotte's Web* by E. B. White, and these I read without fail. But in making my selections, I try to keep in mind the very real differences between children's reading tastes and mine.

Amy Hest's touching story, *The Crack-of-Dawn Walkers*, about young Sadie's special time alone with her grandfather may remind me of Sunday mornings as a child watching my Italian grandmother in her black dress, stockings, and shoes at the kitchen stove stirring a pot of the most delicious meatballs and sauce. But young children who haven't lived long enough to truly value these experiences are often "unmoved" by this story. The more tranquil, subtle books such as this one are often best left to older readers who can appreciate their affectionate humor and use them as models for the kinds of experiences they can write about themselves.

I'm often amused at what children laugh at, respond to—enjoy. It wasn't by chance that Jasmin responded so enthusiastically to *Deputy Dan and the Bank Robbers*, or that Itamar couldn't stop telling the class about the "bathroom emergency" in *Junie B. Jones and the Sneaky Peeky Spying* by Barbara Park that was mistaken for a "real" emergency with actual fire trucks coming to her rescue. These may not be my favorites, but they're sure-fire hits with children.

Now, back to my first goal: to help children become strategic readers.

Read Aloud: Providing Opportunities to Demonstrate Comprehension Strategies

Comprehension is an essential component of reading. Without it, children merely "call" words without understanding what they're reading. When Maky, who could read *Junie B. Jones and the Yucky Blucky Fruitcake* by Barbara Park with 98 percent word accuracy, said: "I don't want to read such long books because I don't understand them. I can't keep everything in my head," she showed a genuine appreciation for this aspect of reading. She didn't want to read what she couldn't understand!

Transitional readers like Maky stand at a threshold. While they're able to read the words accurately, they often can't integrate all the parts of longer, more involved texts. They can't "keep everything in their heads" over several days.

I find it's most effective to start with whole-group demonstrations of comprehension strategies. From my experiences of what's "typical" for children at different developmental stages and my continual assessments of each child's reading during conferences, I can decide which strategies to demonstrate during whole-class sessions, as well as when during the year to demonstrate them.

Some children can apply what I demonstrate during read-aloud sessions to their own reading without a lot of further assistance. Those needing additional demonstrations will receive them later during guided reading and reading conferences.

Comprehension Strategies I Demonstrate During Read Aloud

Of the many comprehension strategies listed in Figure 2–1B on page 10 for understanding text, there are four principle ones that I demonstrate during read aloud. I address the others less formally as the need arises. Figures 7-3A–7-3E list books that support these strategies.

"STOPPING TO THINK" ABOUT WHAT YOU'RE READING

I demonstrate the "Stopping to Think" strategy to help children think at a whole-text level.

I encourage them to pause occasionally to reflect on or discuss what they've read so far and predict what might happen next.

I always start a whole-group demonstration by telling the children what I've noticed in their reading that has led me to show them this new strategy. In the case of the "Stopping to Think" strategy, I explain that sometimes during a reading conference I find that a child doesn't understand what he's read well enough to enjoy it. This may mean he needs an easier book, but not always. And that although he can read all the words, he still might not understand what he's read.

I may even "act out" how I frequently see a child "read and read and read" without ever pausing to think about what he's reading, and then come up to me and say: "I'm done!" But when I ask him to tell me what the story's about, he can't.

Then, I say that I'm going to show them something they can try, and I write these three "steps" on a chart:

1. *What* do I think is going to happen?
2. *Why* do I think this is going to happen?
3. *Prove it* by going back to the story.

This strategy is reminiscent of Directed Reading-Thinking Activities described by R. G. Stauffer in *The Language-Experience Approach to the Teaching of Reading* and later in Jo-Ann Parry's chapter on DRTA in *Teach On: Teaching Strategies for Reading and Writing Workshops*.

"Stopping to Think" About Chester's Way

Chester's Way by Kevin Henkes lends itself to a demonstration of this strategy. Books, like this

one, with strong plots and discernible episodes promote this strategy by providing natural places for readers to stop and discuss the story. I also try to use books the children haven't heard before. If they have, I ask them not to participate in the predictions.

Even though *Chester's Way* is a picture book, I use it because we can read the entire book in one sitting and the children can check the accuracy of their predictions. I demonstrate the "Stopping to Think" strategy with longer books once the children understand how it works. (See Figure 7–3A for a list of books that support demonstrations of "Stopping to Think.")

FIGURE 7–3A Books to Read Aloud That Support Demonstrations of "Stopping to Think"

What to Look for:
a strong story line
some predictability
a story with discernible stopping points
text that elicits a discussion

Some Picture Books:
Don't Need Friends, by C. Crimi
Chester's Way, by K. Henkes
Little Polar Bear, by H. de Beer
Quacky Duck, by P. and E. Rogers
Tacky the Penguin, by H. Lester
Tops and Bottoms, by J. Stevens
Dog Breath: The Horrible Trouble with Hally Tosis, by D. Pilkey
The Real-Skin Rubber Monster Mask, by M. Cohen
Sweet Strawberries, by P. R. Naylor
Wanda's Roses, by P. Brisson
I Don't Want to Take a Bath, by J. Sykes
Stellaluna, by J. Cannon
Timothy Goes to School, by Rosemary Wells
Presenting Tanya, the Ugly Duckling, by P. L. Gauch
The Night Iguana Left Home, by M. McDonald
Where Is That Cat? by C. Greene

Some Chapter Books:
My Father's Dragon, by R. S. Gannett
"Favorite Fairy Tales" series, retold by V. Haviland
No Way, Winky Blue, by P. Jane
The Magic Finger, by R. Dahl
Mary Marony and the Chocolate Surprise, by S. Kline
Half Magic, by E. Eager
The Paint Brush Kid, by C. R. Bulla

FIGURE 7–3B Books to Read Aloud That Support Demonstrations of Story Mapping

What to Look for:
story with conflict/resolution format, i.e., one main problem that's introduced at the beginning and resolved at the end
books with discernible story elements, i.e., character, setting, problem, main events, and resolution

Some Picture Books:
Bernard Bear's Amazing Adventure, by H. de Beer
Chrysanthemum, by K. Henkes
Rachel Parker, Kindergarten Show-Off, by A. Martin
Lunch Bunnies, by K. Lasky
McDuff and the Baby, by R. Wells
The Purple Coat, by A. Hest
Happy Birthday to You, You Belong in a Zoo, by D. de Groat
Amazing Grace, by M. Hoffman
Strega Nona, by Tomie de Paola
Dance, Tanya, by P. L. Gauch
The Chicken Sisters, by L. Numeroff
Don't Fidget a Feather! by E. Silverman
Caleb & Kate, by W. Steig
New Shoes for Silvia, by J. Hurwitz
Grandpa's Teeth, by R. Clement
Stellaluna, by J. Cannon
Too Many Pumpkins, by L. White

Some Chapter Books:
The Beast in Ms. Rooney's Room, by P. R. Giff
Catwings, by U. LeGuin
See You Around, Sam, by L. Lowry
Dear Mr. Henshaw, by B. Cleary
Muggie Maggie, by B. Cleary
Fantastic Mr. Fox, by R. Dahl

FIGURE 7–3C Books to Read Aloud That Support Demonstrations of Character Mapping

What to Look for:
a story where the character's personality is a bit out-of-the-ordinary
a character who "changes" as the story progresses, changing his behavior or learning about himself
a story where the character's personality or behavior is predictable
a character that's featured in other stories

Some Picture Books:
Tacky the Penguin (and other "Tacky" books), by H. Lester
Elmer (and other "Elmer" books), by D. McKee
Lily's Purple Purse (and other "Lily" books), by K. Henkes
Odd Velvet, by M. Whitcomb
Chocolatina, by E. Kraft
Insects Are My Life, by M. McDonald
The One in the Middle Is the Green Kangaroo, by J. Blume

Some Chapter Books:
"Horrible Harry" series, by S. Kline
"Pinky and Rex" series, by J. Howe
"Mary Marony" series, by S. Kline
"Adam Joshua" series, by J. L. Smith
"Nora" books, by J. Hurwitz
"Amber Brown" series, by P. Danziger
The Beast in Ms. Rooney's Room, by P. R. Giff
Fish Face, by P. R. Giff
The Chocolate Touch, by P. S. Catling
Beany (Not Beanhead) and the Magic Crystal, by S. Wojciechowski
Class Clown, by J. Hurwitz

First, I ask the children to think about how the title and cover illustrations might help them predict what the book is about. With so little to go on, they thought that perhaps Chester always wanted to get his own way, and that's why he was standing alone without any playmates. But once I started reading, they learned about Chester's best friend Wilson, disproving their initial prediction. Chester and Wilson, it turns out, were like "two peas in a pod," like "two mittens on a string."

When Lily came into the picture (they remembered her from when I read them *Julius: The Baby of the World* by Kevin Henkes), they predicted that Chester and Wilson were not going to like her and why they thought so. Here's how our conversation went:

Alexis: Chester and Wilson aren't going to like Lily because she's kind of mean.

Teacher: Why do you say that? (As I asked this question I pointed to number "2"—Why do

FIGURE 7–3D Books to Read Aloud That Support Demonstrations of Using Writing to Deepen Understanding

What to Look for:
a story that lends itself to different
    interpretations
text that elicits questions and discussion
text that makes the reader wonder
text relating to age-appropriate issues, such as
    going to school and relating to friends or
    family members

Some Picture Books:
Sam and the Lucky Money, by K. Chinn
Captain Snap and the Children of Vinegar Lane,
    by R. Schotter
A Bad Case of Stripes, by D. Shannon
Grandmother's Pigeon, by L. Erdrich
The Crack-of-Dawn Walkers, by A. Hest
The Rainbow Fish, by M. Pfister
Grandfather's Journey, by A. Say
Daniel's Duck, by C. R. Bulla
Oma and Bobo, by A. Schwartz
Begin at the Beginning, by A. Schwartz
The Sweetest Fig, by C. Van Allsburg
The Summer My Father Was Ten, by P. Brisson
The Ant Bully, by J. Nickle
Fantastic Mr. Fox, by R. Dahl

Some Chapter Books:
Annabelle's Un-Birthday, by S. Kroll
Anna, Grandpa, and the Big Storm, by C.
    Stevens
The Hundred Dresses, by E. Estes
Miss Lily and the Statue of Liberty, by C. Stevens
My Name Is Maria Isabel, by A. F. Ada
The Poppy Seeds, by C. R. Bulla
The Islander, by C. Rylant
The Birchbark House, by Louise Erdrich

FIGURE 7–3E Books to Read Aloud That Support Demonstrations of Making "Before and After" Charts

What to Look for:
books on topics about which children have
    some background knowledge
topics children are exploring in science and
    social studies
fictional texts that give factual background
    information in addition to telling a story
books with graphic organizers, such as tables
    and charts, so the children can continue to
    gather new information as they reread the
    text

Some Books:
Dinosaur Days, by J. Milton
Arctic Son, by J. C. George
Beavers, by H. M. Moore
Animals in Winter, by H. Bancroft & R. Van
    Gelder
Penguins! by Gail Gibbons
Fingers, Forks, and Chopsticks, by Patricia
    Lauber
Meet the Octopus, by S. M. James
Thinking About Ants, by B. Brenner
Backyard Animals ("Eyes on Nature" series), by
    K. Archer
Cats and Kittens, by K. Starke
It's an Ant's Life: My Story of Life in the Nest, by S.
    Parker
*I Didn't Know That: Crocodiles Yawn to Keep
    Cool and Other Amazing Facts About
    Crocodiles and Alligators,* by K. Petty
Finding Out About Birds of Prey, by M. Wooley
    and K. Pigdon
If You Lived in Colonial Days, by A. McGovern
The Life and Times of the Apple, by C. Micucci

you think this is going to happen?—on our list.)

Alexis: She was mean to her brother and to her cousin in *Julius*, so I'll bet she's going to be mean to Chester and Wilson too.

Georgie: I think Chester and Wilson are going to do the same thing to Lily that Lily did to her brother. She got her brother confused by saying the ABCs and numbers the wrong way. 'Cause whatever goes around, comes around.'

Fiona: Now she's going to copy them. She's going to turn into their best friend. Like the Three Musketeers.

Teacher: Why do you think so? . . . (When Fiona couldn't give a reason to support her prediction, I suggested we continue reading to find out what happened.)

Throughout our discussion, I led the children to think more carefully about the story we were reading, and *why* they made the predictions they did. When Alexis and Georgie justified their predictions by referring to Lily's behavior in *Julius: The Baby of The World* and when Georgie offered the adult sentiment that "whatever goes around, comes around," they were making the kinds of connections I want to promote. Children's predictions should be based on evidence, whether it's from hints in the current book, from their first-hand recollection of another book they've read by the same author, or from their own experiences or "received wisdom."

After the children have made their predictions and offer reasons why they think so, I always refer them back to the text to "prove it." Although Fiona couldn't explain why she felt Chester, Wilson, and Lily would all be friends in the end, "like the Three Musketeers," I felt she may have been alluding to the "happy endings" of most stories. I might have pursued this, but this time I suggested that we "read to find out" what actually happened.

Although I encourage children to make predictions based on their general knowledge about stories, on specific books and authors, and on life experiences they've had, I always lead them back to the text to support their positions.

I try not to interrupt the read aloud too many times to guide the children through "Stopping to Think" activities. A good strategy can be overused! I can tell when I've overdone it: the children become restless and disinterested. When this happens, I cease and desist. The use of this strategy should never be at the expense of the children's enjoyment of the story.

"Stopping to Think" About Factual Texts

When reading factual texts aloud, I often "stop and think" about the content and how it's organized. At the end of a chapter, we may consider what we've learned about the topic so far and what we expect to learn next. We may skim subtitles in the next chapter and spend time studying the illustrations and captions. Reflecting on text, instead of racing through without much thought about what we're reading, is a powerful strategy for readers regardless of the genre they're reading.

STORY MAPPING

I demonstrate story mapping to help children think about how the different story elements—characters, setting, problem, main events, and resolution—work together.

By applying this strategy to stories that are read to them, they develop a tool to use when they begin to read chapter books independently.

I try to keep my initial demonstrations as clear and focused as possible by selecting books with distinct episodes, obvious problems, and only a few characters, so that children can easily identify each story element and consider how they work together to "create" the story. I also look for books where one central problem is introduced at the beginning and followed through to the end. *'Gator Girls* by Stephanie Calmenson and Joanna Cole, where Allie Gator is going to summer camp without her best friend, Amy, and *Fantastic Mr. Fox* by Roald Dahl, where Mr. Fox needs food for his family but three farmers try to stop him, are good examples. (See Figure 7–3B for a list of books that support demonstrations of story mapping.)

Some chapter books, such as *No Way, Winky Blue* by Pamela Jane, contain several minor problems that are resolved *as* the story develops. I save books like this one (it's one of my favorites) to help children distinguish between the main plot and subplots.

Introducing Story Mapping with a Picture Book

I sometimes introduce story mapping with a familiar picture book, as I did with *Chrysanthemum* by Kevin Henkes. I knew that by demonstrating story mapping with this more "manageable" and familiar text first, I would have an easier time explaining the story elements, and the children would be more successful applying the strategy to other stories later on.

After we read the story, I asked several children to illustrate a scene representing the "Characters," "Setting," "Problem," and "Resolution" on pieces of 14″ × 17″ paper, each labeled with the name of one of the story elements. (See Figure 7–4 for Shiori's illustration of the "Problem.") For the "Main Events," the children dictated and I wrote a sentence about each important development: "1. Chrysanthemum loved her name. 2. The children at school made fun of her because she was named after a flower. 3. Chrysanthemum started to hate her name . . ."

We stapled these pages together, made a cover, and hung this story-map book in the classroom as a reminder of a strategy to use as for reading *and* writing. These same story elements can help writers organize their ideas before beginning to compose their stories. (See Figure 13–7 for the Story Map Brittany made to plan her story.)

FIGURE 7–4

Shiori's illustration of the "Problem" in *Chrysanthemum* by Kevin Henkes

Story Mapping with The Beast in Ms. Rooney's Room

Once the children are familiar with story mapping, they can apply the strategy to longer texts. Sometimes I have them make a Story Map of the first book in a series, knowing that this exposure might motivate them to read other books in that series after having worked with the first book in a whole-group setting. (See Appendix L for a list of series books I use in my classroom.)

Before making a Story Map of *The Beast in Ms. Rooney's Room* by Patricia Reilly Giff (the first book of fifteen in "The Kids of the Polk Street School" series), I explained that my purpose was to help them think about how the parts of a story fit together so they can understand it better. In addition, the actual Story Map itself could help them hold the story "in their heads" since we could refer to it each day to refresh our memory of the story before reading the next chapters.

I prepared the outline for a story map on chart paper in advance, with the elements: "Characters," "Setting," "Problem," "Main Events," and "Resolution," as headings of the boxes to fill in as we read. (See Figure 7–5 for a completed Story Map of *The Beast in Ms. Rooney's Room.*)

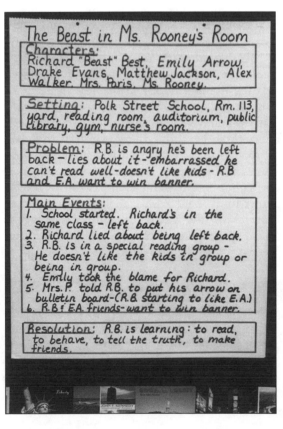

FIGURE 7–5

Story Map of *The Beast in Ms. Rooney's Room* by Patricia Reilly Giff

After reading the first chapter, we stopped to discuss which of the characters that we'd "met" so far were most likely to be central figures in the story and listed them in the "Character" box. Then I wrote down where the story is taking place in the "Setting" box.

I used to just ask the children: "What is the problem?" and was often surprised when they thought I meant what problem they themselves were having. I've learned to be more careful about the way I ask questions. So instead, I asked them, "What problem is *Richard Best* having?"

When some children had trouble identifying the problem, Georgie said: "Maybe we should have read a 'Nate the Great' book because they have a lot of problems to solve!" But eventually the children realized that Richard Best was upset that he'd been "left back," and was in the same class as the "babies in Mrs. White's class." The children decided I should write: "Richard Best is angry he's been left back" in the "Problem" box.

For the next few days, we read two chapters each day and continued to fill in our story map. When we finished the book, the children and I discussed how the story had been resolved, and I recorded this in the "Resolution" box. I always try to push the children to think about *how* the resolution of the problem came about. At first, they're satisfied stating *what* the change was— "Now Richard Best likes school"—instead of describing *how* it happened.

I explain that it's not as though Richard Best woke up one morning and "all of a sudden" started liking school and the kids in his class. But rather it was his experiences with Emily Arrow and Matthew Jackson being kind to him that brought about the *realization* that Ms. Rooney's class wasn't so bad after all. Most times it's a change in the character's attitude brought about by some event (as when Rosie almost loses Winky Blue and *then* realizes he's special just the way he is), and not a change in the actual situation itself, that brings about the resolution of the problem.

CHARACTER MAPPING

I demonstrate character mapping to help children focus on how the main character's personal traits often direct the action of the story.

The children use what they learn about the main character in the early chapters to consider what may happen later in the story.

When demonstrating this strategy, I try to select books whose central characters have distinct, observable characteristics. (See Figure 7–3C for a list of books I use to demonstrate character mapping.) Children just learning to use this strategy have an easier time focusing on "exaggerated" qualities than on more subtle ones.

Making a Character Map of The Chocolate Touch

In my video series, *A Close-Up Look at Teaching Reading*, the children and I make a Character Map of John Midas in *The Chocolate Touch* by Patrick Skene Catling (see Figure 7–6).

I show the children how to use what they know about John Midas from the first chapter and from the similarities they see between him and the fabled King Midas to anticipate what might come later in the story.

After reading aloud the first chapter, I ask them to tell me some things they've learned about John Midas. Of course, they begin by telling me what he "does." I explain that I'm hoping they can think about what John "al-

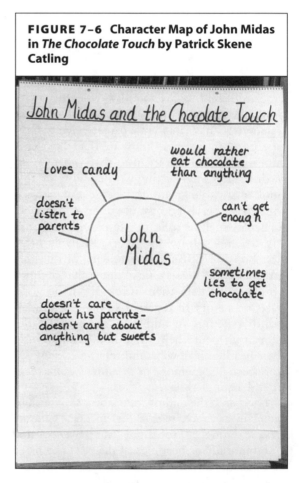

FIGURE 7–6 Character Map of John Midas in *The Chocolate Touch* by Patrick Skene Catling

John Midas and the Chocolate Touch

John Midas

loves candy

would rather eat chocolate than anything

doesn't listen to parents

can't get enough

sometimes lies to get chocolate

doesn't care about his parents - doesn't care about anything but sweets ways does" because this will help us understand what kind of boy he is.

It's often difficult to direct children from thinking about events in the story to thinking about a character's "pattern of behavior." So when I'm first demonstrating this strategy, I list whatever the children say about the character and then highlight the most telling attributes. In this case, I list that John Midas: "loves candy," "loves chocolate more than anything," maybe even more than his mother, and "lies to get chocolate." These are the qualities that eventually get John into a lot of trouble. As we learn more about him in the following chapters, we continue to add to our map.

Helping children use what they already know to learn new things is important whether it's using the first chapter of a book to think about the second, or applying what they know about other stories to the one they're currently reading. The children who had read about "King Midas and the Golden Touch" applied its lessons to John Midas and his "chocolate touch." And it was these very same children who were "insiders" as they listened to *Chocolatina* by Erik Kraft. They *knew* she was asking for trouble!

USING WRITING TO HELP UNDERSTAND WHAT YOU'RE READING

I help children use writing to think more deeply about what they're reading.

I show them that by writing down what they're thinking as they read, they're having a "conversation with themselves" about the story, factual text, or poem. This helps them better understand what they're reading.

Demonstrating Writing About Fiction

Although I can use any well-written, thought-provoking text to demonstrate this strategy, I select fiction that also has strong emotional appeal and characters who act in surprising ways. (See Figure 7–3D for books to help children write about their reading.) I want readers to be immersed in the story, feel for the character, and wonder why he's acting as he is.

When I read a book aloud, I sometimes demonstrate how I can read a few pages or a chapter, and then take a short break to reflect on what's happened and write down my thoughts.

After reading the first chapter of *Anna, Grandpa, and the Big Storm* by Carla Stevens, I wondered out loud: "Anna's grandpa is sure acting strange. He says he wants to go home. Why doesn't he enjoy visiting with his family?" Then I wrote on chart paper at the easel: "I'm wondering why grandpa's so grumpy. He doesn't seem to enjoy visiting his family. Doesn't he love them?" demonstrating to the children that their written responses don't need to recount what happened in the story, but can relate to what the story is making them think.

Then Alexis raised her hand and said: "I get homesick too. Once I had a sleepover at my friend's house for two whole nights. I haven't had one since. I'm surprised a grandpa would get homesick like me."

We recorded Alexis's comments after mine on the chart, read another chapter, and then stopped to reflect and record our thinking again. We continued like this, reading one or two chapters each day until we finished the book. (When I feel it's taking too long to record our comments on the chart, I write them on my clipboard and then record some of them on the chart later.)

Children's Early Attempts at Written Responses to Text

As I demonstrate "writing about text" to the whole class, I encourage the children to practice themselves when they read independently and tell them that writing a little might help them better understand what they're reading. They write in their response notebooks, which are kept in their reading folders.

My most fluent readers and writers are generally the ones who use this strategy to its full purpose. Less skilled readers and writers sometimes approximate this strategy by recording *what happened* at the end of a chapter before going on to the next, without considering *why*. I accept these efforts as steps in the right direction.

For example, when Samantha was just starting to read chapter books, I suggested that, after each chapter, she write one or two sentences about what she was thinking (see Figure 7–7). Even though Samantha's "thinking" about the story was more a listing of the main events, this was a process she could refine when her thinking went beyond just recapping the important parts of the story.

When children write about what they read and then read it back later, it helps them understand that they don't need anyone but themselves and a notebook to have a "dialogue"

FIGURE 7–7

Samantha's Writing About *Mary Marony and the Snake* by Suzy Kline

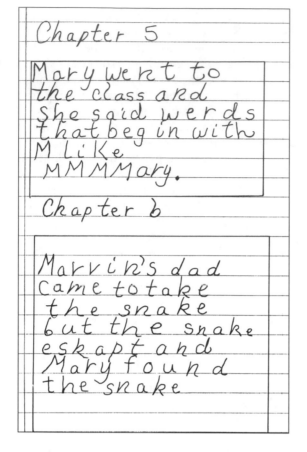

Mud, more mud, add mud, good mud
> You pat
> I gnaw
> I pile
> You store
This stick   here
That stick   there
> Mud, more mud, add mud, good mud
> You guard
> I pack
> I dig
> You stack
That stick   here
This stick   there
> Mud, more mud, add mud, good mud
> I trim
> You mold
> To keep
> Out cold
This stick   here
That stick   there
> Mud, more mud, add mud, good mud

After we talked about the "war" between beavers who "need" to cut down trees and the people that want to stop them, Katie formulated her own opinion by writing: "Beavers should be allowed to cut down trees if they need to. It's how they get food. Would you want someone to stop you from getting food? And besides if they didn't gnaw on wood, their teeth would grow very very long, and then they'd die. And that's why I think beavers should be allowed to cut down trees!" Sean, whose grandparents live in the country, disagreed. Wanting to settle things once and for all, he wrote: "Would you want beavers to chop down the trees around your house?"

* * *

Read alouds provide opportunities for me to demonstrate comprehension strategies to the whole class, strategies I want them to use as they read alone. They're also ones that I'll reintroduce during guided reading. Read alouds set the stage for us to explore ways to help children understand what they're reading

about the story. It also provides them with some distance from their original comments and can foster more thoughtful responses.

Written Responses to Factual Texts and Poetry

When children read factual texts and poetry, their worlds become "larger." Not only do they learn new information, they also experience different authors' perspectives and have a chance to come up with their own.

As part of our social studies curriculum, we read a lot about beavers since so many fur trappers came to our area in pursuit of beaver skins. As we read the Big Book *Beavers* by Helen H. Moore, we learn how beavers make their lodges and dams from the logs and branches they so doggedly cut down. And Marilyn Singer's nononsense poem, "Beavers in November," further conveys their persistence in their gnawing, stacking, and building. Can't you just see the busy beavers at work, doing what they do best in the following lyrical lines:

This stick   here
That stick   there
> Mud, more mud, add mud, good mud
That stick   here
This stick   there

Shared Reading: Demonstrating Strategies to Figure Out Words

While reading aloud gives me the chance to read books *to* the children that are too difficult for them to read on their own, shared reading allows them to read texts *with* me. This provides more support than if they were reading alone, but more challenge than read aloud since they're actually reading the text. (Refer to Margaret E. Mooney's *Reading To, With, and By Children.*) And in shared reading I can show children a variety of ways to figure out words they don't initially know. (See Figure 2–1A on page 10 for a list of strategies I demonstrate to help children figure out unfamiliar words.)

Shared reading offers numerous opportunities to show children what reading is all about. Take page 5 of the Big Book, *The Old Man's Mitten* retold by Yevonne Pollack, for example. By referring to just this one page, I can highlight many features of print, language structure, convention, and letter-sound relationships that children need to know as they develop as readers (see Figures 7–8 and 7–9).

Of course the strength of each "observation" rests on how effectively I relate it to other examples. (Here it's critical that I know my books well enough to select ones that demonstrate what my children need to learn.)

Margaret Moustafa, in *Beyond Traditional Phonics: Research Discoveries and Reading Instruction*, stresses the importance of shared reading in its "whole-to-part" approach: "Shared reading is a powerful teaching strategy that enables early readers to become proficient readers." Its "... predictable stories can enable children to acquire the letter-sound system faster and more effectively than traditional phonics instruction."

Shared reading helps children learn about:

- *Print*—how it "moves" from left to right, how there's a one-to-one match of speech to print, how words are made up of letters that are ordered in a consistent way, and how words can be "chunked" together to make reading sound more fluent
- *The structure of language*—how there are grammatical "rules" governing how printed words are organized in relation to others
- *Conventions of language*—how there are "rules" of spelling and punctuation that help convey meaning
- *Letter-sound relationships*—how letters and letter combinations represent sounds that are combined to represent spoken words

Strategies and Skills Go Hand-in-Hand

Strategies are problem-solving thought processes initiated by readers to make meaning from text. Skills are the knowledge they apply strategi-

FIGURE 7–8

Page from *The Old Man's Mitten* retold by Yevonne Pollack

cally. Both are important. I can't very well ask children to look through a word to the end and listen for the sounds the letters make, without also teaching them about letters and their sounds. On the other hand, I'm not going to wait until I've *presented* all the letter-sound relationships before asking children to "look through a word to the end." (And even if I did, there's be no guarantee they'd "know" and apply them.) Right from the start, I encourage them to use a variety of strategies together—considering what makes sense, sounds right, and looks right. When they look at the letters in a word, they should also "consider" the other two cueing systems as well.

For example, the picture illustrating the sentence, "On Thursday we went to the lake," helps the child with the sounds represented by the letters in "lake." (See Figure 7–10 for a page from *A Week with Aunt Bea* by Judy Nayer.)

As he looks through the word (and at the picture—which is a semantic cue—of "Aunt Bea" rowing a boat in a *lake*), he notes that "a-k-e" in "lake" says /ake/. The child reasons: "It's got to be 'lake' and not a river because 'river' has an /r/ sound at the beginning and end. There's no letter in 'lake' that makes that sound."

FIGURE 7–9 List of Text Features, page 5 of *The Old Man's Mitten* retold by Yevonne Pollack

Some features I can show readers are that:

- A line of print moves from left to right, and from top to bottom.
- There's a one-to-one match between spoken and written words.
- Written words are spelled consistently.
- Sentences begin with capital letters.
- Declarative sentences end in periods.
- Quotation marks show "conversation."
- Pronouns refer back to other words, i.e., "it" refers to "mitten."
- The inflection "ed" is sometimes added to a baseword to show past tense *without*

changing the word, i.e., "looked," "curled," and "squeaked."
- Sometimes the final consonant of a baseword is *doubled* before adding "ed," i.e., "hopped."
- When "ed" is added to a baseword, it can make a /t/ sound, i.e., "looked," "squeaked," and "hopped."
- When "ed" is added to a baseword, it can made a /d/ sound, i.e., "curled."
- The compound word "inside" is made from the words "in" and "side," which both relate to its meaning.

FIGURE 7–10

Page from *A Week with Aunt Bea* by Judy Nayer

Neither phonetic investigations nor the demonstrations of strategies children need to apply can stand alone. They work together, supporting children's efforts to figure out words they don't know. The illustrations in the previous example actually helped to teach phonics!

LETTER AND SOUND EXPLORATIONS

After the children and I have read a shared text together for several days and the children know it well, we often begin a letter or sound exploration. By looking for individual letters or spelling patterns, and by listening for sounds in the text we've read, we explore letter-sound relationships, form hypotheses about how they work, and revise them as needed.

In letter explorations, the children *look* for words with common letters or spelling patterns. We list and later group them to highlight the similarities and differences in what we find. In sound explorations, they *listen* for particular sounds in words and then find examples of words containing those sounds, first in the shared reading text and later in additional text around the classroom and in their own reading and writing. See Figure 7–11 for a description of my letter and sound explorations.

STRATEGIES TO HELP CHILDREN FIGURE OUT UNFAMILIAR WORDS

See Figure 2–1A on page 10 for a list of strategies I demonstrate to help children figure out unfamiliar words.

When I want to demonstrate a strategy, I always:

1. Begin by telling the children why I've selected a particular strategy.
2. Show them how to use this strategy on a shared text I've selected.
3. Allow them opportunities to practice the strategy as we "read together."
4. Remind them to practice this strategy when the need arises as they read independently.

In shared reading, I highlight a featured strategy (for demonstration purposes) while reminding children that there are other strategies they should also consider. Here are several key strategies I demonstrate:

Attending to the Initial Letter/s and the Sound It Represents

I show children how to use the sound represented by the initial letter, or letters (when there's a consonant

---

FIGURE 7–11 Letter and Sound Explorations

1. *Decide on the letter/s or sound for which you want the children to search.*

   After we've read a shared text many times throughout the week, and perhaps dramatized it or read it chorally, we "look for" a specific letter or spelling pattern, or "listen for" a sound—but not both. (It's important to give accurate directions to the children, asking them to *look* for letters or *listen* for sounds.)

2. *Start a list of words.*

   Then we read over the text looking for a letter (or spelling pattern) or listening for a sound, and start a list of words that contain it on chart paper. Children offer additional words they know. We continue collecting words from texts we read into the next week or longer, depending on the children's interest or the relative "importance" of the exploration. For example, listening for words with a long /i/ sound might warrant a longer study than listening for words with an /f/ sound.

3. *Add to the list.*

   I explain to the children that as they read throughout the day, they may come across other words for our list. If they happen to find a "particularly interesting" word, they can write the word and their name on an adhesive note and attach it to the chart. (I make it clear that their primary job is to *read*, not find words to add to the chart.) During

   subsequent shared reading sessions, we discuss whether words they've found fit the category and add some to our list.

4. *Sort the words into categories to demonstrate similarities and differences.*

   As our list begins to grow, children notice how the words are different or the same. For example, sometimes the featured letter might be at the beginning of the word, and in other words, it may come in the middle or at the end. Or they might note that one sound, for example, the /er/ in "father," can be represented with different letter combinations, such as "ir," "or," "ur," "ar," and even "ear" as in "earth."

   We highlight the words in each category by "boxing" them with colors we've established in our key, or by starting a new sheet for each category. We might continue adding words to these sheets for several days or weeks.

5. *Remind the children to use their knowledge of letter-sound relationships to read new words.*

   When I send children off to read independently after a shared reading session, I remind them to use what they know about letters and sounds to figure out new words. All the work we do together looking for spelling patterns and listening for sounds is of little use if they don't apply it as they read.

blend or consonant digraph), to figure out an unfamiliar word.

While this may seem obvious to us, it isn't always so for young children. Those at the beginning of the emergent stage need to be reminded to look closely at the first letter/s of the word and think of the sound it represents. It's important that children know enough of the surrounding words to support their "sounding out" of the new one.

Using the Illustrations

I show children how to use the pictures to figure out what a word might be.

I use Big Books where the illustrations and print are closely matched to show emergent and early readers how to look carefully at the pictures to get a sense of what the print says. If they come to a word they don't know and have given it a try, they can refer to the pictures for help. In fact, emergent readers generally look at the pictures first.

Looking Through the Word to the End

I show children how to look through the entire word to figure it out.

Once they understand that they need to first look at the initial letter for the sound it represents, I show them that they need to also look through the rest of the word to the end. After the initial sound, it's sometimes the final sounds they hear most clearly and most frequently know.

Looking for a Familiar Spelling Pattern

I show children how to use a spelling pattern they know to get a word.

Even though words are written from left to right, they're not always "attacked" this way. It's a mistake to ask children to look only from left to right. Sometimes children see a spelling pattern in the middle or at the end and use it to get the rest of the word.

Using "Skip and Return"

I show children how to skip a word they don't know, read on to the end of the sentence, and then return to the word for another try.

Or if the unknown word is the last word, they can read the next sentence. When they do, they have the meaning of the entire sentence (or the next one) as support.

I make it clear that I don't mean they should just "skip words." They must always come back to the word they "skipped" and use what they've learned from the rest of the sentence to figure out the word they didn't initially know.

Using Meaning, Structure, and Graphophonic Cues in Combination

I show children how to combine the use of meaning, structure, and graphophonic cues when they come to a word they don't know.

I want them to ask what makes sense, what sounds right, and what looks right.

In shared reading sessions, I generally use cloze procedures—covering up words or parts of words—to highlight the cueing system I want the children to focus on:

- If I want children to pay attention to meaning—to what makes sense—I cover some *content words*, such as "river," with adhesive notes. Then when we read the sentence "The boys went to the *river* to fish," they consider what word would make sense.

- If I want children to pay attention to structure or grammar—to what sounds right—I cover *function words*, such as "also," "under," "when," "but," and "her" to help them consider what would be syntactically correct. By covering the word "but" in the sentence "I wanted to go camping, *but* she didn't," the children can focus on that word's conjunctive role in the sentence.

- If I want children to pay attention to letter-sound relationships—to what looks right—I cover up *letters* or *letter clusters* and then gradually "uncover" them as the children consider the sound that each letter or group of letters represents. By covering the word "another" in the sentence "My sister got *another* present for her birthday," and by revealing it a little at a time, they can attend to the sounds represented by individual letters and spelling patterns.

Monitoring, Cross-Checking, and Self-Correcting

I show children how to "listen to themselves" as they read to make sure that it makes sense, sounds right, and looks right.

When their reading fails to meet any one of these criteria, they need to use additional cueing systems and self-correct so that it does.

* * *

At the end of each demonstration, I always remind the children to practice the strategies

I've demonstrated. They understand from our *many many* discussions of reading strategies and how to use them that I don't want them to practice "using strategies" for the sake of drill or use them when it's not necessary. Strategies are not "activities" to add on to their reading, but tools to help them understand what they're reading or figure out unknown words *when they're having difficulty*.

Conclusion

On the same "Today Show" segment mentioned earlier, a teacher from California expressed her view on how children learn to read. Wanting to make the point that her teaching is systematic and explicit, she explained that she starts by teaching children sounds and then builds up to words, then sentences, and finally paragraphs. She was emphatic that letter-sound relationships had to be taught *in order* to ensure children wouldn't miss something.

I believe in being "systematic," but in wise ways—in ways that make sense to children. Children don't need strategies and skills pre-sented in specific order, but in relation to their needs as they arise in the course of reading and writing. A system is parts working together as a whole. Insisting on an arbitrary order to teach reading skills and strategies decontextualizes a context-laden process and often turns children off to reading when they should love it.

Learning is a recursive process: Children read. They notice things. They ask questions. They write. They ponder how things are similar, yet different. Relate one thing to another. Make hypotheses. Revisit old "learnings." See new things. Ask more questions. Revise their hypotheses. These behaviors are as natural as beavers cutting down trees to build dams. It's what children do!

Teaching, too, is also a recursive process: We support children's investigations, showing them connections and helping them make new ones. The strategies I demonstrate during read aloud and shared reading are the same ones I present during guided reading and one-on-one conferences. I demonstrate the same strategies "again and again." It's through these repetitions of the same strategies in different contexts that children grow stronger and more confident in their use. It's how they learn and how, I'm convinced, we should teach.

Guided Reading: Demonstrating Strategies in Small-Group Settings

ONE WEEKEND LAST FALL, WHEN MY SON Matt, his wife Clarisa, my husband Ted, and I were at our house in Vermont, I decided to make pancakes. I found the recipe for "Griddlecakes," and pulled the mixing bowl down from the cupboard.

Then, as I started measuring the ingredients and mixing them together, I kept stopping to take the butter out of the refrigerator so it would soften for spreading on the pancakes, make the coffee, set the table, warm the maple syrup, pour the orange juice... What first seemed simple enough had turned into a test of my planning and organizational skills. I hadn't made pancakes in a while, and had forgotten how much coordination it takes!

That's when it occurred to me that doing guided reading is a lot like making a pancake breakfast. Mixing the ingredients and frying the cakes are the easy part. Getting everything to the table at the same time takes more effort.

And so it is with guided reading. There's so much more to it than just guiding a group of children through a text. I've got to cluster children with similar needs, select a book at the right level of difficulty that supports the strategy we're focusing on, and engage the rest of the children in meaningful reading work. Leading the actual group itself is "a piece of cake," or "*pan*cake," as the case might be.

What Guided Reading Is and Isn't

Guided reading is a key component in my reading program in which a small group of children (usually between three and six) reads multiple copies of the same text under my guidance. The text is one the children can *almost,* but not quite, read on their own, and supports their practice of a reading strategy I want them to acquire. I allow the children as much independence as they can handle, but I'm there to provide as much assistance as they need.

Guided reading stands alongside read aloud, shared reading, independent reading, word study groups, and writing as one means of helping children acquire the strategies and skills they need to become fluent readers. It provides me with *another* opportunity to demonstrate what reading is all about—this time to a small group of readers—and *another* opportunity for children to practice.

Guided reading groups are not last ditch efforts to make sure some children "get" a skill others in class have already acquired. There are other ways to provide direct demonstrations of phonetic skills, such as letter and sound explorations (see Chapter 7) or word study groups (see Chapter 9). Rather, guided reading is a way to help children understand how reading works and learn techniques to figure out words and comprehend texts that are just a little too challenging for them to read without support.

Grouping Children for Guided Reading

Years ago, I assigned children to work in small reading groups very differently than I do now. I used to give each child an informal reading inventory during the first week of school to determine his reading level. Then I assigned him to one of three or four ability groups. These groups met daily and remained together throughout the year. After my initial assessments, I rarely reevaluated my children's needs. (I wrongly assumed I didn't need to!) I just followed the sequence of stories and skills the basal series prescribed. The completion of a basal text signaled passage to a new level, and the children moved on together.

Today, I still cluster readers with similar strengths and needs, but they aren't locked into the same group for the entire year. Instead, at the end of each month, when I organize my four guided reading groups for the coming month, I reflect on each child's reading to see if any changes have occurred to warrant his working with different children. Although children may end up working with many of the same classmates for several months—as there are natural clusters of children capable of reading the same text—there's more flexibility now regarding how children move among the groups.

I schedule guided reading two or three days a week and reading conferences on the other days. (Refer to Chapter 4 for how I set up my schedule). On each "guided reading day," I meet with only *two* of the four groups. Each group works together for about twenty minutes. Although there are always a couple children who aren't in a guided reading group in a particular month, I'm confident I'm meeting their needs through all the other components of my balanced literacy program. And when I work with these children during reading conferences, our one-on-one work may be seen as a customized "guided reading group" of sorts.

I continue to meet with these same two groups for one or two more days that week and, if needed, on additional days the following week, until we've completed the book and the children have practiced the strategy I've demonstrated. Then, each group is disbanded and different groups convene. Consequently, only two of the four groups are meeting within the same time frame.

This overview of how I do guided reading describes *what* you'd see if you visited my classroom. But the question that teachers most frequently ask is: *How?* How do you group children for guided reading? How can these groups reflect a child's stage in reading development and his needs, yet be flexible enough to allow him to work on occasion with different children? How do you decide what strategies children need to acquire the most, which books to use, when to disband a group? How do you make sure the "other" children, the ones not working in a group, are engaged in independent reading work that will add up to more proficient reading? How are you certain the few children who are not meeting in a guided reading group at all that month are getting what they need?

To provide a framework and clarify my procedures, I've prepared a time-line of action steps related to grouping children for guided reading. (See Figure 8–1.) This time-line will help you follow the sequence of steps within each month and note the slight variations in procedures between September and October and the rest of the year.

Conferring to Gather Data

I don't do guided reading at all in September. Instead, I spend the first two to three weeks of school getting to know my children as readers and helping them find "just-right" books for their book bags. Once my schedule of alternating "guided reading days" with "reading conference days" begins, the children who aren't working with me will need books in their bags that they can read on their own. (See Chapter 3.)

During the fourth week of school (for me, the last week in September), I schedule an individual conference with each student to consolidate the information I've gathered thus far so I can group him or her for guided reading in October. I'm able to meet with all my children within this one week because, throughout September, I'm using *both* the reading and the writing workshop time every day to confer with readers.

Up until the fourth week, I've been observing each child's reading for how it aligns with characteristics that are typical of children at various stages in reading development. (See Figure 2–2 on page 14 for details on these characteristics.) Now, I consider his or her "place" on this continuum of behaviors to determine the array of readers in my class and the potential groupings for guided reading. I need to see what clusters of readers, with similar strengths and needs, emerge.

USING THE PLANNING SHEETS

During our conferences in the last week in September,

I begin using my Guided Reading Planning Sheets (see Appendixes N, O, P, and Q), which I keep on a clipboard, to sort the children according to their stage in reading. These four sheets—for the emergent, early, transitional, and fluent stages—provide a place for me to summarize each child's reading on the sheet designated for her developmental stage. By combining the use of assessment notebooks for detailed notes on each child's reading and

FIGURE 8–1 Time-Line for Planning Guided Reading Groups

September		October		November through June	
		Beginning of Month	Select a book that the children in each group can read with support. Select a strategy the children need to acquire. Record the title of the book and the strategy on which each group will focus, on the Guided Reading Group Sheet.	**Beginning of Each Month**	Select a book that the children in each group can read with support. Select a strategy the children need to acquire. Record the title of the book and the strategy on which each group will focus, on the Guided Reading Group Sheet.
Weeks 1–3	Confer with children to assess their needs and match them with books for independent reading. Record notes about their reading in their assessment notebooks.	**Weeks 1–4**	Confer with children to assess their needs and match them with books for independent reading. Record notes about their reading in their assessment notebooks *and* on the planning sheets. Confer with each child several times throughout the month, continuing to record information about his reading.	**Weeks 1–4**	Confer with children to assess their needs and match them with books for independent reading. Record notes about their reading in their assessment notebooks *and* on the planning sheets. Confer with each child several times throughout the month, continuing to record information about his reading.
Week 4	Confer with each child: Record his name and a note about his reading on the September Planning Sheets to plan for October guided reading groups.				
End of Month	Based on what you've learned about the children by conferring with them throughout the month, organize them into four guided reading groups of readers with similar needs. Each group will have between three and six children. List the children in each group on a Guided Reading Group Sheet. Make plans for the few children who do not fall into one of the four guided reading groups, either because the groups would be too large or because their needs are different from the other children in the group.	**End of Month**	Use notes on the planning sheets to organize the children into four guided reading groups for November. Make plans for the few children who may not be working in a guided reading group for this month. Use the information on the planning sheets and any additional information you have about the child to decide on which sheet—emergent, early, transitional, or fluent—to record his name for the coming month.	**End of Each Month**	Use notes on the planning sheets to organize the children into next month's groups. Make plans for the few children who may not be working in a guided reading group for this month. Use the information on the planning sheets and any additional information you have about the child to decide on which sheet to record his name for the coming month.

planning sheets for summaries, I can track each child's needs, and think about her similarities to other children in class. (See Figure 8–2 for a September Emergent Stage Planning Sheet.) Although this may sound time-consuming, it

actually takes only a minute to write a phrase or two about the child's reading. And it's time well spent!

The listing of the children on the planning sheets and the notes I write alongside their names help me decide how to group them for guided reading the following month. For example, I use the notes I've made at the end of September and throughout October to plan my guided reading groups for November. They also help me decide which strategy to focus on because I've preprinted some possible strategies at the top of each planning sheet. I find this procedure more efficient than going through each child's assessment notebook at the end of the month for information.

At the end of each month (beginning with October),

I sit with the four *old* planning sheets and go through them, taking a "fresh look" at each child's reading and the progress she's made. Then I enter each child's name on a planning sheet for the month that's just beginning. (I form my guided reading groups using the information on the last month's planning sheets and any new information I've acquired.)

When I confer with a child during the coming month, I find her name on the planning sheet and record the date and observations about her reading alongside it. This helps me identify the children with whom I still need to confer. For example, from the December Emergent Stage Planning Sheet in Figure 8–3, I can see that I've met with Mikey on December 8 and Taha on December 7, but that I still need to schedule conferences with Sasha and Tiffany.

Organizing the Children into Groups

At the end of each month,

I sit down with the four planning sheets from the month just ending (see Figure 8–4) and a "worksheet" to organize the children into guided reading groups (see Figure 8–5). The worksheet is simply a blank piece of paper to help me think through possible ways in which to group the children.

I start by jotting down the names of children with similar strengths

---

Guided Reading Planning Sheet (Sept for Oct.) Emergent Stage

Some Strategies to Demonstrate:
- tracking print
- noting patterns in text
- using pictures to predict the story and words
- attending to visual cues (especially the beginning and ending letters)
- looking through the word to the end

9/24 Jack – identifies initial sound – then guesses – recognizes just a few high freq. words.

9/24 Daniel – works hard at sounding out – doesn't consider other cues

9/24 Sasha – uses meaning but needs to attend to letter-sound relationships

9/25 Brittany uses meaning or visual cues but doesn't often consider both (she may be more an early reader?)

9/28 Tiffany – at beginning of stage – needs lots of support and direction

9/28 Scott – at beg. of stage – needs lots of supp.

9/28 Mikey – at beg. of stage – very serious about work/reading

9/28 Taha – uses pictures a lot to predict – at beginning of stage.

FIGURE 8–2

Guided Reading Planning Sheet (Sept. for Oct.) Emergent Stage

---

Guided Reading Planning Sheet (Dec. for Jan) Emergent Stage

Some Strategies to Demonstrate:
- tracking print
- noting patterns in text
- using pictures to predict the story and words
- attending to graphophonetic cues (especially beginning and ending letters)
- looking through the word to the end

Sasha

12/8 Mikey – tracks print consistently – attending more closely to letter-sound relationships – tries to look all the way through word – not just at beginning.

Tiffany

12/7 Taha – nice progress – tries to match letters and sounds but isn't consistent.

FIGURE 8–3

Guided Reading Planning Sheet (Dec. for Jan.) Emergent Stage

Guided Reading Planning Sheet (*Nov.* for *Dec.*)   **Emergent Stage**

Some Strategies to Demonstrate:
- tracking print
- noting patterns in text
- using pictures to predict the story and words
- attending to graphophonetic cues (especially beginning and ending letters)
- looking through the word to the end

11/10 Sasha – matching sounds to letters – beg. to
11/16 look through word to end – more practice

11/4 Tiffany – looks at beginning but not end
11/10

11/2 Daniel – needs to focus on meaning as well
11/16 as letter sounds – knows a lot but needs to
relax so he can use it altogether.

11/10 Mikey – is beginning to figure out many
11/20 words himself – uses pictures and sounding out

11/24 Scott – works hard on books in bag – good
improvement – has difficulty pronouncing
many ed words – Tries to give all the
/ed/ sound. (Move to early stage.)

11/9 Taka – trying to make sense and look
closely at letters (skips lines occasionally –?)
reading sometimes "choppy" – even when knows
text well.

Guided Reading Planning Sheet (*Nov.* for *Dec.*)   **Early Stage**

Some Strategies to Demonstrate:
- noting spelling patterns
- monitoring and self-correcting
- using meaning, structure, and graphophonetic cues together
- chunking words into phrases
- "Skip and Return"

11/2 Chelsea – doing nicely – self-corrects a lot –
encourage to do more – close to trans. stage –
11/19 at first didn't want chapt. bks – now asks.

11/4 Brittany – looking thru word to end – steady
progress – self-corrects more consistently.
11/16

11/19 Nick – needed easier books (in g.r.g. for
11/30 past two wks)

11/12 Fanny – won't ask for conferences – I need to!
– has been in a lot of g.r.g. – needs a lot of
11/30 exposure to spoken & written Eng. – more time
with books on tape

11/30 Dana – beg. to monitor and self-correct –
11/12 likes folk tales – trying to "Skip & Return."

11/9 Alexis – just moved from emergent stage –
11/19 needs to monitor and self-correct more

11/30 11/4 Thomas – self-correcting more consistently
11/9

11/4 Jack – working hard – focused – at beg. of
11/9 early stage

Guided Reading Planning Sheet (*Nov.* for *Dec.*)   **Transitional Stage**

Some Strategies to Demonstrate:
- "Stopping to Think"
- making a Story Map
- making a Character Map
- using a "Before and After" Chart
- retelling chapters in writing
- rereading to clarify meaning

11/20 Shiori – reading M&H – good understanding – confident
11/24

Georgie

11/2 Jordan – needs more comprehension strategies – can
11/16 read M&H "okay" on own – but probably needs
easier text ?

11/2 Mary – just entering stage – needs to read a lot –
11/16 discuss stories/text – think – talk – can retell what
she's read (she selected "Arthur" books)

11/9 Jena – needs to focus on comprehension strategies –
inferences – discussions

11/2 Jimmy is reading longer books – but needs
11/12 a lot of support with comprehension – tried
Polk Street School but didn't understand.

Jordan T.

Guided Reading Planning Sheet (*Nov.* for *Dec.*)   **Fluent Stage**

Some Strategies to Demonstrate:
- "Preview and Predict"
- using text features to aid comprehension
- researching---taking notes---making data charts
- writing to deepen understanding of stories, factual texts, and poetry
- webbing "What I Knew/What I Know Now"

11/12 Molly – enjoys reading – confident – good comprehension
11/20 – reading Pinky & Rex

11/10 Fiona – confident – needs to read more factual text
11/20

11/2 Sophia – needs to read more factual text –
11/30 independent worker

11/12 Rafe – likes chapter books – but not "ones that
11/24 are too long"

FIGURE 8–4   Guided Reading Planning Sheet (Nov. for Dec.) Emergent, Early, Transitional, and Fluent Stage

and needs. These are usually children who can read the same text with a word accuracy rate between 92 percent to 97 percent. Although, in many instances, these clusters of readers mirror their placements on the planning sheets, I do make adjustments in response to their progress from one stage to the next. For example, Daniel and Scott were listed as emergent readers on the November Emergent Stage Planning Sheet (see Figure 8–4), but my notes indicated they had progressed to the early stage and could be grouped with early readers in December. In addition, to make each group as close to six children as possible (for management purposes), I sometimes consider whether a child can work successfully with readers in an "adjacent" group. Often a child at the "top" of one developmental stage can read quite successfully with the children who are at the "lower end" of the next stage.

When I reviewed my November Planning Sheets and considered possible guided reading groupings, here's how the December groups took shape (see Figure 8–5 for worksheet):

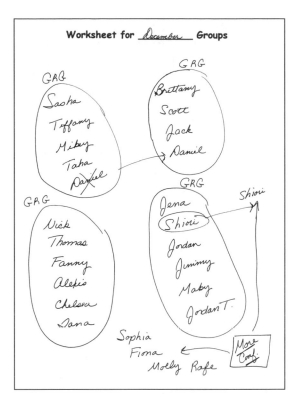
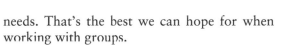

FIGURE 8–5

Worksheet for December Groups

There was one emergent group. Sasha, Tiffany, Mikey, and Taha could work together and benefit from the attention a smaller group affords.

They had made steady progress since September, when they were just starting out. They had learned more words and were beginning to attend more closely to letter-sound relationships.

There were two early groups. I noted that my ten early readers (eight on the Early Stage Guided Reading Planning Sheet, plus Scott and Daniel, who had just moved into the early stage) would require *two* groups.

I decided to put Chelsea, Fanny, Iana, Thomas, Alexis, and Nick, the "stronger" early readers, in one group, and Daniel, Scott, Brittany, and Jack, in another.

There was one transitional group. I saw that Jena, Georgie, Jordan, Jimmy, Maky, and Jordan T. could work together to learn strategies to better understand longer, more complex text.

While it was unlikely that every member of the group would need precisely the same thing at the same time, the fact that each of the children was a transitional reader meant that many of their needs were similar. This, in addition to the notes I took on the planning sheets, helped assure me that I was addressing, as much as possible, both their shared and individual

needs. That's the best we can hope for when working with groups.

The planning sheet also indicated that neither Georgie nor Jordan T. had conferred in November, although they had met quite regularly in guided reading groups. Since they weren't initiating conferences themselves, I would have to pursue them more aggressively. I circled their names on next month's planning sheets as a reminder. I also planned to write a note in each of their assessment notebooks the next time we conferred to remind them to: "Ask for more conferences."

Early in the year, I'm particularly careful not to advance children ahead to the next stage until I'm confident they belong there. That's why in September, October, and November there were so many readers on the Early and Transitional Stage Planning Sheet, and so few on the Fluent. I'm reluctant to identify children as fluent readers until I've had time to assess both their word knowledge *and* their comprehension, as well as their overall attitude toward reading.

There were five readers who could work "on their own."

- *Four fluent readers* Sophia, Fiona, Molly, and Rafe were the most fluent readers in class. If I hadn't already decided on the four groups described previously, I might have grouped them to work on refining some of their strategies for reading longer, more complex text, or to help them read factual text with better understanding. But since I'd met with them in guided reading groups during the month just ending, I was comfortable letting them "sit out" the month and giving them additional conferences and more independent work. I put an asterisk (*) alongside their names on the planning sheet to remind myself they needed some extra attention.

- *One transitional reader* That left Shiori. Because I already had a group of six transitional readers and because of Shiori's confidence and skills, I decided that she could work "on her own" for the month, and then work in a guided reading group the following month. I put an asterisk (*) alongside her name on the December Planning Sheet to remind myself to give her more conferences and additional support.

I'm more willing to allow more proficient readers like Shiori, Molly, Fiona, Sophia, and Rafe to *occasionally* forgo working in a guided reading group than children who are just beginning to acquire reading skills. Although self-improving readers like these still need guided reading to help them refine and extend their reading of fictional text, as well as to become more skilled at reading factual texts and poetry, they can also consolidate their skills by working independently. Children at the other end of the continuum need closer, more direct support.

In fact, occasionally, during the first independent reading session when I typically meet with children for word study groups, I sometimes hold an "extra" guided reading group instead. This gives the readers who need more assistance some additional time with me. It also gives me a chance to meet with children who are not in a formal guided reading group that month.

Listing the Groups

Once I decide on my four groups for the month, I record the members' names on a Guided Reading Group Sheet (see Appendix R). Before we meet for guided reading, I select a book they can read with 92 to 97 percent accuracy and a strategy I want to demonstrate. Ideally, the book supports this demonstration. I also record the name of the book and the strategy on the sheet. Then, each time the group meets with me to read, I record the date (see Figure 8–6).

Each time the group meets during that month to read a *new* book, I list the children's names and the book and strategy they'll be working on

again on a new sheet. By the end of the month, I often have three or four pages of Guided Reading Group Sheets on my clipboard.

Selecting a Book and a Strategy

Maintaining a Core Collection

I keep sets of books to use for guided reading in my classroom. Although our school has a resource room that houses multiple copies of texts, I prefer having my own core collection.

I keep these sets separate from the rest of my books. Since I often want to discuss what might happen next in a story, how a character's behaviors drive the plot, or predict what information might be included in a factual text, I prefer texts the children haven't read. I organize them according to what readers at the emergent, early, transitional, and fluent stage are likely to be able to read. My husband Ted made me a bookcase with four shelves so that I could store my books accordingly.

The range of books you have in your classroom will depend upon the grade you teach. Kindergarten and first-grade teachers will need many more books for emergent and early readers; while second- and third-grade teachers will want more books for transitional and fluent readers. In addition, teachers of these older children will need to collect sets of books to use for book discussion groups. These groups are different from guided reading groups in that they focus more on helping children interpret texts, such as Beverly Cleary's *Dear Mr. Henshaw*, and less on guiding children step-by-step through the actual reading of them. For information on how to organize book discussion groups, I recommend Joanne Hindley Salch's *In the Company of Children*.

I put a rubber band around each set of six books so they're together when I need them. I don't collect the books until a week or two after groups have disbanded so that the children can continue to practice reading them. If I find that a set is incomplete, I put it on the right side of the shelf to remind myself to locate the missing copies.

When I select a text for a group to read, I use the following criteria:

(1) It must be worth reading.
(2) Everyone in the group can read it with the required rate of accuracy.
(3) It supports my demonstrations of the strategy I want the children to acquire.

FIGURE 8–6

Guided Reading Groups (Month of December)

Guided Reading Groups	Month of _Dec._
Book: *Tiger Is a Scaredy Cat*	**Book** *Norma Jean, Jumping Bean*
Strategy: *Looking Through Each Word to the End*	**Strategy:** *"Skip and Return"*
Dates: _____	**Dates:** _____
Children: 1. *Sasha* 2. *Mikey* 3. *Tiffany* 4. *Taha* 5. 6.	**Children:** 1. *Daniel* 2. *Brittany* 3. *Scott* 4. *Jack* 5. 6.
Book: *Beavers*	**Book** *M & M and the Halloween Monster*
Strategy: *Monitor and Self-Correct*	**Strategy:** *Story Mapping*
Dates: _____	**Dates:** _____
Children: 1. *Nick* 2. *Thomas* 3. *Fanny* 4. *Alexis* 5. *Chelsea* 6. *Jana*	**Children:** 1. *Jena* 2. *Georgie* 3. *Jordan* 4. *Jimmy* 5. *Maby* 6. *Jordan T.*

THE BOOK MUST BE WORTH READING

I'm as choosy about the books I use for guided reading as I am about the rest of my books. After all, they are the "hooks" that motivate children to want to read more. Without children's engagement in reading, everything else is to little avail. Therefore, when deciding whether to include a title in my guided reading collection, I ask:

• Will it appeal to children?
• Will it motivate them to read more?
• Is it attractive?
• Does it convey a compelling or important message?
• Is it respectful of people's differences?
• Will it foster good discussion?
• Does it relate to children's experience or background knowledge?
• Does it present a nonstereotypical view of ethnic groups and gender roles?

THE CHILDREN CAN READ THE BOOK WITH SOME GUIDANCE AND SUPPORT

When selecting a book for a specific guided reading group, I aim for one the children can read with a 92 percent to 97 percent word accuracy rate. If the book is more difficult, it's harder for children to monitor their reading for meaning and accuracy. I say "aim" because it's far too easy to overestimate a child's reading ability. I have to keep reminding myself that it's better to err on the side of the book being too easy rather than too hard.

THE BOOK SUPPORTS MY DEMONSTRATION OF THE STRATEGY THE CHILDREN NEED TO ACQUIRE

When selecting which book to use during a guided reading group, I consider the strategy I want to present and how the book will support

---

FIGURE 8–7A Some Books and Strategies for Emergent Readers

Strategies to Demonstrate:	Text and Book Features That Support Readers and My Demonstrations:
• tracking print • noting patterns in text • using pictures to *predict* the story and words • attending to graphophonic cues (especially the beginning and ending letters) • looking through the word to the end	• consistent placement of text • font and spacing between words and lines that help children focus on the print • pictures that closely match the text • book language that matches children's spoken language • predictable text and language structures

Some Books I Use for Guided Reading:

There's a Mouse in the House, by A. Trussell-Cullen (Mondo) *Is This a Monster?* by S. Lovell (Mondo) *Cool Off,* by N. Diaz (Mondo) *At the Zoo,* by P. and S. Sloan (Sundance) *I See,* by C. A. Olsen (Mondo) *Honk,* by Sue Smith (Mondo) *Buzz Said the Bee,* by W. C. Lewison (Scholastic) *A Week with Aunt Bea,* by J. Nayer (Mondo) *My New Boy,* by J. Phillips (Random House) *I Eat Leaves,* by J. Vandine (Mondo) *The Three Goats,* by I. Douglas (Storyteller) *Winter,* by R. Weber (Storyteller)	*There's No One Like Me,* by R. Gunther (Wright Group) *How Many Pets?* by C. Montgomery (Mondo) *Who Lives in the Sea?* by S. M. James (Mondo) *Chickens,* by D. Snowball (Mondo) *Who Can?* by E. Montgomery (Mondo) *What Animals Eat,* by P. and S. Sloan (Sundance) *Lili's Breakfast,* by H. Upson (Storyteller) *Tarantulas Are Spiders,* By N. Platnick (Mondo) *Clever Little Bird,* by I. Douglas (Storyteller) *What Comes First?* by L. Swanson-Natsues (Mondo) *Animal Habitats,* by P. and S. Sloan (Sundance)

---

my demonstration. See Figure 8–7A, B, C, and D for some strategies to demonstrate, some book and text features supporting my demonstrations and the children's reading of the text, and some suggestions of books to use at different developmental stages.

Identifying a Book and a Strategy

The following are the books I selected for each guided reading group in Figure 8–6, and the thinking that went into my decisions. I consider how well the book will promote the children's overall reading, and if it will help them acquire the strategy I want to demonstrate. In most instances, I select the strategy from those listed at the top of the Guided Reading Planning Sheet that best fits the needs of each group of readers.

For the emergent group: *Tiger Is a Scaredy Cat*/**Looking Through the Word to the End**

I wanted to encourage Sasha, Tiffany, Mikey, and Taha to look from the beginning of

the word to the end to make sure that what they say matches the letters. Although the pictures in *Tiger Is a Scaredy Cat* by Joan Phillips were supportive of the text, the children couldn't predict what the text said from the pictures alone.

They needed to pay close attention to the letters and the sounds they represent, looking all the way through the word to the end. They couldn't say "steps" for "stairs" or "sad" for "sorry," just because they make sense and start with the same letters.

This group of emergent readers was "advanced" enough so I could demonstrate only one strategy at a time. Often, at the *beginning* of the emergent stage when children are new to reading, it's difficult for me and them to isolate one strategy from all the others they need to acquire. They're just learning about reading, and so they need to become conscious of doing it all—looking at the pictures, trying the initial and ending sounds, pointing with their fingers. Readers at other stages "do it all"

FIGURE 8–7B   Some Books and Strategies for Early Readers

Strategies to Demonstrate:	Text and Book Features That Support Readers and My Demonstrations:
• noting spelling patterns • monitoring and self-correcting • using meaning, structure, and grapho-phonic cues together • chunking words into phrases • "Skip and Return"	• pictures that support and extend text • text that is chunked into phrases • adequate spacing between words and lines • language that reflects children's oral language • books about topics children can relate to and about which they have some background knowledge

Some Books I Use for Guided Reading:

Too Many Rabbits, by P. Parish (Dell)
Ashes for Gold, retold by K. Maitland (Mondo)
Nina, Nina Star Ballerina, by Jane O'Connor (Grosset & Dunlap)
The Surprise Party, by A. Prager (Random House)
Big Boss, by A. Rockwell (Aladdin)
Minnie & Moo Go to the Moon, by D. Cazet (DK Publishing)
Beavers Beware, by B. Brennar (Byron Press)
Off to Squintums, adapted by G. Collins (Mondo)
The Best Teacher in the World, by B. Chardiet and G. Maccarone (Scholastic)
King of the Playground, by P. R. Naylor (Aladdin)
Well I Never, The Story Box (Wright Group)
Norma Jean, Jumping Bean, by J. Cole (Random House)

Beaver's Home, by C. Butterworth (Steck-Vaughn)
Beaver's Day, by C. Butterworth (Steck-Vaughn)
The Shortest Kid in the World, by C. D. Bliss (Random House)
Snow Day, by C. D. Bliss (Random House)
Er-lang and the Suns, by T. Cuo and E. Cheung (Mondo)
Happy Birthday, Little Witch, by D. Hautzig (Random House)
Ice-Cold Birthday, by M. Cocca-Leffler (Grosset & Dunlop)
Small Wolf, by N. Benchley (Harper Trophy)
Small Pig, by A. Lobel (Harper Trophy)
The Missing Tooth, by J. Cole (Random House)

too, but they're more able to focus on one strategy while applying the others with less deliberation.

For the first early group: *Norma Jean, Jumping Bean*/"Skip and Return"

Daniel, Scott, Brittany, and Jack needed to continue learning new strategies to figure out unfamiliar words, such as reading past a word they don't know after attempting it and then coming back for another try. Children just beginning to acquire reading skills often resist "skipping" words, insisting on a word-by-word progression. This works fine when they can figure out each word, but when they can't, their reading may come to a halt. "Skip and Return" is a helpful strategy for this group to try.

Although any book that meets the criteria I described earlier would help the children

practice this strategy, I selected *Norma Jean, Jumping Bean* by Joanna Cole for this group because they'd enjoy the story and have a lot to say about Norma Jean's unusual situation.

For the second early group: *Beavers*/Monitoring and Self-Correcting

Chelsea, Fanny, Iana, Thomas, Alexis, and Nick needed to become better at monitoring their reading for sense and accuracy, and self-correcting as needed. They needed to "listen to themselves read" to make sure they were indeed reading what the author wrote. I felt *Beavers* by Helen M. Moore would be particularly appropriate since we had learned so much about beavers in our study of New York City, enabling the children to bring this background knowledge to their reading. Although this book is listed in Figure 8–7C as a book for transi-

---

FIGURE 8–7C Some Books and Strategies for Transitional Readers

Strategies to Demonstrate:	Text and Book Features That Support Readers and My Demonstrations:
• "Stopping to Think" • making a Story Map • making a Character Map • making a "Before and After" Chart • retelling chapters in writing • rereading to clarify meaning	• longer text with chapters, sections, or an episodic structure • characters with interesting yet predictable personality traits • balance of narration and dialogue • straightforward plot • book features to access information, e.g., tables of contents, chapter titles, charts, tables, and glossaries • series books • books on familiar topics

Some Books I Use for Guided Reading:

Deputy Can Gets His Man, by J. Rosenbloom
Could We Be Friends: Poems for Pals, by M. James (Mondo)
Grandpa Comes to Stay, by R. Lewis (Mondo)
Young Cam Jansen and the Missing Cookie, by D. A. Adler (Puffin)
Cam Jansen and the Mystery of the U.F.O, by D. A. Adler (Puffin)
Pinky and Rex and the School Play, by J. Howe (Aladdin)
The True Story of Pocahontas, by L. R. Penner (Random House)
Thinking About Ants, by B. Brenner (Mondo)
Beavers, by H. M. Moore (Mondo)
M & M and the Halloween Monster, by P. Ross (Penguin)

Fish Face, by P. R. Giff (Dell)
Six Things to Make, by R. Green (Mondo)
Lionel and Louise, by S. Krensky (Puffin)
Where's Molly? by U. Waas (North-South Books)
The Banana Split from Outer Space, by C. Siracusa (Hyperion)
Edwin and Emily, by S. Williams (Hyperion)
Spider, the Magazine for Children (Carus Publishing Co.)
The Best Older Sister, by S. N. Choi (Hyperion)
Emily at School, by S. Williams (Hyperion)
My Home in the Netherlands, by D. Bailey (Steck-Vaughn)
Beauregard the Cat, by R. P. Rhodes (Mondo)

---

tional readers, I thought it would be appropriate for this group of early readers because of their background knowledge of the topic.

My primary focus here was to help children monitor their reading and self-correct if needed. Whereas with the group of emergent readers attending to letter-sound relationships throughout the word, my prompt to check what they're reading against meaning and structural cues was parenthetical and secondary to the main strategy I was highlighting.

For the transitional group: *M & M and the Halloween Monster*/**Story Mapping**

Jena, George, Jordan, Jimmy, Maky, and Jordan T. needed to acquire strategies for understanding the longer, more involved texts they were beginning to read. *M & M and the Halloween Monster* by Pat Ross helped them think about how the story elements—character, setting, problem, main events, and resolution—work together to "create" the story. (See Figure 8–8 for the Story Map Jena made while in this group.)

FIGURE 8–7D   Some Books and Strategies for Fluent Readers

Strategies to Demonstrate:	Text and Book Features That Support Readers and My Demonstrations:
• "Preview and Predict"	• books on topics of interest to readers
• using text features to aid comprehension	• stories that lend themselves to multiple interpretations
• researching—taking notes—making data charts	• texts requiring inference
• writing to deepen understanding of stories, factual texts, and poetry	• books in different genres
• webbing "What I Knew/What I Know Now"	• books about topics related to children's science and social studies investigations

Some Books I Use for Guided Reading:

The 'Gator Girls, by S. Calmenson and J. Cole (Beech Tree)

Cobblestone Magazine (Cobblestone Publishing)

Corn Is Maize, by Aliki (Harper Collins)

Air Pollution, by D. R. Stille (Children's Press)

Water Pollution, by D. R. Stille (Children's Press)

The Netherlands, by K. Jacobsen (Children's Press)

Planning a Birthday Party, by F. Bolton (Mondo)

Beany and the Magic Crystal, by S. Wojciechowski (Candlewick Press)

Hilary and the Troublemakers, by K. Leverich (Beech Tree)

Beavers, by E. Lepthien (Children's Press)

No Way, Winky Blue, by P. Jane (Mondo)

Take a Bow Winky Blue, by P. Jane (Mondo)

If You Lived in Colonial Times, by A. McGovern (Scholastic)

Sugar Cakes Cyril, by P. Gershator (Mondo)

The Stories Julian Tells, by R. Smith (Knoph)

The Stories Huey Tells, by R. Smith (Knoph)

The Adam Joshua Capers: The Kid Next Door, by J. L. Smith (Harper Trophy)

Mary Marony Hides Out, by B. Sims (G. P. Putnam's Sons)

Birds of Prey, by M. Woolley and K. Pigdon (Mondo)

Busybody Nora, by J. Hurwitz (Puffin)

Superduper Teddy, by J. Hurwitz (Puffin)

New Neighbors for Nora, by J. Hurwitz (Puffin)

Meet Benjamin Franklin, by M. Scarf (Random House)

A Kid's Guide for New York City, Gulliver Books (Harcourt Brace Jovanovich)

Leading the Group

On "guided reading group days," I announce the two groups with whom I'll be working at the end of the morning meeting. As a reminder, I record the name of one child in the group on our dry-erase schedule board, e.g., "Daniel's group."

The children know that if their group is meeting first, they should come directly to the meeting area with their reading folders and bag of books. If their group is second, they should read independently while the first group meets. Children who are not in either group have their independent reading and other reading-related work to do (see Chapter 12).

The children and I sit in a circle. They take their assessment notebooks out of their folders and place them in the center of the circle so that, once the group gets underway and it's convenient, I can record in each of their notebooks: the date, the title of the book, and the strategy they're practicing. The children put their reading folders and book bags behind them so they're not in the way.

Guidelines for Conducting Guided Reading Groups

During each session, I guide the children through the text and encourage them to try the

FIGURE 8–8

Jena's Story Map

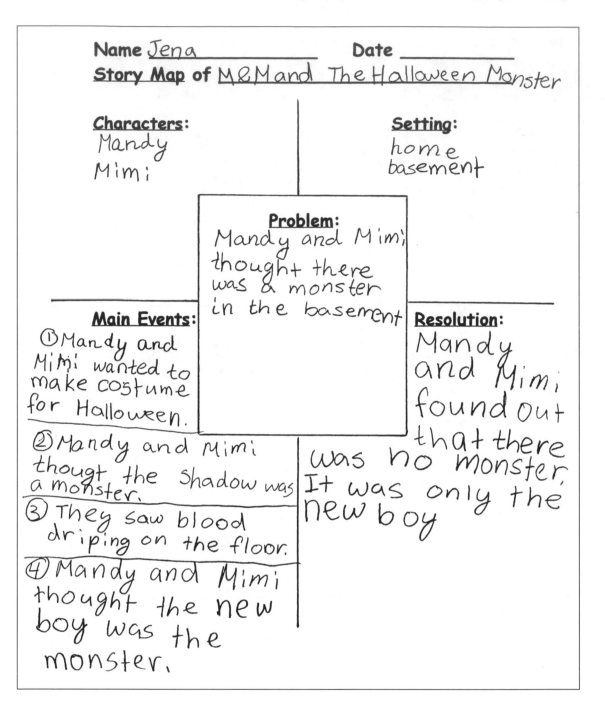

Name Jena   Date _____
Story Map of M&M and The Halloween Monster

Characters:
Mandy
Mimi

Setting:
home
basement

Problem:
Mandy and Mimi
thought there
was a monster
in the basement

Main Events:
① Mandy and
Mimi wanted to
make costume
for Halloween.

② Mandy and Mimi
thougt the Shadow was
a monster.

③ They saw blood
driping on the floor.

④ Mandy and Mimi
thought the new
boy was the
monster.

Resolution:
Mandy
and Mimi
found out
that there
was no monster.
It was only the
new boy

strategy I'm demonstrating. Although I don't know *exactly* what I'll say from one moment to the next, I do know that it will be in response to what I've learned about them, what I observe them doing, and what I'd like them to do differently.

The following guidelines provide a predictable framework for each session:

- I explain why I called the group together.
- I introduce the text.
- I demonstrate the strategy.

- I provide opportunities for the children to read the text and practice the strategy.
- At the end of each session, I remind the children to practice the strategy as they read independently.

Knowing that I'll move from explaining why I called them together at the beginning to reminding them of what they should do when they're reading independently, I can concentrate my attention on what the children are saying and doing, and how I might respond.

EXPLAINING WHY I CALLED THE GROUP TOGETHER

When I meet for guided reading, I always tell the children why I called them together by referring back to what I've noticed about their reading. I try to be as explicit as possible in regard to what I've learned, how I plan to help them, and what they need to do.

The following excerpts from the four guided reading groups I've been describing are representative of how I start out my group meetings.

Emergent Readers

Teacher: I've noticed that you don't always match the words you read with words in the text. You start out great. You get the beginning sounds, but then you're not as careful that the other sounds match too. For example, if the book says "small" and you say "smart," you're partly right because you got the first part—"sm" represents the /sm/ sound—but the rest of the sounds also need to go with the letters.

Taha: You mean like for my name, you can't say "Thomas" because there's a "h" and an "a" at the end of "Taha."

Teacher: Exactly. I'm going to show you how to pay closer attention to letters and the sounds they make all the way to the end of the word.

First Group of Early Readers

Teacher: Let me explain why we're working together. First of all, I'm really pleased with how you're trying a lot of different strategies to get words you don't know. You try to look closely at the letters and think of what sounds they represent. You look at the pictures. You think about what makes sense. But there's something else I'd like you try. And that's—skipping a word you can't get, and then coming back to it to try it again. Now I know your moms probably say: "Don't skip words," but this time it's okay. Because you'll be doing it on purpose to help yourself understand what the whole sentence is about. Then maybe that will help you get the word.

Jack: You showed us that when we read that Big Book.

Teacher: And now we can practice it some more.

Second Group of Early Readers

Teacher: I've noticed that lots of time when you read for me during conferences, you say something that doesn't make sense and doesn't match the letters and you keep right on going. For example, you might say, "The dog *stuffed* the grass," instead of "The dog *sniffed* the grass." When you do this, you aren't really listening to yourself read. Today you're going to practice a really important strategy. You're going to listen to what you're reading to make sure it matches the letters and makes sense. And when it doesn't, you're going to correct yourself so that it does.

Iana: I try to do that sometimes when I read.

Thomas: I do too.

Teacher: Yep. Sometimes you do. But it's so important that you've got to keep working at it.

Transitional Readers

Teacher: You guys should be really proud of yourselves. You're starting to read longer books. It's fun reading chapter books, isn't it?

Jordan: I'm reading them at home too.

Teacher: That's great. But sometimes it's hard to understand how all the parts of longer stories go together. So today I'm going to show you a strategy we've worked with before when I read books aloud. It's called story mapping.

Georgie: Like we did with *Chrysanthemum*?

Teacher: That's right. When we thought about the characters, setting, problem, main events, and resolution, it helped us think about how the whole story worked. And now you can use that same strategy to understand your chapter book better and remember it from day to day.

INTRODUCING THE TEXT

I always introduce children to the text before they start reading it. My introductions vary according to their stage in reading:

- *Emergent readers* usually need to be "walked through" their book (which is typically only eight or sixteen pages), as they look carefully at each picture and discuss what's happening. When talking about what's on each page, I try to use the same language patterns and some of the exact words as the text. I want the children to be so familiar with what the print says that the words practically pop out of their mouths when they go to read them. The children finish the book during one session, but will reread it and may do extension activities related to the book on follow-up days.

- *Early readers* still need fairly detailed introductions, but don't need to be "walked through" the text before they read it. For one thing, their books are longer (around thirty-two pages). We may look over a couple of pages before reading them, but I don't try to preview what the text says. That's their job. They're beginning to focus more on the print, using the pictures now to confirm what the text says. It might take them two or three days to complete a text.

- *Transitional readers* need even briefer introductions. Their challenge is understanding longer and more complex text, holding it in their heads over several days and integrating the story elements. Their introductions might include looking at the back of the book for information about the story, examining the table of contents to see what clues it offers, recalling other books in the same series or by the same author, or recalling events in their own lives that may be similar to those suggested by the title, cover, and jacket information. It takes them several days to complete a text.

- *Fluent readers* can begin reading fictional texts with minimal introductions. I usually try to help them refine and internalize some of the strategies they used more "deliberately" as transitional readers, or interpret what the text has to say. Their books also take several days to complete.

When guiding children through factual texts, I direct them to examine some text features before they begin reading the book, such as tables of contents and indices; and others, such as glossaries, section headings, captions, and illustrations, while they read. The process of reading factual text is more specific and goal-oriented than reading fiction. Children may only need to find an answer to a question or gather information about a topic they're researching.

DEMONSTRATING THE STRATEGY

After I've introduced the book, I demonstrate the strategy we'll be focusing on. Although I generally don't use the guided reading text itself for this demonstration, I may use a text that's familiar or simple enough so not to distract the children's attention from what I'm trying to show them. For example, if I want to illustrate how to "chunk words into phrases," I may use a poem the children know from shared reading where the lines contain phrases reflecting the way the poem should be read. If I used an unfamiliar text, the children's attention would be drawn to the content, making it harder to focus on the strategy I'm highlighting.

There are times, however, when I use the first few pages of the text they'll be reading. If, for example, I want to show beginning emergent readers how to use the pictures to *predict* what the text says, I might have them examine the first couple pages and describe what they see, cueing them in to what the text says. And then I show them how they can use the pictures throughout the rest of the book in the same way. Regardless of the text I'm using or the strategy I'm demonstrating, it's important to show children just what it is that they need to try.

If I'm working with transitional or fluent readers and we are going to use a strategy sheet (see Appendixes G, H, and I), I show them how it works. Most often, my explanation is actually more of a reintroduction of the strategy than a description of a new procedure, since I already demonstrated the strategy to the whole class during shared reading or read aloud. (It's important to remember that the children use strategy sheets *while* they're reading a text to support their use of a particular reading strategy, not after they've completed it, which would be more of a response.)

For example, when I met with a group of fluent readers to read *The Adam Joshua Capers: The Kid Next Door* by Janice Lee Smith, I wanted them to understand how critical the characters' personalities are to this story's plot. So I explained they would make *two* story maps—one for Adam Joshua and the other for his best friend Nelson—*as they read* the book. (See Figure 8–9.)

It is the *differences* between Adam Joshua and Nelson that provide much of the story's tension. Although I usually demonstrate character mapping to transitional readers, given the needs of this particular group of fluent readers I felt it would be a helpful strategy due to the story's nature.

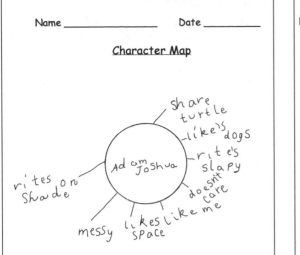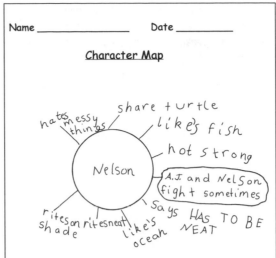

FIGURE 8–9

**Itamar's Character
Maps of Adam Joshua
and Nelson**

When another group of fluent readers gathered, I directed them to use a "Before and After" Chart as they read *Water Pollution* by Darlene R. Stille. This encouraged them to use what they already knew about the topic and then record new information they learned (see Figure 8–10 for Fiona's "Before and After" Chart.)

Once I've introduced Strategy Sheets during guided reading, the children sometimes ask to use one as they read a book from their bag. I keep extra copies of these sheets on file for the children to take as they need them.

PROVIDING OPPORTUNITIES FOR READING THE TEXT AND PRACTICING THE STRATEGY UNDER MY GUIDANCE

Finally—the children read the text, and I give them whatever help they need. I used to worry a lot about what to say, wondering if I was saying the "right" things, asking the "right"

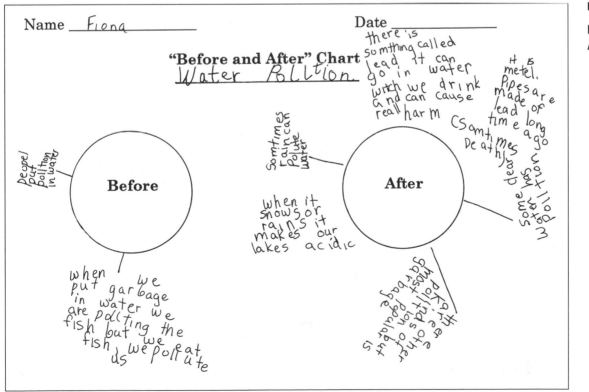

FIGURE 8–10

Fiona's "Before and After" Chart

questions. This was probably a carry-over from my days of using a basal reader when everything was prescribed (regardless of whether it met my children's needs). Now I know that guiding children through the text is the easy part; the hard part—organizing the groups, deciding what to teach and which book to use—has already been done.

Georgia Heard once told me that before she goes into a classroom to work with children, she lets go of her anxieties and fears about remembering all the best practices regarding how to teach children to write poetry. She stops trying to "hold on" to *what* she knows, and instead, tries to be the very best person she can be. Georgia knows that by doing this, the truly important things will come to her. I try to follow Georgia's wise advice.

When I sit down with my children for guided reading, I stop worrying about what the "best" or "right" thing to say might be, knowing there *isn't* one best or right way. In truth, if several teachers were to sit down with the same group of children each lesson would be different—and they'd each be valid, as long as the teacher was responding to what the children had said or done, and trying to respond to them in wise ways. Here is some advice to consider as you guide children through text:

Encourage children to use the demonstrated strategy as needed.

It's important that children understand that they should try using the strategy I've demonstrated, along with others they know, *only if they need to*. We must teach them to become strategic readers not just users of reading strategies. In *Knowing Literacy: Constructive Literacy Assessment*, Peter Johnston writes that we should help children understand when and where to use strategies, and not to just apply them indiscriminately.

Elicit discussion.

Far more important than asking children to respond to preset questions about what they've read is getting them to take the initiative to talk about the book. We want them to talk before, during (if an important issue arises), and after reading the assigned selection. The children's discussion about what they've read, what might happen next and why, what the character might do, how certain text and book features help readers, and how this story is different from others by the same author are the kinds of dialogue that engage children in reading.

Encourage "silent" reading.

Of course, the reading behaviors of the group and kind of support I offer differ depending on the developmental stage of the readers. When emergent readers and those at the beginning of the early stage read "silently," they can't read in their heads. They need to voice their reading, making it more palpable. They need to hear what they're reading so they can begin to monitor their reading and self-correct. So when they begin together, it is very noisy. But oddly, hearing what each other is reading actually supports them and helps the less confident readers get started. Before long, they're on different pages and the children eventually finish the book at different times.

As readers grow more confident and skilled, they learn to internalize their reading (with the help of my reminders to: "Try to read as quietly as you can.")

See how each child is doing and give them assistance if needed.

Once the children start reading, I move from child to child, asking each one how he's doing and seeing how I can help. If the child is an emergent or early reader, I listen as they read out loud. I want to see if they're having trouble with the book or using strategies wisely.

If they're transitional or fluent readers, I go to each one to ask if they're having trouble, and I only ask a child to read out loud if I have any questions about his reading. Interrupting them would be particularly bothersome since they're trying to understand more difficult text.

Encourage the use of context to figure out the meaning of unfamiliar words.

I used to prepare children to read the text by introducing new vocabulary words at the onset of the story. Now I know that figuring out the meaning of new words from the surrounding text is a skill they need to acquire. I usually give the children a chance to work at figuring out a word themselves, and then we discuss it when we pause to talk. My awareness of words that are likely to present a challenge helps me give the children what they need.

Recording

Each day the group meets, I take a moment to record in their assessment notebooks the date, the title of the book, and the strategy they worked on. Then I give the notebooks back to the children and they put them into their reading folders.

REMINDING CHILDREN TO PRACTICE THE STRATEGY AS THEY READ INDEPENDENTLY

Before I disband the group, I remind the children that when they read by themselves, whether at home or in school, they should use the strategy they've been working on (in combination with others) if the need arises.

Reading should be a pleasurable endeavor. The strategies are there to help them out when they hit a snag. Using strategies is not an end in itself, but a means to more fluent reading. Although the children begin the journey along the developmental continuum as emergent readers, deliberately and "concretely" applying strategies, they should end as fluent readers, combining them, internalizing them, and, most importantly, knowing when to use them.

Keeping the Rest of the Children Engaged in Meaningful Reading Experiences

The question, "What are the other children doing?" while you're meeting with guided reading groups, is one that teachers ask me a lot. Although Chapter 12, "Independent Reading," deals with this question in more detail, there are a few points I'll make here.

As discussed in Chapter 3, virtually all the decisions I make in my classroom—my room arrangement, schedule, materials, teaching practices—are aimed at helping children work independently while I'm conferring with readers or leading guided reading groups. Here are some examples of what the other children are doing:

- *reading books from their book bags*—Each child has a set of five to ten books that were chosen because they interest him and can be read by him with at least 95 percent accuracy.
- *filling in their reading logs for the day*—They write the title and author of a book they've read that day on their "Weekly Reading Log." They also color the box to correspond to the genre of the book. If they've read sev-

eral books, they select the one they feel is "most important" to record.

- *recording on the back of their logs*—On Friday of each week, they record what they were successful at that week and what they plan to do next week.
- *responding to books*—They write responses to some of the books they've read in their response notebooks. The frequency and types of responses vary according to children's fluency in both reading and writing.
- *reading Big Books, listening to and reading along with books on tape, or reading with a partner*—Emergent and early readers often engage in these more collaborative reading experiences for a portion of their independent reading time.
- *working on strategy sheets*—Sometimes children work on strategy sheets they started in their group or one they're using while reading a book from their bag.
- *extension activities that grow out of the guided reading groups*—When children work on a book for several days, they sometimes continue working on related activities for one or two more days. They may listen to a book on tape. They may work with sentence strips, arranging them in the order they were presented in the story, or they may sort words from the story into different categories.

Conclusion

We have to be easy on ourselves during guided reading more than at other times of the day. It's challenging—grouping children, selecting suitable books and strategies to teach, making sure we're saying wise things to the group, and getting children not working in groups to read independently. We need to give ourselves room to make mistakes, because they're inevitable.

Many a time, when the group begins reading, I realize that my selection is too hard. There are times I've even wondered why on earth I put a particular child into a group: "He really can't keep up as I'd hoped." On occasion, I've had to disband a group prematurely because the book I'd selected and the group I convened didn't match. I've even had visitors in my class when this has happened. I had to "cut my losses," finish the book as a read aloud, and tell the children I'd need another day or two to find a better book for them to read.

But I'm okay with that. I can't see how it can be any other way. In fact, I can relax about the fact that not everything goes as planned, that I make mistakes—and that I'll keep making them. For teaching, like learning, involves learning from your mistakes, assessing what's working and what isn't, revising your thinking about the best way to proceed, and knowing that you'll get better.

Word Study Groups: Analyzing Words for Their Phonetic, Structural, and Morphemic Features

IT WAS THE LAST TEN MINUTES OF THE READING workshop—the time when the children reconvene at the meeting area to share strategies that worked for them that day. Jack sat on the rocking chair, waiting for his classmates' attention. Once he had it, he began: "Today when I was reading, I came to a word and at first I didn't know it. The word was 'now.' Then I remembered what I did this morning in my word study group. We were thinking of words that had "o-w." Some words had an /ō/ sound and some had an /ow/ [like cow] sound. At first I tried the /ō/ sound, but that didn't make sense in the story. So then I tried /ow/, and it did."

Jack had used what he'd learned in his word study group that morning to figure out a new word he was trying to read, and felt good about it. Making this connection evoked a sense of accomplishment like the one he experiences making a clay pot, building a city out of blocks, or writing a story.

In part, Jack made this connection between what he knew and what he was learning because we'd set the stage for it. In his word study group, we examined the different sounds represented by "o-w" and practiced using this skill to read unfamiliar words. I scheduled independent reading to follow these demonstrations so the children could make more connections on their own. And by creating a time for sharing in our day, all the children knew that we'd share what we learned and learn from one another.

The Thinking Behind and Activities of Word Study Groups

Three or four times a week, at 8:40 a.m., as soon as the children put their coats away and place their homework in the basket, I call five or six children over to the small meeting area alongside the chart wall for a fifteen minute word study group. These are *informal* gatherings of children who, in general, need some extra time with me to study the same sorts of things. The children aren't grouped painstakingly as they were for guided reading, with careful regard to who might work best together or what strategies they need to acquire. There are no word study group sheets to keep track of the groups or assessment notebooks to list when each group met and what they did. They don't need their folders or their book bags.

I identify the children with whom to meet from the assessments I do of their reading during conferences. I might call some emergent readers (or early readers, if it's later in the year and they're the ones needing more support), or transitional and fluent readers who need to study words at a more advanced level than would be appropriate for the rest of the class.

The group sits around the edge of the carpet, and I sit facing them. The children who aren't meeting with me read books from the table book pots, from our nonfiction library, or from those set around the easel that I've read aloud, used for shared reading, or referred to during science or social studies.

Since I generally "teach to the middle" during shared reading and writing sessions, I welcome this time to focus my attention on a small group of readers requiring additional or special support. I strive to help children, especially those at the lower end of the developmental continuum, improve their reading *as quickly as possible.* It's not only important that they make progress, but that their *rate* of growth be rapid enough to minimize the gap between them and the highest achieving readers.

As children move from kindergarten through twelfth grade, the less-skilled readers who don't catch on in the early grades face a widening gap with their higher achieving counterparts. By the third grade, the gap may be five grade levels (Crevola and Hill, 1999). Of course, there will always be differences in achievement; that's the nature of things. But we must make every effort to help accelerate children's growth early on (optimally in kindergarten and first grade, or before they turn eight).

It's important that transitional and fluent readers make strides in reading as well. Even though they're starting from a different place, they still have a lot to learn. Word study groups are one way to give the kind of demonstrations they may not otherwise receive.

What We Do in Word Study Groups

Phases of Phonic Learning

In *Whole to Part Phonics*, Henrietta Dombey and the staff at the Center for Language in Primary Education report on Uta Frith's work on the sequence of children's phonic learning. Frith's conceptual framework confirms many of my own observations and informs my work with children during word study groups.

Frith's three overlapping phases describe the progression of children's phonic learning from ages four through eight:

- **Logographic Phase**—In the logographic phase, children begin to recognize *whole* words that have special significance for them, such as their own names and the Mc-Donalds or Toys 'R Us signs. They cue in to a word's size, color, and shape.

As children are exposed to print-rich environments at home and at school, they begin to

recognize more and more whole words. They may read the labels around the classroom or on food containers in their kitchen cabinets. They may also begin to identify words from their shared reading and writing texts.

Toward the end of this phase, children start to notice initial letters in words and the sounds they represent. This awareness is key since it supports their learning of new words by analogy—the hallmark of the next phase.

- **Analytic Phase**—As children's knowledge of whole words and letter sounds increase, they move into the analytic phase, marked by the *associations* they make between the spelling patterns in words they know and new words they encounter.

Children's reading "takes off" as they realize that they can use what they know to learn new things. If they can read "pet," they can also read "met," "let," and "bet." Similar associations occur in their writing, although it's a while before they're able to confidently and *consistently* apply what they know about spelling patterns to their writing.

- **Orthographic Phase**—In the orthographic phase, children come to recognize words almost automatically, no longer needing to "work at" making connections between them. They can *rapidly identify* an increasingly large number of words because they know a lot about the structure of words and how they're spelled.

I've found that this automaticity best occurs when children have had phonetic instruction that takes into account the importance of learning by analogy, and helps them apply what's learned to new situations. This, coupled with many daily opportunities to read, helps children consolidate their learning and learn "new" letter-sound relationships. Children at the orthographic phase can monitor their reading more consistently and self-correct when there's a discrepancy between the text and how they've read it.

Implementing the Conceptual Framework

Frith's phonic phases correspond to the emergent, early, transitional, and fluent stages of reading as follows: The logographic phase, where children learn whole words in context, largely from cueing into their length, structural features, and visual patterns, corresponds to the beginning of the emergent stage. The analytic phase describes the word analysis behaviors of more advanced emergent readers and early readers, while the orthographic phase reflects transitional and fluent readers' rapid recognition of most words.

When working with emergent and early readers, I focus on elements of phonic learning that help them analyze words for their letters, spelling patterns, and structural components, and then use what they know about words to learn new ones. By addressing single consonants and consonant clusters, spelling patterns, inflectional endings, compound words, common prefixes and suffixes, vowel digraphs and diphthongs, and long and short vowels (once they have the support of other phonic learning to handle them), I can help children move through the analytic phase of reading into the orthographic.

I must emphasize that progressing through these phonic phases and developmental stages is a goal over the course of several years, not one or two. Building on what the children know, I may introduce new spelling patterns, vowel combinations and short and long vowel investigations, knowing these will be reintroduced again and again. Children's learning is not linear, it's recursive—falling back on and going over again what's been learned to catapult them to new levels.

When working with transitional and fluent readers, I focus on helping them use what they know about the structure and spelling of words to learn new words. Once they can recognize most words quickly, readers can direct their attention to other aspects of words, such as less common prefixes and suffixes and learning about the word derivatives.

In the following I describe some of the activities that make up my word study group sessions. Although I present each activity as it is used with either "small," "bigger," or "difficult" words, the activities under each category can be adapted for any of the three categories. We can *sort* "bigger" and "difficult" words as well as "small" ones. And we can *make* "small" words as well as "bigger" and "difficult" ones. I select words containing features I want to highlight from our shared reading, shared writing, and guided reading texts, or those I've identified through the children's writing that they need to focus on.

Although I refer to these as "activities," they are never isolated from the rest of our work. The children understand why I'm meeting with them, they recognize the sources of the words

we are "studying," and they know that they must apply what they're learning in the group to their own reading. Word study groups are effective only to the extent that the children see these connections.

WE EXAMINE "SMALL" WORDS

Emergent and early readers need lots of opportunities to examine monosyllabic words with two, three, and four sounds, or phonemes. (A phoneme is the basic sound unit of speech. For example, "on" has two phonemes, /o/ and /n/; "will" has three phonemes, /w/, /i/, and /l/; and "small" has four, /s/, /m/, /a/, and /l/.) The practice in study groups of analyzing words for their phonetic and structural features, and then writing them down, solidifies children's learning.

Sorting Words—This activity helps children attend more closely to different features in words and to generalize about letter-sound relationships.

When working with monosyllabic words, I ask children to group words by either:

- their length
- their common letter/s
- their common sound
- their spelling pattern

I sometimes make an "other" category for words that don't fit the categories we're examining. For example, when sorting words containing spelling patterns representing the /ī/ sound (the long i sound) and our categories are "igh," *i-consonant-e*, and "*y*," I make an extra column for words that don't fit any of the other categories, such as "I" and "eye." At later stages, in addition to sorting words by their letters or sounds, children might also sort "bigger" and "difficult" words by their syntactic (structure-related) features or their morphemic (meaning-related) features.

Before the children gather, I write ten-to-fifteen words on oaktag strips and place them randomly on the sentence strip holder. These are usually words I've taken from a Big Book we've shared or a language-experience chart we've made.

Then we begin to sort the words—perhaps by where a particular letter is located in a word. If we're focusing on whether the "d" comes at the beginning, middle, or end of a word, we place all the words with "d" at the beginning under a key word, "dog" for example. Words with "d" in the middle or end might go under other key words such as "ladder" and "red," respectively. As the children read the words and categorize them, they might notice (and if they don't I help them) that although the "d" is sometimes in the middle of the word, as in "ride," it's the last sound we *hear*, helping children begin to generalize that many times "e" at the end of a word is silent. (But many times it is not, as in "be.") There are always blank cards available for adding new words.

Children can also think up their own categories. For example, the same words we sorted according to where the "d" was located might also be arranged according to how many letters there are in the word, or whether the "d" is followed by a consonant or a vowel. For more about sorting words see *Phonics They Use* by Patricia Cunningham.

Extending Our Work with the Spelling Pattern Word Wall—This activity helps children see common spelling patterns.

They learn that if they know how to read, write, and spell one word, they can read, write, and spell many others.

We have a "dependable" spelling pattern word wall where I highlight spelling patterns that usually represent only one sound. For example, we can expect "-ame" to represent /ame/ and "-eat" to represent /eat/. See Figure 9–1 for a photograph of the word wall, a list of thirty-seven "dependable" spelling patterns (corresponding to the thirty-seven "dependable" rimes—the *sounds* represented by the spelling patterns—reported by Wylie and Durrell, 1970), and a description of how the word wall is used during whole-class sessions.

Although we start out working as a class, I use the word wall with word study groups to extend the children's learning. Before the children arrive in the morning, I look through the poems hanging on the chart wall for one containing a spelling pattern that's also on the word wall, and post it at this meeting area. It's not that I've identified a specific spelling pattern on which they all need to work, it's more to explore the relationship between letters and sounds. In doing so, it helps them appreciate that they can use what they know about words to learn new ones.

After explaining to the children why I called them together, we read through the poem where the spelling pattern originated once for "old times sake." Then we read it again, looking for words containing the "featured" spelling pattern, and draw a box around the words in the poem with that spelling pattern.

We list the words from the poem on chart paper, and think up new words to add to the list. As we do, I give the children time to write them on their individual chalk boards that are stored in this meeting area. By starting with a text the children know, and then focusing on a spelling pattern contained in the text, children understand how what we're doing in the word study groups fits into the "whole" of learning to read.

Before ending the group, I write one or two "new" words containing the featured spelling pattern on a chalkboard, and I ask the children: "If you were reading and came across these words, how would you know them?" The children usually explain how they would use what they know about that spelling pattern and its related sound to read the words.

Occasionally, the group might work on a spelling pattern *before* the class does, giving them an edge when we do it as a class. In addition, toward the end of the year, when I realize that I won't get to all the spelling patterns on the word wall (I never do), I work with the children who need more coaching in relating letters and sounds than those children who have made more of the connections on their own.

WE EXAMINE "BIGGER" WORDS

When children analyze words for their graphophonic, structural, and meaning-related features (in contrast to just synthesizing sounds), they're more likely to learn new words by analogy since they're examining the whole word and not just piecing together the parts.

Clapping Syllables—This activity helps children understand that each syllable in a polysyllabic word can be analyzed for its spelling patterns in the same way as monosyllabic words.

It's more important that children know that there are smaller units (syllables) to analyze than it is for them to know precisely where to divide the word.

I usually choose a poem from the chart wall that we've shared and know well. As we read it, the children clap out the beats and I put a tic (/) above each syllable. For example, the first line of Charlotte Zolotow's poem "Winter Day" would look like this—"The world is cold today."

Then, with the letter cards I use for "Making Words" (see next section), I make one of the polysyllabic words, e.g., "today," on the sentence strip holder hanging on the wall. We "divide" each word into syllables by pushing the letters apart and inserting a blank oaktag strip to separate the syllables. Then we examine each

FIGURE 9–1 "Dependable" Spelling Pattern Word Wall

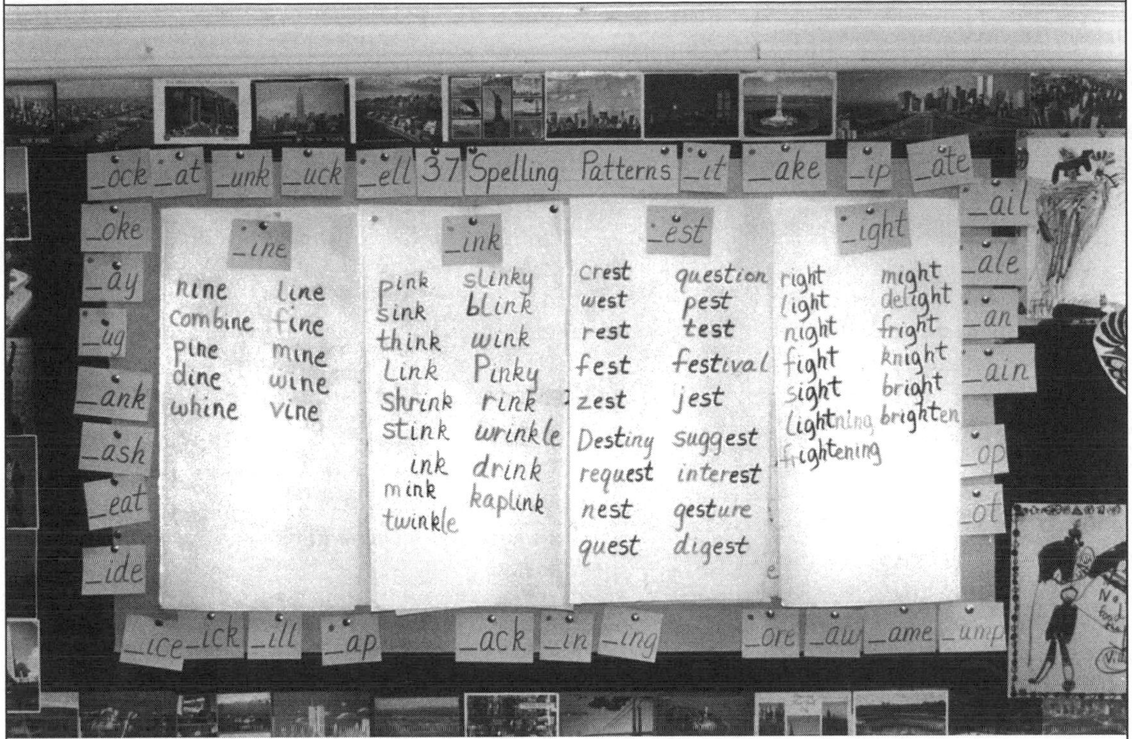

Thirty-seven dependable spelling patterns that make up nearly 500 primary-grade words. (These are the spelling patterns that represent Wylie and Durrell's thirty-seven "dependable" rimes.)

ack	ail	ain	ake	ale	ame
an	ank	ap	ash	at	ate
aw	ay	eat	ell	est	ice
ick	ide	ight	ill	in	ine
ing	ink	op	ir	ock	oke
op	ore	or	uck	ug	ump
unk					

Description of how I use my spelling pattern word wall:

To make this word wall, I staple a piece of 3′ × 5′ butcher block paper to my bulletin board. Then I attach the thirty-seven spelling pattern cards (cut from sentence strips) around the border with thumbtacks, so I can remove the cards to work with them at the meeting area during shared reading.

When deciding which spelling pattern to highlight, I try to select one that's in a poem we're using for shared reading. For example, when reading Marci Ridlon's poem "Love," I noted it contained three words with the "ick" spelling pattern, "icky," "sticky, "licky" and two words with the "ail" spelling pattern, "pail" and "tail." We might "investigate" one of these.

Once I decide on a spelling pattern, I remove the corresponding card from the word wall. Then I take a 1′ × 3′ piece of a different color butcher block paper. (If my background is tan, I use white for the 1′ × 3′ pieces.) I tape the spelling pattern card to the top of the narrow end of this sheet and bring it to the meeting area. When we're ready to start our investigation, we read the poem and identify the spelling pattern with which we'll be working.

Then the children try to think of other words with the same spelling pattern. I write them on the spelling pattern sheet, using a different color marker to highlight the spelling pattern within the word. Some words the children might come up with for "ick" are "stick," "lick," "pick," "flick," and "slick." We add to our list until the paper is full, which might take two days. Then I attach the completed spelling pattern sheet to the word wall. I'm only able to fit four spelling pattern sheets side-by-side on the word wall, but I can cover them with new ones. I put a small dot on the word card to remind myself that we've worked with that spelling pattern, and return it to the border of the word wall once the spelling pattern sheet has been covered with a new one.

syllable for spelling patterns we know. As we work with several more words, I let the children write the word on their individual chalkboards and then "divide" it by inserting a line between the syllables.

Making Words—This activity helps children understand how letters can be rearranged, added, or removed to make new words, focus on letter sequence, and recognize spelling patterns in words.

Because of the deliberate way in which the children decide which letters to change, in addition to considering the left-to-right sequence, they are also analyzing them.

I generally select words to "make" from one of Patricia Cunningham and Dorothy P. Hall's *Making Words* books. Basically, I pick a "secret" word and build up toward the creation of that word through smaller words within it. I choose words to make that include some of the spelling patterns we're investigating in whole-class sessions or ones with which the children need to work. For example, if I know that by making the word "parking," they'll get to work with the "ain," "ink," and "ank" spelling pattern, I may select it as our secret word. The "sequence" of words to make is outlined in the lesson description and the index, so I can see in advance the spelling patterns involved in making each word. (See *Making Words* for a full description of this activity.)

I give each child a letter holder that I've made by folding up the bottom third of a manila file folder and taping the ends to form a shallow pocket, and letter cards they'll need to make the secret word. (Each 2″ × 6″ oaktag card has a letter written along the top so it's visible when the card is in the pocket.) If the "secret" word is "skate," I give each child an "a," "e," "k," "s," and "t." On one side of the card, the letter is written in lower-case letters and on the other it's capitalized. Consonants are "blue" and vowels are "red." The children keep the letters on the floor in front on them and only put them in the holder when they're making a word.

We start with two-letter words and progress to longer ones—eventually getting to the secret word. As I give each direction, e.g., "Take two letters and make the word 'at'," the children select and arrange the letter cards in their folder to make the word. Then I write the word on a small chalkboard so the children check their word against it. They correct their word if they need to, and say it slowly as they run their fingers under it. Since we're sitting close together, I can see who's "getting it" and who needs extra help. Then we continue. This time I may direct them to: "Take one letter away and add one letter to make the word 'as.'" We proceed in this way, making three-, four-, and five-letter words until we get to the word "skate," which the children have been trying to guess all along.

While we do whole-class word analysis activities during shared reading, I don't do "Making Words" with the whole class because not all the children need this focused practice. Doing it with small groups means all the children have the opportunity to get more of what they need. Those who need to "make words" get my full attention, while the others get to read more. (Figure 9–2 shows the holder I've made to store the letter cards when they're not being used.)

Splitting Compound Words—Working with compound words helps children understand how bigger words are often made up of smaller words which can be analyzed for their letter-sound relationships and meaning.

I distinguish between true compound words which contain smaller words related to the meaning of the larger word, e.g., "birthday," and those containing two smaller words whose individual meanings don't contribute to the overall meaning of the word, e.g. "today."

Before the group meets, I write five to ten compound words on oaktag cards and arrange them on the sentence strip holder. Then, after we've read the words, I cut each one into its two smaller words and randomly place them back on the sentence strip holder as separate words. The children take turns rearranging the small words back into the original compound words. They may also find ways to make new compound words. For example, if we started with "birthday" and "bookmark," the children might realize that they can also make the word "birthmark." I keep blank cards at this meeting area so we can add to our bank of words.

Sometimes we extend this activity as follows: I write the phrase, "If I can spell . . ." at the top of a piece of chart paper. Then we select one of the compound words and try to make as many other words as we can using parts of that word. For example, if the word is "raindrop," we could write "rainbow," "droplet," "raining," "dropping," "rainy." It's fun see how many words the children know, and to understand a basic principle of learning—that you can use what you know to learn new things.

Exploring Common Prefixes and Suffixes—Children learn that by removing the prefix and/or suffix from the base word, they can figure out words they don't know. They can also understand what words mean by considering the meaning of the prefix and/or suffix.

FIGURE 9–2 Illustration of Where I Store My Letter Cards

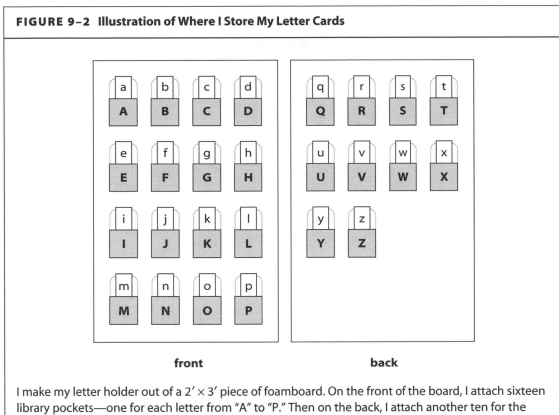

front   back

I make my letter holder out of a 2′ × 3′ piece of foamboard. On the front of the board, I attach sixteen library pockets—one for each letter from "A" to "P." Then on the back, I attach another ten for the letters "Q" to "Z." I write the letter name on each pocket and secure each row of cards with clear bookbinding tape. I make twelve cards for each letter. On the front of each 2″ × 6″ strip, I make a capital letter, and on the back I make a lower-case letter. Consonants are written in blue and vowels are written in red.

Analyzing words with inflectional endings, such as "-ed," "-ing," "-s," "-es," "-er," and "-est" is a powerful strategy for early readers whose texts are beginning to include more complex words. Although we generally initiate our study of inflectional endings during whole-class letter and sound explorations, we often revisit them in word study groups.

We may identify some words from a Big Book we've read that match the inflectional ending we're investigating, e.g., "-ing" or "-ed," and list them on a chart. Then I cover up the ending, highlighting the base word. We read the base word, uncover the ending, and read the whole word. Then we do the same with some new words. This activity is especially helpful for English-language learners who often have trouble with endings on English words.

We also analyze words containing common prefixes and suffixes—prefixes such as "un-," "mis-," and "re-," and suffixes such as "-ful," "-ly," and "-tion." I write a word containing the focus prefix or suffix on the wipe-off board, e.g., "untie," and I record additional words the children suggest. Together we consider how the prefix or suffix contributes to the word's overall meaning. The children write the words on their individual wipe-off boards.

I remind the children that their knowledge of prefixes and suffixes can help them read and understand the meaning of unfamiliar words they meet as they read independently.

WE EXAMINE "DIFFICULT" WORDS

When working with transitional and fluent readers, I try to focus on more complex aspects of words that we might not get to in whole-group sessions.

Analyzing Words with Less Common Prefixes and Suffixes—Here the focus is more on using prefixes and suffixes to understand the meaning of a word than to help children figure out how to read it.

Although I introduce common prefixes and suffixes as children begin to explore "bigger" words, I save the more uncommon ones for when they're reading at the transitional or fluent stage and are reading about content-area topics in greater depth.

Some prefixes I'm likely to examine at these stages are: "dis-," "il-," "im-," "ir-," "in-," "mis-," "anti-," and "under-." Some suffixes are: "-ist," "-ast," "-ment," "-hood," "-age," "-ance," and "-ive." See Snowball and Bolton's *Spelling K–8: Planning and Teaching* for a comprehensive list of prefixes and suffixes.

Analyzing a word for its prefix and/or suffix helps children figure out the meaning of the whole word. I follow the same procedure for analyzing words with less common prefixes and suffixes as I did for words with common ones: isolating the prefix or suffix from the base word, identifying the base word and exploring what the prefix or suffix means, putting it back together to examine the meaning of the whole word, and coming up with related words.

Analyzing Words Sharing a Derivative—We attend to a word's derivative to understand its meaning and its relationship to other words.

Sometimes during shared reading and read aloud, we encounter words that share a common etymology with many other words. For example, when reading that beavers, like all rodents, gnaw at things with their teeth, I explain that the word derivative, "dent," is found in many other words related to teeth. ("Dens/dentis" is the Latin word for teeth.) I write the word "dentist" and elicit others, such as "denture" and "dental." The children see that even "indent" is related since the first line of a paragraph looks like a "bite" might have been taken out of it. I then draw the children's attention to how the derivative "dent" helps give these words their meaning.

Sometimes I postpone a lengthy investigation of a word until I'm working with children in word study groups. At this time we might recall where the word was first introduced and make a web of words sharing a derivative. (See Figure 9–3 for a web from the word derivative "auto.")

The children working in the group share the web with the class during our meeting, and we hang it in full-view so that the whole class can be on the lookout for other words to add.

But again, it's not the investigation of any particular word derivative in itself that's most important. It's children's understanding that if they know something about where the meaning of a word originates, they can figure out what other words mean. Underlying all of our word explorations, whether in whole-class or small-group settings, is the realization that words are fascinating. It's fun to see how they're made up, and how they relate to one another. And it's essential that this sense of wonder is kept alive in the classroom.

* * *

At the conclusion of each word study group, I demonstrate how the children can apply what they've learned to their own reading and writing. Although some children make these connections naturally, others need frequent reminders.

I write on a small chalkboard a word the children haven't seen before that exemplifies a spelling pattern or word category we've been exploring, e.g., "pickle," if we'd been focusing on the "-ick" spelling pattern. Then I ask: "If you came to this word, how would you figure it out?" The children might say that they'd try to sound it out and then notice the "ick" and remember that it says /ick/. Then they'd put the /p/, the /ick/, and the /le/ together to get "pickle."

If I want children to focus on how to spell a word they're trying to write, I say the word instead of writing it: "If you wanted to write 'shopping,' (assuming we'd been attending to the '-ing' at the end of words), how would you do it?" They might have some idea about doubling the final consonant at the end of a consonant-vowel-consonant word, but the exact generalization is developed as their experience grows and my demonstrations elicit their observations.

Although I always emphasize the importance of looking through the entire word they're trying to read for clues that might help them, I want children to understand that sounding out a word from left-to-right isn't the only way to approach an unfamiliar word. Instead, they can also look through the word for parts they know and use that to get the rest of the word. As Snowball and Bolton point out in *Teaching Spelling: A Practical Resource*: ". . . blending, or synthesizing sounds in a word is a more difficult task than analyzing a word into its sound components."

FIGURE 9–3

Web of Words with "Auto" Derivative

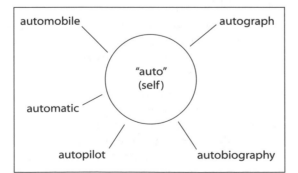

What About Vowels?

The view that children learn to read primarily by blending sounds together in a step-by-step, letter-by-letter process is deeply rooted, going back to the time of Socrates (Moustafa, 1998). Those who share this viewpoint believe we need to teach the sounds represented by graphemic units, e.g., single consonants, short vowels, long vowels, consonant and vowel clusters, and then ask children to blend them together to make words. They reason: "How else would children read a word, 'cat,' for example," than by blending the sounds of the letters together—/c/, /a/, and /t/ to make "cat"?

However, this perspective ignores the absence of a one-to-one correspondence between letters and the sounds they represent. For example, there are five speech sounds for the letter "c," i.e., "cent," "cage," "cheese," "Christmas," and "suspicious" and the sound of the letter "a" is highly dependent on the adjacent letter/s, e.g., "same," "hair," "apple," "say," "read," "part."

To cope with this lack of a one-to-one match between letters and sounds, many perceive a need to limit young children to texts that contain only the sounds to which they've been formally introduced. For example, in Chapter 1, it's unlikely that Billy would have been given a text to read that contained words with a long vowel sound until he learned all the short vowels and had been formally introduced to long vowel sounds by his teacher. With this constraint, it's unlikely the word "cat" and "cheese" would appear in the same beginning text—the assumption being that children could never handle it.

However, this rigid control over text becomes unnecessary when we recognize that we can help children use what they know—whether it's letter-sound relationships, their knowledge of the topic, the cues provided by the illustrations, or the structure of language itself—to learn more. This is not to say that no control of text is needed; we understand the importance of supporting children's reading progression. But the choice of text is based on a different understanding of how children learn to read.

Consider the following incident: When administering a city-wide assessment to my children, I asked Chelsea, a first grader, to give the sound of letters I pointed to. She confidently gave each consonant sound, but when she came to the vowels, she said /ah/ for each one. "E"

was /ah/, "o" was /ah/, "i" was /ah/, and so on. She sensed this was wrong as she wriggled from side to side in her chair.

However, Chelsea's face lit up when I pulled out the next task card and asked her to read the list of words. She practically jumped up and down with delight as she said: "Oh, I can do that. I can read really good!" And indeed she read every word correctly.

The fact that she didn't know the vowel sounds in isolation didn't detract from her reading one bit. I've found that many of my children have learned to read without being sure of the vowel sounds *beforehand*, despite the fact that the six primary vowels account for 39% of the characters in written text. In *Beginning to Read: Thinking and Learning About Print*, Marilyn Adams writes: "As for the vowels, . . . it may be their presence rather than their identities that is most important for the purposes of word identification. It may matter more that you know that there is one than that you know what it is with certainty."

That doesn't mean I don't ever teach vowel sounds—I do! But I try to be as wise about how and when I introduce vowels as I try to be about the rest of my teaching. Here are some guidelines:

Guidelines for Working with Vowels

Avoid introducing vowels too early.

I'm careful not to introduce the vowel sounds (either long or short) before the children are able to handle them. By presenting the more regular, easily heard letter sounds first—like consonants, consonant clusters, and spelling patterns—we can prepare children to successfully work with vowels.

Start with what's easier.

Smaller phonemic units aren't necessarily easier for children to handle than larger ones. Rather than separating the vowel from the letters alongside it, work with spelling patterns, for example in "ran," focus on the /r/ and /an/, and not /r/, /a/, and /n/, until the children are better equipped to hear and manipulate the individual vowel sounds.

Introduce vowels in a supportive whole-group setting.

I generally initiate my work with vowels during letter and sound explorations, which precede my demonstrations of related skills during word study groups. Children are better able to handle new information when it's presented initially in whole-class sessions, and when they have lots of opportunities to read and practice the skills and strategies they're trying to acquire.

Conclusion

Although I make every effort to teach phonetic skills wisely, I have seen that learning the letter sounds isn't the sole determinant of how easily a child catches onto reading. For in the end, learning to read has as much to do with process—making connections, using what we know to learn new things—as it does with content—learning the actual sounds of the letters.

Try not to panic when you see you can't get to every sound or spelling pattern. For example, at the start of the year I "intend" to get to each of the thirty-seven spelling patterns on my Spelling Pattern Word Wall, but I find that late in the year I have usually only "done" a little more than half. But this doesn't mean that I have to race through the rest, because all along I've been teaching my children how to use what *they* know to make new connections *themselves*. So even if we don't do the "-ore" spelling pattern formally, "more" has been on our high-frequency word wall all year. If the children can spell "more," they are also likely to be able to read and write words like "store" and "tore."

When Jack shared how he'd used what he'd learned about the sounds "o-w" represents in combination with what made sense to figure out the word "now," he shared a growing awareness of the value of making these connections.

Teaching Reading Strategies One-on-One

A T THE END OF OUR MORNING MEETING when I ask: "Who needs a conference?" hands shoot up. Molly wants help finding new books. Daniel complains I haven't met with him in a "very long time" (his sense of a week). Fiona has finished her response to a "Mary Marony" book and wants to show it to me. Georgie's reminder note says he should ask for more conferences, and so that's what he's doing.

And as much as I try to discourage it, every year I find children huddled together over their assessment notebooks, comparing the number of times they've met with me for a conference.

Seeing them covet our one-on-one time, I can't help but remember the very first conferences of the year when many children were apprehensive about meeting with me—not knowing what to expect and, perhaps, a little fearful of what I'd uncover. Now they love this time together, and I love it too.

The Importance of One-on-One Time

Individualized instruction is invaluable when learning a new skill. As adults we all experience this, whether at work, in an art class, at a gym, or learning to use the computer. Group instruction alone isn't enough. We need the "expert" to watch what we're doing, and then show us a better way. And so we seek out the personal trainer, the consultant, the coach.

But children who are acquiring reading skills generally don't know how to get the help they need. In fact, those just starting out might not even realize they're having difficulties, often unaware that what they read should make sense,

sound right, and match the letters. They struggle with strategies that don't work or select ones that don't meet their needs.

Some even try to mask their problems. Not wanting to be identified as a "poor" reader, they try to keep their difficulties to themselves. Consequently, their problems may go unidentified and become increasingly complex, precipitating poor attitudes about reading or even full-blown reading problems. Without intervention, these children have no way of knowing that there are alternative strategies and cueing systems to use.

This chapter shows how working one-on-one with children provides opportunities to reacquaint them with strategies I may have demonstrated initially in large- and small-group sessions and helps them understand the concepts about print, text, and books that underpin their reading. While I have described many of these strategies in earlier chapters, they take on a different quality when it's just the child, the book, and the teacher.

Rules of Thumb for Optimum One-on-One Instruction

There are several key practices that make my individual work with children more effective:

Provide the Time, the Place, and the Materials

Years ago when I met individually with a child, my work was often "hit or miss." I would scout the room for children with whom to confer, and when I finally settled down alongside a child, our encounter conveyed a casualness that belied the very importance of the work at hand. Now that I see this work as part of a larger picture, feeding into and being fed by each of the other components of my reading program, I give it a much more deliberate setting.

I hold reading conferences, which are usually five-to-ten minutes long, at the back table, while the other children read books from their book bags. I have an established time and place to meet, and materials to use (a reading folder, an assessment notebook, and a bag of books) that support our interactions. These organizational tools are essential to making our work more productive.

Start with What the Child Is Doing Well

We all need our successes affirmed before we can "hear" where we need to improve. Children need to know the progress they're making, so they can stand on what they're doing well to reach higher ground.

When I saw how Taha figured out a word he didn't know, I congratulated him on the skillful way he monitored and self-corrected his reading—not in those words, of course—and encouraged him to do more of the same. (He was reading the sentence "Blue Sky climbed down," and at first read "clipped," instead of "climbed." He explained that once he saw the word "down," he knew the other word must be "climbed.") When his conference was over and he exchanged seats with the child next to him, I overheard him whisper in his classmate's ear: "Sharon said I was 'too cool.'"

I actually did say that, along with telling him: "I like the way you tried to sound the word out and then realized it couldn't be 'clipped' because of the word that came after it. 'Clipped down' wouldn't make sense, and it certainly doesn't match the letters. It was so smart of you to listen to yourself read and then correct what was wrong. You can do that whenever you read! Taha, you're too cool!"

Give Children Honest Feedback

I don't sugarcoat my comments about their reading. If I can't show them directly what they need to do better, as well as what they already do well, who can? Honest and specific feedback is appropriate and necessary for children's development.

Sometimes visiting teachers are surprised by my frankness with children. They say they doubt they could ever be that truthful for fear of hurting their children's feelings. My response is always: "How could I not be truthful?" It's because I want them to succeed that I tell them what I see. If the book is too hard, I tell them. If they're approaching text in a problematic way, I point it out.

The key, however, is that my assessments and interventions are done within a supportive and respectful relationship. I work hard from the first day of school to create an environment that allows the children and me to interact in mutually respectful and considerate ways. I can be honest with them without fear of offending them because my responses accurately reflect their behaviors and don't generalize about their ability or motivation. And I always offer alternatives to their less effective ways of dealing with text.

Send the Children Off to Practice

It's a basic fact of learning that you cannot acquire a new skill without the opportunity to practice it. So after I demonstrate a strategy, I send the child off to read.

Independent reading allows children to try out and eventually refine the reading strategies they need to acquire. Practice is essential to move from using strategies with deliberation to applying them *automatically*.

Once when Daniel was sharing a strategy at the end of the reading workshop, he summed up how important it is to practice reading by simply stating: "If you don't read, you won't get better." He's right.

Deciding What to Teach and Why

My decisions about what to teach depend upon my observations of what the child is doing well and what she can do better. As I listen to her read, I assess the way she handles problems that arise or how she recounts a text she's read. I talk with her about her reading, asking about the kinds of books she enjoys and her favorite authors. I'm able to pinpoint strategies she needs to learn or understandings about print or books she needs to acquire, because I'm *observing* her reading. No predefined scope and sequence of skills can replace five or ten minutes of watching a child read or listening to her talk about her reading, and then deciding how best to proceed.

Helping Children Understand Print, Text, and Book Features

Before children can apply strategies to improve their reading, they must understand how print, text, and books work. While whole-group sessions may be the most efficient way to demonstrate these features to the class, one-on-one conferences are the most *targeted,* because they allow the teacher to respond directly to what the child is doing.

PRINT FEATURES

As young children move from the pre-emergent stage (in which they "role-play" reading with little regard for the actual text) into the emergent stage, they begin to focus on print. But before they can learn to attend more fully to its semantic, syntactic, and graphophonic features, they must have a basic understanding of how print works (Clay, 1991). It's futile to try to teach a child about letter-sound relationships, or that text should make sense and sound right, when she doesn't yet understand what a "word" is or how print moves from left to right across a page. See Figure 10–1 for a list of some concepts about print that children need to acquire.

We can help children learn these concepts of print by observing them as they handle books and "role-play" reading them. Then we can show them what they need to do. If a child starts reading a book from the back cover to the front, we can guide her to start at the front. When she "reads" without looking at the words because she's memorized the story, we can read the book to her as we run our finger under the line of text. When we see a child "jumping around" the page as he reads without regard for left-to-right directionality, we can show him the direction in which print moves.

I try to give children oral directions to accompany my demonstrations: "When you come to the end of a line, always sweep your finger back to the left side." Or "Every time I *say* a word, it matches a word in the book. Watch." These demonstrations are enormously effective because I'm speaking directly to the child about what I see him doing and showing him what he needs to do differently.

FIGURE 10–1 Some Concepts About Print

Children need to understand:

- print conveys meaning
- the message remains constant throughout repeated readings
- print moves from left to right
- print moves from top to bottom
- what a letter is
- what a word is
- there are first letters and last letters in words
- you can choose upper- or lower-case letters
- there are spaces between words
- different punctuation marks have meanings

TEXT FEATURES

Text has many features that must initially appear foreign to children. Besides the letters they eventually learn to name—there's all the other curlicues, squiggles, dots, and dashes. While we recognize these as punctuation marks, they mean little to children. They don't know at first that those two frontward "c"s and two backward "c"s at the top of some words mean someone's speaking—in fact, they may not even distinguish them from the rest of the text. They don't know that the "?" "." and "!" mean that a sentence is ending. How could they? They don't even know what a sentence is yet. There's a lot they don't understand, and yet they trust that these "marks" are there for a reason, and that eventually we'll help them figure them out. See Figure 10–2 for a list of some text features.

But before we can help children out, we need to know what they're thinking. As we conferred one morning, Tiffany said that some of the books in her bag were "too hard." When I asked her to read one, wanting to see what she meant, I was pleasantly surprised at how well she read it and asked why she thought she needed an easier book. Tiffany explained that she couldn't read some of the words.

It turned out that the name "Broody Hen" was giving her trouble—and *every time* she came to it, she had trouble! To Tiffany, this reoccurrence added up to her not knowing "some" of the words. I often say to the children: If you're having trouble reading too many of the words you may need an easier book, but

---

FIGURE 10–2 Some Text Features

Children need to understand:

- a period marks the end of a "telling" sentence; a question mark is used at the end of a sentence that asks a question; an exclamation mark is used to express surprise or excitement

- a capital letter begins sentences and the names of persons, places, or things—they're also used in the first word and usually all "important" words in a title

- bold, italicized, or underlined text is often used for emphasis

- quotation marks show dialogue

- a hyphen breaks a long word into syllables at the end of a line of text—they're also used in some compound words

- a dash (—) shows a break in a sentence, indicating a parenthetical element or omission

- an ellipse (. . .) shows an omission or break in thought or time

- a text break (***) shows a change in time, place, or situation

- a paragraph in nonfiction shows a new point is being made

I never imagined—although perhaps I should have—that a child might interpret this to mean the same word repeated several times. I learned about Tiffany's misconception only because I had scheduled time to meet with her alone.

I told her the word "Broody" and explained that it's the name of one of the characters, noting that "Broody Hen" is capitalized just like "Duckling" is. In this instance, I didn't focus on helping her sound the word out or on explaining its meaning. Instead, I made the point that she should notice words in a sentence that begin with a capital letter and know they may indicate a character's name. I also wanted her to know that in the future, she shouldn't get "hung up" on names, reasoning: "After all, look at how well you read the book even though you couldn't get Broody Hen's name."

When we looked at some other books in her bag, we found several more examples of how an animal's generic name had become a character's name. In *Rhino and Mouse* by Todd Starr Palmer, the rhino's name was "Rhino" and the mouse's name was "Mouse."

Meeting one-on-one also gives children opportunities to ask questions they have about text. When Shiori met with me after reading *Bee My Valentine* by Miriam Cohen, she wanted to know why the sentence "Everybody must send a card to everybody else in first grade" was underlined. I explained that it's to show the exaggerated way in which the author wanted it to be read, and that other publishers may show this by italicizing words or using bold print. Shiori could ask this question and I could answer it because I'd provided a personal time for us to interact around text.

As a result of our conferences, both Tiffany's and Shiori's understanding of text features grew more complete. Although I had highlighted these same features earlier during shared reading, both children understood them more fully after our conference since I was responding to their specific needs.

BOOK FEATURES

The more opportunities children have to examine books alongside an adult who points out their features, the more comfortable they'll be handling books themselves. This is especially important for children who come to school without having had many experiences with books and the delights of reading. These children need plenty of opportunities in school to learn what other children have been introduced to at home.

While features such as the title page, front and back cover, and dedication are common to all books, there are also differences among books, especially those written in different genres, that affect the reader's interaction with the text. In factual texts, photographs, labels, captions, sidebars, graphs, and maps extend the reader's information about the topic and support his comprehension. He can skim pages and read the parts that interest him, or look at the pictures and read the captions first, to get a better idea of what the text says.

Young readers also need to become aware of the features that can help them acquire specific information they're seeking. For example, the index helps the reader locate key terms, and the glossary defines the book's key concepts. Poetry anthologies are often organized according to theme, and some of their indices are organized by subject, author, or first line. While many of these book features can be explored during read aloud, shared reading, and guided reading sessions, my one-on-one time with children is a forum for additional demonstrations. See Figure 10–3 for a list of some book features.

FIGURE 10–3 Some Book Features

Children need to understand the general features of books and those particular to specific genres:

General:
- front and back cover
- title and half-title page
- dedication page
- table of contents
- prologue and epilogue
- foreword and afternotes

Factual Books:
- labels and captions
- glossary
- index
- headings and subheadings
- charts and diagrams
- sidebars

Poetry:
- author, subject, and first-line indices

Considering What Makes Sense, Sounds Right, and Matches the Letters

After taking several running records of a child's reading, I'm able to identify which cueing systems he uses consistently and the ones he needs to attend to more closely. Emergent and early readers tend to focus either on meaning, without adequate attention to the visual (graphophonic) information, or they over-attend to the visual cues, at the expense of meaning. They must learn to integrate their use of all three cueing systems—semantic, syntactic, and graphophonic.

SEMANTIC CUES

When children use meaning to predict what the text says, the relevant information and the words used to "convey" that information "rise to the surface" of their consciousness, thinning out their pool of possible responses. For example, in Chapter 1, the child reading about dinosaurs was not likely to substitute "tiger" for "triceratops" because she knew to expect a "dinosaur-related" word.

When children come to a word they don't automatically know, they need to try to figure it

out in light of their life experiences, background knowledge, and what they've learned so far from reading the text. By cross-checking graphophonic cues against semantic (and syntactic) ones, they become better equipped to self-correct their reading.

When a child reads a sentence that doesn't make sense, such as "He blew out the <u>candy</u> on the cake," I can prompt her to consider the semantic cues by asking:

- "You said, 'He blew out the <u>candy</u> on the cake.' Does that make sense?"
- "If someone said, 'He blew out the <u>candy</u> on the cake,' would you know what he meant?"
- "Would you write that?"

See Figure 10–4 for a list of prompts I use to help children consider semantic, syntactic, and graphophonic cues. (Although prompts similar to these have been written about extensively in

---

FIGURE 10–4 Prompts to Help Children Attend to Semantic, Syntactic, and Graphophonic Cues

Prompts for Semantic Cues:
- You said (child's attempt). Does that make sense?
- If someone said (child's attempt), would you know what he meant?
- You said (child's attempt). Would you write that?

Prompts for Syntactic Cues:
- You said (child's attempt). Does that sound right?
- You said (child's attempt). Can we say it like that?

Prompts for Graphophonic Cues:
- You said (child's attempt). Does that match the letters?
- If it were (child's attempt), what would it start with?
- If it were (child's attempt), what would it end with?
- Look at the first letter/s . . . the middle letter/s . . . the last letter. What could it be?
- If you were writing (child's attempt), what letter/s would you write first? . . . What letter/s would you write next? . . . What letter/s would you write last?

professional literature, I first heard Diane Snowball describe them as she worked with teachers in New York City public schools.)

SYNTACTIC CUES

In addition to text making sense experientially with regard to what's "possible" or likely, certain types of words "sound right" together, while others don't. The sentence, "The <u>children plays</u> in the yard" doesn't sound right. Not because we can't imagine what it might mean, but because "plays" doesn't *go with* "children," while "play" or "played" would. It's just how English grammar works!

Children understand syntax because they use it when they speak. It's the glue that holds language together. When they read, they have to apply their understanding of grammar to texts. When reading a sentence that doesn't "sound right"—where the words in the sentence don't go together—they have to recognize that it's not right and then consider how to fix it.

In prompting a child to attend to syntactic cues, I might say:

- "You said, 'The <u>children plays</u> in the street.' Does that sound right?"
- "You said, 'The <u>children plays</u> in the street.' Could you say it like that?"

While it's not difficult for children whose first language is English and who share the dialect represented in most published texts to cue into English grammar, it's harder for English-language learners and children speaking other English dialects to use syntax to attempt an unfamiliar word or to self-correct. They haven't had enough experience hearing English spoken to use this cueing system as they read. Or they don't hear and speak the same dialect at home. They need a teacher who is sensitive to their issues to guide them through this process.

GRAPHOPHONIC CUES

Pre-emergent readers who make up the story as they read or recall one they've memorized, exhibit behaviors appropriate for their stage and beneficial to their overall language development. However, as they become emergent readers, they must understand that the author's message to the reader is conveyed through print.

When I showed Nick his running record and reminded him to listen carefully to what he reads, looking to see if it matches the letters, he nodded knowingly, and added that Alinda, his four-year-old sister, "just makes up the story." Nick understands that his reading must be different from Alinda's, and I need to help him transform this understanding into specific behaviors.

When I read with children, I often prompt them to use graphophonic cues. If he reads, "The bug was <u>great</u>," instead of "The bug was <u>green</u>," I might say:

- "You said 'great.' Does that match the letters?"
- "If it were 'great,' what letter would it end with?"
- "Look at the 'n' at the end of the word. What could the word be?"
- "Look at the 'een' spelling pattern. What could the word be?"
- "Look at the two 'e's together. What could the word be?"

As children internalize these prompts, they develop an awareness of different information sources they can use as they read. When I ask children to explain how they got a word that initially troubled them, they're usually very clear about what they did. This self-awareness is essential to their becoming self-improving readers.

* * *

When prompting children to attend to semantic, syntactic, and graphophonic cues, I sometimes appeal to experiences they've had writing their own stories. When children read something that doesn't "make sense" semantically or syntactically, I might say: "You know a writer would never write something that doesn't make sense. You wouldn't, and neither would this writer." Or when what they've read makes sense, but doesn't match the letters, I might remind: "If you read something that makes sense, but doesn't match the letters, it's not what the author wrote. This is his story, not yours."

Figuring Out Unknown Words

While most strategies for figuring out new words are introduced during shared reading, they also lend themselves to one-on-one demonstrations. While I've already listed some strategies in Figure 2–1 on page 10 to help children figure out words and understand text that gives them trouble, I've included some of the same strategies here as a reminder.

During conferences, I may show children how to:

- look closely at the initial letter/s
- look at the pictures
- consider what makes sense and sounds right
- look through the word to the end
- rerun the sentence, making their mouths ready to say the word
- look for spelling patterns they recognize
- look for smaller words within the word
- skip the word and return
- take the ending (e.g., "ing" or "ed") off and try the word

Reintroducing reading strategies during conferences helps children better understand how and when to use them. For example, emergent readers are generally hesitant to "skip words and then return to them." Their moms, babysitters, or older siblings probably cautioned them against it. However, during a conference, I can show them how it's often helpful to read past the difficult word to the end of the sentence (or the next sentence, if the problematic word is at the end of the sentence) and *then come back* with the additional information they've acquired.

And in some instances, I help clarify a child's understanding of how to apply a strategy. Initially, Sam thought it was just fine to skip a word he didn't know and read on. In fact, when I met with him—he'd just finished reading *Just This Once*—and asked him to read for me, I learned that he had skipped the word "vacation" throughout the entire book. And now, at the end, he still didn't know it. When I reminded him that he needed to skip the word, read to the end of the sentence, and then come back to the word, Sam informed me that "'vacation' *is* the end of the sentence." In his view, he had done as I'd asked. However, he had forgotten a most important piece—to figure the word out! Our conference gave me a window into his thinking, allowing me to help convert his partial understanding of what the strategy actually means into a workable version.

Likewise, while "looking for smaller words" within a word is sometimes a helpful strategy, it can also create additional problems for readers. When Brittany read "nowhere" as "now" and "here," she was following the strategy, but in an incomplete way. For she failed to "get" a word that both matches the letters *and* makes sense in the text. The smaller words that Brittany had found were the wrong words. Children need to try different strategies, but then always cross-check cues and self-correct when things still don't make sense and match the letters.

Achieving More Fluent-Sounding Reading

Early readers eventually come to realize they must integrate graphophonic cues with semantic and structural ones. But as they focus on each word, their reading often acquires a stilted quality. Reading conferences are a perfect time to show children proper phrasing and fluency and let them try these out for themselves.

When Miles read aloud during his conference, I was simultaneously struck by his accuracy and the halting quality of his reading. He pointed to each word he read, probably because he'd learned to do this as an emergent reader. But now this print-tracking strategy was no longer helpful. In fact, it was interfering with his growth.

I pointed this out to Miles, and then read from his book to show him how it should sound with the same fluency, expression, and phrasing that I use when speaking. Miles immediately noticed the difference and asked if he could try it himself. He tried chunking his words into phrases as he read, and was quite successful.

We even noted how the "I Can Read" book he was reading was actually designed to support the reader's fluency and phrasing because each line of text is arranged by phrases. When Miles left the conference, he had a new strategy to practice and an awareness of how book formatting can enhance his reading.

Books for emergent readers can also support proper fluency and phrasing. Many of these books contain repetitive language patterns that, in addition to "freeing them up" to attend more fully to words they don't know, also helps them read in a more natural sounding way. Working with children one-on-one during conferences allows me to encourage them to practice this, and then go off to try it themselves.

Learning Strategies to Better Understand the Text

Although comprehension strategies are best demonstrated initially in whole- and small-group sessions where there's more time to devote to them, I can use the conference time to remind children of what they should try and to review a strategy they may be neglecting. I might remind them to:

- stop to think about what they're reading
- reread the confusing parts
- think about how the characters, setting, problem, main events, and resolution work together to "create" the story
- think about how the character's "way of acting" can help to predict what might happen
- "create a picture" in their mind of what they're reading
- read on a little and then come back to think about the part that confuses them
- write about what happened at the end of each chapter
- preview the book by examining the table of contents, section titles, charts, illustrations, and captions

When I met with Jack for a conference, he had just completed his first "Nate the Great" book. I was very curious to learn how he did since this book marked his entry into reading "longer texts." In retelling the story, he gave enough details, and a good explanation of the book's "problem" and how it was resolved, to demonstrate he understood it. I was very impressed with his reading and told him so.

When I asked what he does when he comes to a part he doesn't understand, Jack said he usually "stops to think" for a while about what's happened and what might happen next. He also said he often rereads the part that gives him trouble. I confirmed that these were both very important approaches to take. I didn't have the time to show him another strategy to try, but I could affirm the one he was already using.

I wrote a reminder note in his assessment notebook—"Continue to stop and think, and reread the parts that don't make sense"—and sent him off to read with a refreshed awareness that he's on the right track.

Sometimes when I notice children having difficulty understanding what they're reading, I suggest they use a strategy sheet if it applies. For example, if a transitional reader is having difficulty holding together all the parts of the story from one day to the next, she might use a story map to record and think about the different story elements. (See Figure 8–8 on page 108 for Jena's story map.) However, I make it clear that she should only use this, and other strategies, if she needs to. There's no reason for children to respond to a text at the end of each chapter or make a character map unless it will help them resolve a difficulty they're experiencing.

Conclusion

Working one-on-one with children is my favorite time of day. I love seeing the smiles on their faces when they do or say smart things. I love the serious attention they give me when I show them other ways to do things. And I love the lilt in their voices when reading starts to make sense.

Taha didn't stop at telling one classmate that I said he was "too cool." He told Shelley and his mother and anyone in class who would listen. Taha entered school in September as an emergent reader, and by March prided himself on the progress he'd made. He'd read Stephen Vincent Benet's poem "Indian," just for the asking—a poem I shared related to our study of Native Americans because it was too beautiful to resist—and willingly explained how he "gets" words that are hard at first. One day, Taha told me he'd read that poem eleven times during our first independent reading time, and couldn't wait for our second reading time because he had a whole bag of "Nate the Great" books he hadn't read. He still wants to keep his first one though. He said he wants to read it over: "There still might be parts I can get better at." Taha has "arrived." He's becoming a self-extending reader and I'm so proud. Clearly, for Taha, the sky's the limit! As his teacher, I also know there are "parts I can get better at." And meeting with children one-on-one is one way to learn what I need to do.

PART FOUR

Offering Children Opportunities for Practice and Response

CHAPTER 11

Matching Children with Books for Independent Reading

W HEN I MEET WITH PARENTS TO DISCUSS reading, I always emphasize the importance of selecting books that support their child's development. I joke that picking out books for their child is different from buying him clothes. We choose jackets and pants big enough to last more than one season. But with books they'll read on their own, we want a fit that's just right, *right now*.

Matching children with books they can read independently is a primary concern. That's why I devote all my reading and writing conferences during the first three weeks of school to getting to know the children as readers and matching them with books, and why finding "just-right" books continues during reading conferences throughout the year.

The Benefits of Choosing "Just-Right" Books

I find that children, even very young ones, can read independently for extended periods of time when they are matched with books they can read with a 95 percent or higher word accuracy rate. They are also more successful with books that interest them.

Children Engage in Reading

Engagement is a process by which the learner sees himself as capable of learning a particular skill and decides to do whatever is necessary to acquire it. In *The Whole Story: Natural Learning and the Acquisition of Literacy in the Classroom*, Brian Cambourne writes that engagement is essential if children are to accept our demonstrations. They must want to learn the skills and strategies being taught and see themselves as potential doers of that activity.

When I sat down alongside Emily during the first independent reading time, she moved closer to show me the page she was reading. She said: "I found out this word myself. I looked at the picture and asked, 'What is she (the teacher) doing?' Then I saw 'i-n-g' at the end. I said the word slow—'p-p-point.' And then I put the 'ing' back and said 'pointing.' That's how I got the word."

Emily's description shows the responsibility she has assumed for learning and her recognition that she needs to work even harder. Because the book she's reading appropriately supports and challenges her, she appreciates the meaning-making nature of reading. Consequently, she is motivated to read more and become even more engaged.

One day I was telling my friend Sue Slavin about the progress my children had made since the start of the year, and she asked why I thought the children were doing so well. At first, I said it was the amount of independent reading my children do—they read in class for more than an hour each day. Then I qualified it to include the degree to which they are engaged—they *want* to read better! Even if we set aside large blocks of time for independent reading, our gains will be limited unless children read books that are right for them.

Children Can Use a Variety of Strategies

Children are capable of using a variety of reading strategies if their books offer the right amount of supports and challenges. Semantic and syntactic cues cannot be accessed when books are too difficult and children are forced to rely on graphophonic cues. When they should be using *three* information sources, they can use only one.

When Chad first came to our school, it was painful listening to him read, relying solely on phonetic cues with little idea that what he reads must also make sense. He always went for books that were too hard. A major part of my work with Chad that year was to direct him to more appropriate books and show him how to use meaning, syntax, and graphophonics together.

Children Read for Extended Periods of Time

When children are engaged and can work out difficulties along the way, they are more likely to enjoy reading and want to read more. Reading good books, discussing them with classmates, and relating them to their own experiences empowers readers. Reading becomes a satisfying experience that they want to repeat.

Consequently, we must recognize that most teachers need more books in classroom libraries that match children's needs and interests. We must also try to select books that are worthy of their time, books they will gravitate to again and again because of their excellence.

Setting the Stage for Matching Children with Books

Knowing my books and my children, and making a match between them, is one of the most important things I do—and one of the most demanding. It is exacting work that has led me to adjust my priorities in how I use my planning and class time.

Years ago I spent hours each week writing detailed lesson plans, making gorgeous bulletin boards, and correcting stacks of homework papers. Although I still plan, value a beautiful workplace, and review children's work to see who needs additional support, I now spend my preparation and class time in ways that add up to more effective instruction.

I think about the children I am teaching and their needs. I think about how the books in my classroom support and challenge readers. And I think about which books are most likely to make a difference in each child's reading life.

Know Your Books

Having an ample supply of books is essential. But having more books than we can know well and use effectively is almost as problematic as having too few. I have visited classrooms where the books are out of control and stored everywhere—under tables, packed in boxes, jammed into closets. When there are too many books and they are inaccessible, these resources have little effect on children's learning.

Unfortunately, most schools have the opposite problem: There are too few books to support the needs and interests of the full range of readers. Book allocations are used to purchase class sets and accompanying workbooks. Teachers scrounge for additional reading material for their children.

While there is nothing wrong with frequenting garage sales and one-dollar stores, cashing in on book club award points, asking parents to donate books, and sponsoring fund-raising events, there should be enough money in school budgets for each teacher to have a core set of books to meet her children's needs. Yes, we can share with other teachers on grade and have book rooms to store our common books, but there must be enough books *in each classroom* to accommodate the changing needs and interests of our children.

I believe that 1,500 is about the right number of books to have in each classroom. This may seem shockingly high until you consider how quickly those eight-page books and sets of guided reading texts add up. And think of how fast your collection might grow if year after year money was spent building up your classroom library. We must teach out of abundance, not poverty.

HOW BOOKS SUPPORT AND CHALLENGE READERS

Readability formulas have characteristically considered word difficulty, word frequency, word length, and sentence length to determine how easy or difficult a book is. However, we need to apply a broader range of criteria that take into account all the cues readers use. See Figure 11–1 for these criteria.

Books for Emergent and Early Readers

Emergent and early readers who are acquiring and refining basic skills need different supports and challenges than transitional and fluent readers. Since they are just learning about print and letter sounds, their books must help them

---

FIGURE 11–1   Criteria for Determining Text Difficulty

Emergent and Early Readers:

- Font size, spacing, and background
- Number of words and lines per page
- Consistency of text placement
- How closely illustrations support the meaning of the text
- Repetition of language patterns and predictable text structures
- How closely the writing reflects children's oral language
- How closely the content relates to children's interests and prior experiences
- Word difficulty

Transitional and Fluent Readers:

- Book length
- Character and plot complexity
- The degree of support offered at the beginning of the book and chapters
- Age-appropriateness of concepts
- Book features that help children access information
- Familiarity of topics and experiences
- Balance of narration and dialogue
- Change of setting/time cues
- Age-appropriateness of humor
- Whether or not a book is part of a series

---

focus on words, integrate semantic, syntactic, and graphophonic cues, and use what they know about words to learn new ones.

I consider the following criteria when matching them with books:

- **Font size, spacing, and background.** Print must be large enough and well-proportioned to the spaces between words and the lines of print so that the reader can easily distinguish one word and line from the next. For example, bigger print with tighter spacing between the lines of print (or leading) can be more difficult to read than smaller print with more leading. In addition, a black typeface is harder to distinguish on a colored or dark background than on a white field.

The spacing between letters, words, and lines of text is as much a reading cue as the print is. Appropriate spacing helps the reader know where words begin and end, and focuses him on a single line of text without having his eyes wander. When selecting books for beginning readers, I weigh these features before any others to determine how supportive a book is (or isn't). Regardless of the content, I don't consider the text further if it fails to meet these criteria.

- **Number of words and lines per page.** Children who are just beginning to understand top-to-bottom, left-to-right directionality, and the one-to-one match of oral words to

print need books with few words on each page.

While they often begin reading caption books with one or two words labeling each illustration, they should also be reading books with full sentences on each page. Sentences are often easier to read than quick phrases that don't closely match children's oral language or the picture. The sentence: "The girl is walking in the rain" (where there is a simple picture to accompany it) is very supportive of beginning readers.

- **Consistency of text placement.** Text is more supportive when it appears at the same place on each page. When it is less consistent—sometimes at the top and sometimes at the bottom—a beginning reader is more likely to miss it. Children will learn to anticipate a change in the text's location as they become more skilled, but initially they are better supported when text *always* appears at either the top or the bottom.
- **How closely the illustrations support the meaning of the text.** Illustrations that closely match the text help children figure out what it says. Although we don't want emergent readers to "read" the pictures instead of the words, as they did at the pre-emergent stage, we do want them to use pictures as an aid to *predict* what print says. They can use their

growing knowledge of letter sounds to try the word first, and then confirm or reject their hypothesis based on how closely their attempt matches the printed word and the illustrations.

Illustrations help children combine, even extend, what they already know about letter sounds. Seeing a picture of a kitten and its relationship to the word, they associate the letter "k" with the /k/ sound. They're less likely to settle on "cat" because they'll note that the /t/ in "kitten" comes in the middle and not at the end of the word, where there is an "n."

Simple, clear pictures are more supportive than elaborate, detailed ones, which often confuse children and distract their attention from the word/s the picture is meant to illustrate.

- **Repetition of language patterns and predictable text structures.** Repetition and predictability are children's allies. Most children love hearing stories again and again. Even when they know what will happen, they are just as satisfied by the story's outcome as the first time they experienced it.

When language patterns are repeated and text structures are predictable, a child can participate more fully in the book and proceed more confidently. In *I Eat Leaves* by JoAnn Vandine (see Figure 11–3), the structure of the two sentences on each page is consistent throughout the book, allowing readers to focus on the one new word. This pattern doesn't change until the last page, when children are better prepared to meet this challenge.

- **How closely the writing reflects children's oral language.** The more closely writing mirrors the way children speak, the easier it will be for them to read it. They can cross-check structural cues against semantic and graphophonic cues. After attempting an unfamiliar word, they can reason: "This can't be right because this is not the way I would say it." Or: "Yep. This must be the word. It sounds right to me."

Children who speak different languages have a more difficult time using structural (and semantic) cues than readers whose primary oral language is the same as the book's language. However, as their experiences with English increase, they'll be able to integrate all three cueing systems more effectively.

- **How closely the content relates to children's interests and prior experiences.** Children can better understand what they are reading, and make reasonable predictions at the word and text level, when their books reflect their experiences. Texts about typical childhood experiences, such as *The Shortest Kid in the World* by Corinne Demas Bliss and *My Tooth Is Loose* by Martin Silverman, engage readers and extend their thinking. Readers can use a combination of cues and self-correct more easily.
- **Word difficulty.** Of course, the words themselves are central to considering how easy or difficult a text might be. Generally, children are able to read monosyllabic words more easily than polysyllabic ones. Rhyming words are often more predictable and therefore easier, while words with inflectional endings and prefixes and suffixes may be more challenging.

* * *

When all of the preceding criteria are taken into account in selecting books for the classroom, children don't need to be locked into a strict progression of reading very easy books first and moving ahead, baby-step-by-baby-step, to the more difficult ones. Children can move along more naturally, drawing on the many sources of support the text provides.

Books for Transitional and Fluent Readers

Transitional readers have acquired basic reading skills, but are challenged by the longer, more complex texts they are beginning to read. And as fluent readers, they'll be asked more often to interpret the author's message, compare books on similar themes, and research topics of interest.

I consider the following criteria when matching them with books:

- **Book length.** Longer books are generally more demanding than shorter ones. In fact, one of the biggest challenges facing children at the beginning of the transitional stage is learning to handle a text over the several days it may take to read it. Where they were once able to begin and end a book (even several) in one sitting, they must now carry their reading of a single text from one day to the next. When they come back to it on the second or third day, they must recapture their momentum.

Although many series books for transitional readers, such as "Nate the Great" and "M & M," are more involved than texts for early readers, they are also shorter than those for fluent readers. Most children can read them in a day or two, enabling them to grow into this new experience.

- **Character and plot complexity.** As children's reading skills evolve, so does the complexity of their books. The characters in texts for transitional and fluent readers are multidimensional and more interesting than characters in emergent and early texts. Their personalities and desires often create a tension that drives the plot.

In addition, the main problem in a story may not be as obvious as it once was. The setting may change from chapter-to-chapter or even within a chapter. There may be more characters (and consequently, more dialogue), and more events building up to the resolution.

Where stories once ended "happily ever after" with the good or handsome prince (Yeah!) winning the good and beautiful princess, and the bad and ugly villain (Boo!) banished forever from the kingdom, the resolution may now rest on the character adjusting his own attitudes upon realizing that he can't change the external situation.

- **The degree of support offered at the beginning of the book and chapters.** Books that begin by clearly setting the stage and introducing the characters are more supportive than those that do not. *Pioneer Sisters* (adapted from the Laura Ingalls Wilder "Little House Books") opens with the lines: "Laura had two sisters. Mary was the oldest, and Carrie was the youngest. Laura was right in the middle. They all lived with their Pa and Ma in the Big Woods of Wisconsin in a little gray house made of logs." These crisp, clear sentences ground young readers, letting them know exactly who the story is about and where it is taking place.

In contrast, books and chapters that begin more vaguely, often with a lot of dialogue, force readers to work harder to get oriented.

- **Age-appropriateness of concepts.** Sometimes children (and their families) confuse word accuracy with true reading in which the reader grasps an author's concepts. Consequently, they think they should be allowed to read anything, failing to understand that it is much easier to lose interest in a book, especially a long one, without having the conceptual framework for support. While a child's word accuracy may be high, she may be unable to handle, or sustain interest in, the book's more mature concepts and themes.

- **Book features that help children access information.** Children beginning to read factual text need the tables of contents, indices, glossaries, and charts to help them get the information they seek. See Figure 11–5 for how the text features in *Birds of Prey* support fluent readers.

- **Familiarity of topics and experiences.** Reading about familiar topics is easier than reading about things outside our experience. Therefore, I try to provide factual texts about topics children studied last year, or ones we are currently investigating in science and social studies. By giving them both fictional and factual texts they can to relate to, I'm providing enough support so that they can go on to read about less familiar topics.

- **Balance of narration and dialogue.** As plots become more complex, the number of characters increases, resulting in more dialogue. Children have to keep straight "who is talking to whom." Too much dialogue can be difficult to handle.

I look for books with a healthy mix of narration and dialogue, so that the back and forth movement between the two allows the reader to "catch his breath" and note cues that signal a change in speaker.

- **Change of setting/time cues.** Writing that is more supportive tells readers when there are changes in time and place. For example, each page in Patricia Reilly Giff's *Watch Out for Ronald Morgan* begins with scene-setting openings: "It all started when the bell rang," or "After I hung up my jacket. . . ." There is only one scene per page.

Books with transitions within a page from one scene to another often indicate these switches with a series of asterisks or dashes between paragraphs. At other times, there may be extra white space to signal them.

- **Age-appropriateness of humor.** Children love funny books, but often have trouble understanding subtle humor or sarcasm. So at the beginning of the transitional stage, I avoid burdening readers (already facing the challenges of longer texts and increased character and plot complexity) with the additional task of appreciating obscure humor.

My beginning transitional readers, except for English-language learners who are not yet facile with English, love "Deputy Dan" and "Amelia Bedelia" books because of their funny word play. The humor is not hidden, but very obvious. In contrast, when Louise, Lionel's sister in *Lionel in the Fall*, teases him, saying she hopes he's done raking the leaves by Thanksgiving, I expect most children will think she means it literally. And they do. As they become more skilled, they're better able to handle subtle humor because they can infer the character's intention.

- **Whether or not books are part of a series.** Books that are part of a series are generally more supportive than those written to stand alone. Authors of series know that their readers are making the transition from easier books they can read in one sitting to books that may take several days to complete. The books' shared characters, settings, and themes will support readers, just as illustrations and predictable story structures support emergent and early readers acquiring basic skills.

ORGANIZE YOUR BOOKS BY DEVELOPMENTAL STAGES

When I first began to organize my books so I could more effectively match children with them, I had to consider what readers at each developmental stage are like (see Figure 2–2 on page 14). Knowing where children are coming from and where they are headed, helped me identify books to appropriately support and challenge them. So I first sorted my books into four categories—for emergent, early, transitional, and fluent readers—to parallel the major stages of development. Then, as I became more familiar with each book's specific features, I fine-tuned my leveling within each stage.

I use the criteria in Figure 11–1, and whenever necessary refer to Reading Recovery lists and the generous book lists in Pinnell and Fountas' *Guided Reading: Good First Teaching for All Children* and *Matching Books to Readers: Using Leveled Books in Guided Reading, K-3*. But I try to avoid over-relying on outside leveling systems. I've seen classrooms where books are organized into twenty or thirty levels, yet the teachers themselves don't understand what it is about the books that makes them more or less supportive.

I label books at each stage by placing a blue, yellow, red, or green adhesive circle at the upper right-hand corner of each volume, and write "1," "2," or "3" on each circle to show increasing text difficulty within each stage. Books with blue dots labeled "1" are for children at the very beginning of the emergent stage, while books with green dots labeled "3" are for fluent readers at the opposite end of the continuum. See Chapter 3 for a prior description of my system.

Although my book pots are actually pink or white to match my classroom color scheme, the children and I refer to them by the color of the circles on the books they contain. Books for emergent readers are in the "blue pots"; early books are in the "yellow" pots; transitional books, "red"; and fluent books, "green." Within each of the four stages, however, I don't segregate books by degree of difficulty. The yellow pots have 1's, 2's, and 3's mixed together. I label my series books the same way, but keep them sorted by series and store them in separate pots.

Fortunately, the adhesive circles can be easily removed, as I still make many mistakes when leveling my books. And I'm sure I'll always be making corrections to refine my leveling based on new experience.

Develop Your Expertise over Time

If our greatest nightmare is someone sneaking into our classroom at night and removing all the labels from our books, it might very well be that we need to rely less on outside leveling systems and more on our own knowledge of our books. However, this process cannot be completed in several months or even years. It is ongoing, as we are constantly examining our books and replacing worn or less useful books with new ones.

The following are examples of ways books support and challenge readers. Figure 11–2 shows a page from *I Eat Leaves* by JoAnne Vandine, and Figure 11–3 describes the supports and challenges in that text, a book I have leveled "Blue 2." Figures 11–4 and 11–5 do the same for *Finding Out About: Birds of Prey* by Marilyn Woolley and Keith Pigdon, which I have leveled "Green 1."

In addition to these more apparent supports and challenges, there are less obvious qualities that emerge only after repeated examination and use of books. For example, over the years I have learned that *M & M and the Big Bag* and *M & M and the Bad News Babies* by Pat Ross are the easiest in the series, and so I direct children to them before the others—even before the introductory title *Meet M & M*.

FIGURE 11-2

Page from *I Eat Leaves* **by JoAnne Vandine**

Bamboo

I am a panda.
I eat leaves.

3

FIGURE 11–3 Supports and Challenges in *I Eat Leaves*

The supports are:

- Bold print and large font
- Good spacing between letters, words, and lines
- Picture and text match closely
- Natural language structures
- Repetitive text
- Children's natural interest in animals

The challenges are:

- Concept of sentence
- Change in pattern on the last page
- Return sweep
- Label adds information that may be unknown

Know Your Children

This section is much briefer than the previous section "Know Your Books" because I have already discussed the "nuts and bolts" of assessing children's reading through running records, retellings, and reading discussions in Chapters 5 and 6. However, this brevity should not detract from the importance of the topic, for before we can match children with books at the beginning of the year, we need to know at which stages they are reading, and then later, whether they have the skills to move on to more challenging texts.

To review: taking a running record and asking children to talk about the book helps us assess their strengths and needs, and decide if the books are right for them. If they can read with 95 percent or better word accuracy, that is, if they make five or fewer miscues for every hundred words, then the book (and others like it) are at their independent reading level—assuming, of course, that they *understand* what they've read. If they get more than 5 percent of

FIGURE 11–4

Page from *Finding Out About: Birds of Prey* by Marilyn Woolley and Keith Pidgon

What special body parts do they have?

Birds of prey use their powerful hooked beaks and **talons** to gather and tear their food. They have a special part of the stomach called a **gizzard** which grinds up the food.

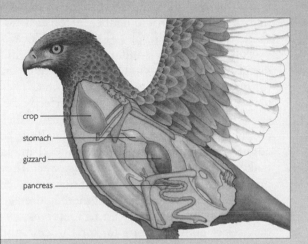

crop
stomach
gizzard
pancreas

The digestive system of an eagle.

The hooked beak of an eagle.

Birds of prey have bones that are paper thin, hollow, and light so that they can fly. Their wings provide power and lift for flying and gliding, and their feathers overlap in special ways to help this. Feathers also keep the bird warm.

These birds have **air sacs** inside their bodies to store the extra oxygen needed for flying.

The talons of a Golden Eagle.

6

the words wrong, then the book is probably too hard and should be put aside for a later time. As children move into the transitional and fluent stage, I take running records less frequently, and instead direct my attention to comprehension.

At the emergent and early stage, I may ask one or two broad comprehension questions as part of our conversation about the book. But since the meaning of the text is generally so literal and accessible, the readers usually understand it. At the transitional and fluent stage, I decide on a book's appropriateness by how well children can retell what happened. If they can recount the text accurately with enough supporting detail, I feel safe in assuming they can proceed on their own. Then I help them find other similar books.

FIGURE 11–5 Supports and Challenges in *Finding Out About: Birds of Prey*

The supports are:

- Larger print than used in fictional text at same level
- Captions that highlight important information
- Chapter titles as questions, e.g., "What are birds of prey?"
- Key words in bold type
- Meaning of key words found in text
- Good mix of diagrams, charts, and photographs
- Consistent use of subtitles throughout text to organize information
- Table of contents
- Glossary

The challenges are:

- Content words with which children might be unfamiliar
- Complex sentence structures
- Paragraphs that are not indented
- Lack of spacing between paragraphs
- Children may not have background knowledge to bring to the text

Matching Children with Books at the Start of the Year

During the first three weeks of school, I help children find their first set of "just-right" books for their book bags. They'll read these books during the second independent reading time, while I confer with other children or work with guided reading groups. I need to confer with each child two or three times during the beginning weeks before I am confident they have a good starting set of books.

Here is what I do during our first conference to match a child with books. I refine these selections during subsequent conferences by following the procedures outlined in Chapters 5, 6, and 7.

Determining the Child's Reading Stage

I try to learn at which developmental stage the child is reading. This steers me to one of the book pots for either emergent, early, transitional, or fluent readers.

Before a child comes for a conference, I ask her to select two books she thinks are "good for her" from the *table* book pots, which, unlike the *leveled* pots, contain an assortment of books for readers at different stages. I explain that these books should neither be too easy nor too hard, but "just right"—like in Goldilocks.

This Goldilocks standard helps most children understand the kind of book I'm referring to, but some do not get it right at first. They may bring books they can read perfectly because of past exposure to them or because they are better readers than they are willing to admit—perhaps wary of the demands I might make if I knew they could read that well. They may also bring titles they have at home or even books they have memorized. Other children go to the opposite extreme: wanting to impress me, they select books that are far too difficult, and then struggle to read them.

I listen to the child read several pages from one or two of her books. If she reads from a book with a "yellow" sticker and it is too hard, she may be an emergent reader or at the beginning of the early stage. If it is too easy, she may be more advanced, unless of course, I learn she knows the book by heart. I note my observations in the child's assessment notebook, but do not take a running record until we are closer to making a final determination of her reading stage.

Then, I give the child the Ohio Word Test (see Marie Clay's *An Observation Survey* and Appendix K) to assess her knowledge of high-frequency words, and thereby, help me zero in on her stage even further. As I point to each word on the list (which I have put into a plastic sleeve and set before the child), the child attempts to read it. Alongside each word on her test sheet, which I keep before me to write on, I either record a checkmark for accurate reading, a dot for no response, or her incorrect response.

I use this score, along with my own observation of the child's reading, to determine the child's stage. For example, if a child reads only three of the twenty high-frequency words in List A accurately, as Amelia did in Figure 11–6, I know she is probably an emergent reader.

Early readers know more words than that, and transitional and fluent readers typically

FIGURE 11–6

Amelia's Ohio Word Test Score Sheet

APPENDIX 1   **OHIO WORD TEST SCORE SHEET**

TEST SCORE | 3 /20 |

Date: _9/5_

Name: _Amelia_   School: _____

Recorder: _____   Classroom Teacher: _____

Record incorrect responses.
Choose appropriate list of words.   ✓ (Checkmark) Correct Response   ● (Dot) No Response

	LIST A 3/20		LIST B 1/5 – 14/20		LIST C
Practice words	can		in		see
and	do	ran	✓	big	
the	✓	it	✓	to	
pretty	book	said	✓	ride	
has	have	her	here (sc)	him	
down	by	find	fad	for	
where	will	we	✓	you	
after	my	they	✓	this	
let	I	live	✓	may	
here	✓	away	way	in	
am	I'm	are	✓	at	
there	the	no	on	with	
over	here	put	pit	some	
little	I will	look	✓	make	
did	be	do	✓	eat	
what	would	who	✓	an	
them	the	then	✓	walk	
one	on	play	✓	red	
like	can	again	✓	now	
could	✓	give	✓	from	
yes	why	saw	sue	have	

know all twenty. In analyzing the score, I keep in mind that children are more likely to do better at reading high-frequency words in context than in the list format of this assessment.

I store copies of the Ohio Word Test until I need them. As each test is given and scored, I place it in the child's reading folder where it remains throughout the year. Follow-up tests (Lists B and C) that measure her progress are recorded on the same sheet.

Depending on her score on this test and her reading of the books she selected, the child and I go to either the emergent, early, transitional, or fluent book pots for books. (When I conferred with Amelia, who brought *The Big Egg* to read and scored 3/20 on the Ohio Word

Test, we started looking in the "blue"—emergent—pots for books.) During these initial assessments, I often keep one pot from each of the four stages on the floor near the conference table, so we don't have to walk across the room for books.

Selecting a "Test" Book and Taking a Running Record

We select three or four books she might be able to read. Then, I ask her to read aloud from one to see how close it is (and, by inference, the others are) to her independent reading level. If it's close, I take a running record on one of them. If not, we keep looking.

First, I record the date, the title of the book, and the level of the pot from which it came. I introduce the book to the extent the child's stage warrants. If I think she is an emergent reader, I might do a quick picture walk to give her a sense of the whole book. If the child is an early reader, the introduction I give may just set up the story before she begins to read it herself. Transitional and fluent readers require even briefer introductions. If I am unfamiliar with the book, I do the best I can, conveying what I have learned by skimming the front and back cover.

Then I take a running record on a hundred word sample, or on the entire book if it's short. In addition to matching children with books, I later use running records to assess which strategies and cues the child uses and the ones at which she needs to improve (see Chapter 5).

Helping a child find her first set of books can be very demanding, taking ten-to-fifteen minutes per child. Consequently, I find I am unable to think wisely about comprehension until the second or third conference when things become more settled.

Putting Several Books in the Child's Bag

Based on the child's running record, we decide if the books selected from the leveled pots are a good match. If they are, we put them in her bag. If they aren't, we keep looking.

I have heavy-duty freezer bags with a piece of colored electrical tape attached to the front ready beforehand, so that all I need to do during the conference is write the child's name on the tape.

Maintaining a Continuous Flow of Books Throughout the Year

I do not set aside specific days to refresh the books in my children's book bags. Nor do I change all the books at one time. This would be unrealistic.

By helping children find new books only as they need them, there are fewer books to replace at each conference. Usually children work with their books for a week or two before they need new ones. Those reading lengthy books often keep theirs even longer. Rereading is a highly regarded strategy whose merits we openly and repeatedly discuss.

When children ask for a conference or I ask to meet with them, they bring their bag of books and their reading folder to the conference table. Here's how I help them exchange too-easy books with new ones.

Sorting Books That Are Too Easy and Those Still Needing Work

I ask the child to remove all his books from his bag and sort them into two piles, those that have become too easy and those he'd still like to work on. It is enlightening watching him decide, seeing him weigh each one, and place it onto one or the other pile: "I want to give back this one, and this one. This one, I want to keep—it's easy, but I really like it! And I need to work more on this and this and this." Done.

If I disagree with a child's decisions, that is, if I think he needs to keep working on books he says are easy, I ask him to read a page or two (usually from somewhere in the middle of the book) while I observe how accurately he reads it. Or I question him briefly.

I try not to be overly exhaustive in this process. If I felt I could never remove or exchange a book unless I had fully assessed the child's word accuracy and comprehension, then this process would grind to a halt. I'd have to routinely ask the child to answer comprehension questions or write responses to books. But experience shows that this tends to distract from reading without giving me what I really need.

I am looking for movement and growth—for children to become self-improving readers—and when I see them acquiring skills and strategies, and moving from one developmental stage to the next, I know that there's enough going well for me and them to keep proceeding as we have been. Teaching involves approximation as much as learning does.

Selecting New Books from the Leveled Pots

I go with the child to the leveled pots to find some new books. As we leaf through the volumes in the pots that match his reading stage, I ask him to be on the lookout for books he'd like to try. He may have seen classmates reading certain books, and wonder if he's ready for them yet. Or there might be a series he's been wanting to try. Eventually, I want the children to be responsible for selecting their own books, but at the start of the year, and with emergent and early readers in particular, I have a very heavy hand in book selection. It makes no sense to allow children to choose books that are too difficult.

I might ask him to read a page from one of the books under consideration. If it seems right, we bring several more like it back to the conference table. If the child asks for a book that I am sure is too hard, I tell him so directly, or I ask him to read a page or two to see for himself. And I caution transitional and fluent readers that their real challenge lies in understanding these longer texts and carrying them across several days to completion.

All the while, however, I am aware of our time constraints. There are still children at the conference table waiting their turn and only fifty minutes to complete four or five conferences. So, while I would love to give each child time to ponder every possibility and read from several books to get a better sense of how he can handle them, I must be satisfied with less-than-perfect decisions—perhaps including the child less than I'd like in the final book selection.

If I know a child awaiting a conference needs new books, I might send him over to the book pots alone while I confer with the child scheduled before him. Or, I may I send him over to browse while I record what happened during the opening minutes of our conference, e.g., who requested the conference and why, what I learned from his running record (if I took one), what concerns me about the child's reading. Then, I join him after a minute or two, or he returns with books he selected on his own. We start with the ones he selected and make our final decisions about these and others based on how well they match his needs.

Taking a Running Record—Or Not

I do not always take a running record when I am helping a child select books to replace the "old" ones in his bag. That depends on how closely I think the books match his independent level, the stage at which he is reading, the number of children I need to confer with, and how well I know the child as a reader.

Most Frequently Asked Questions

How many books are in each child's bag at one time?

The number of books in a child's bag usually depends on his reading stage. Emergent and early readers read shorter books, and so they need more books to keep them engaged. They may have between five and ten books in their bag at a time. Transitional and fluent readers need fewer books, as it may take them several days to read just one.

Figure 11–7 contains a list of books that children at different reading stages had in their book bags at one point in the year. It exemplifies the differences in the number and types of book that are likely among readers at different stages.

What if I don't have enough books?

There is no way to get around the fact that we need plenty of books to effectively teach reading. Building up a healthy supply of books for our classroom library must become everyone's priority. Here are a few things to consider:

- Ask yourself (or whomever orders your books) whether or not it's really necessary to purchase class sets. Wouldn't it be more cost effective to select books that closely match the needs of readers in your class, and then buy six of each title that you really want. Far too often money is spent on class sets of thirty that are only appropriate for a third of the class. And wouldn't it be wise to select Big Books that support your content-area studies as well as help demonstrate reading strategies?

FIGURE 11–7 Books in Children's Book Bags

Books in Amelia's book bag (emergent/early reader):

- *Katie Couldn't* (A Rookie Reader)—R.R. Level 10
- *Katie Did It* (A Rookie Reader)—R.R. Level 13
- *Help Me* (Story Box, Level 2)—G.R. Level H
- *Mike's New Bike* (First Start—Easy Reader)—G.R. Level F
- *Morning, Noon, and Night: Poems to Fill Your Day* (Mondo, trade book)—book with which child is familiar from shared reading
- *Ten Little Bears* (Scott, Foresman)—R.R. Level 11
- *Animals at Night* (First Start—Troll)—G.R. Level I
- *Tarantula's Are Spiders* (Mondo)—G.R. Level F

Books in Joey's book bag: (early reader)

- *The Show-and-Tell Frog* (Bank Street Ready-to-Read, Level 2)—G.R. Level J
- *Bear Shadow* (Simon & Schuster)—G.R. Level J
- *Addie Meets Max* (Harper Trophy)—"Yellow 2"
- *Help Me* (Story Box, Level 2)—G.R. Level H
- *Let Me In* (Story Box, Level 3)—G.R. Level I

Books in Luan's book bag: (early reader)

- *Martin and the Teacher's Pet* (Scholastic, "School Friends" series)—"Yellow 3"
- *Bunny Runs Away* (Scholastic, "School Friends" series)—"Yellow 3"
- *Martin and the Tooth Fairy* (Scholastic, "School Friends" series)—"Yellow 3"

Books in Griffin's book bag: (early/transitional reader)

- *Nate the Great and the Fishy Prize* (Dell)—"Red 1"
- *Nate the Great and the Snowy Trail* (Dell)—"Red 1"
- *Nate the Great and the Tardy Tortoise* (Dell)—"Red 1"
- *Dinosaur Time* (Harper & Row)—G.R. K
- *The Beast in Ms. Rooney's Room* (Dell, "Kids of the Polk Street School" series)—"Red 3" [This is a book I was reading aloud to the class.]
- *Lionel and Louise* (Puffin "Easy-to-Read")—"Red 2"

Books in Maxine's book bag (transitional/fluent reader):

- *Fish Face* (Dell, "Kids of the Polk Street School" series)—"Red 3"
- *Junie B. Jones Has a Monster Under Her Bed* (Dell, series)—"Red 3"
- *Junie B. Jones and the Sneaky Peeky Spying* (Dell, series)—"Red 3"
- *The Secret Secret at the Polk Street School* (Dell, "Polka Dot Private Eye" series)—"Red 3"
- *The 'Gator Girls* (Beech Tree)—"Green 1"

Comments on book bags for children at each stage in reading:

Emergent readers need a lot of books in their bags. Amelia had eight. The books are short, so they can read several during one independent reading session. It would be unusual for all a child's books to be at one level. Usually there's a range. In this instance, one of the books, *Morning, Noon, and Night,* is a poetry anthology that we read together (in Big Book format) during shared reading. Amelia also owns a copy.

Early readers also need quite a few books in their bags, but usually not as many as emergent readers. Their books have more pages, so it takes the children longer to read them. Joey, who hasn't started reading series books yet, has a wider variety of books, while Luan is reading three books from the "School Friends" series.

Transitional readers often want to read several books from the same series, which gives them extra support. Griffin has three "Nate the Great" books. While *The Beast in Ms. Rooney's Room* is certainly too difficult, it's all right in this situation because I'm reading the book aloud to the class and his independent reading of the text is following my read aloud.

Fluent readers can move easily from text to text. Although they no longer need the support of series books, they often choose them because they enjoy reading them. Maxine had five books in her bag—more than she needed—from four different series. She had no trouble moving from series to series as she no longer relied on the series for support. However, she needs to get more factual texts and poetry in her bag.

Thinking about how all the parts of our day and the subjects we teach fit together can help us spend our money more wisely. For example, while I wouldn't expect to find a prepackaged collection on rivers, beavers, eagles, and Native Americans, I can put together customized sets of books to use during guided reading, and have individual copies of others in book pots for the children to read on their own. It makes so much sense to have books on these content-area topics available during the reading workshop to encourage children to use their background knowledge and extend it even further.

- **Go to your principal with a proposal stating what you need and why.** Principals want to provide for their teachers' needs, but are also caught up in the day-to-day pressures of running a school. When approached with a worthwhile specific request, they're more likely to supply us with what we need.

Unless we explain *why* we can't teach reading without a wide-range of books in our classroom and back it up with some prepared book lists in hand, we shouldn't be surprised if money is allocated elsewhere. But we can no longer accept trying to teach reading without enough books to do it right. That would make it unnecessarily hard, and force us to retreat to packaged basal series and programs. We've come too far and know too much to ever go back.

- **Enlist parents' help.** Parents are often very willing to help us out—once they know we need it. However, you'll need to be careful about how you explain to parents that there aren't enough books in your classroom. You don't want to antagonize your principal (who you're also asking for help) or make her job any more challenging than it already is.

Parent associations might organize a school-wide campaign asking for donations of used books, which are often packed away in basements just waiting for a home. Parents might also sponsor fund-raisers to provide each teacher with an extra allowance for buying additional books. Each year our parent association gives every teacher $300 for supplies. We can purchase books or anything else we need.

Fund-raisers don't need to be schoolwide either. Parents in each class can plan monthly events, such as a bake sale or ice cream sale, and donate the proceeds. However, these extra efforts shouldn't take the responsibility from the school districts who allocate budgets. If there's money for computers, why not books?

Do children ever get to explore books they're interested in trying?

During our first independent reading time from 8:40 to 9:00, the children can select any book from the table book pots or those clustered around the easel, regardless of whether they match their independent reading level. They read (or skim) high-interest books, page through factual texts looking at the pictures or reading the captions, try books that are harder than the ones they're reading during the workshop, or even read easy books that present no challenge at all.

Sometimes children read books for homework that are harder than ones I might select. However, I look for assurance from the parents that their child has enough support. Perhaps an older sibling sits alongside him, helping out with difficult words, or the child reads at the kitchen table while his mom is preparing dinner.

What if a child wants to read a book that's too hard?

In these situations, my response to the child is usually the same: "No." Not in a harsh or arbitrary way, but "no" in a helpful, "I-care-about-your-reading-and-this-would-not-be-good-for-you" way. If their books are too hard, children will not get better at reading as quickly as they would otherwise.

For the most part, I'm very insistent about this, but there are no absolutes. Occasionally children demonstrate they have the determination to work hard at a book that may be just a bit above what they should be reading. In these cases, I caution them that they may need to reread it several times, and may need to go slowly—and they do. Or a child may be between two stages, wanting badly to move ahead, and persistently bringing it up. When this happens I have to weigh his ability to handle the book against his maintaining a good attitude about reading. Both are important.

I may allow the child to try the book—just one—but I explain my concerns and caution him that if I see him racing through without understanding it, I'll intervene. And the child knows that I will!

Won't children feel badly if they're reading books that are "easier" than their classmates'?

I work hard to help children understand that we all learn at different rates. Just as they didn't lose their teeth or learn to walk and talk at the same time, there are differences in how quickly and easily they'll learn to read. When this advice is sincerely and consistently given, over time children recognize it as true. They learn to measure their work against their own past performance.

Is it possible to get too hung up on monitoring children's reading levels that the provided books aren't challenging enough?

Yes it is. While it's important to support children's reading, we can overdo it. In these instances, we become so intent on leveling our books and monitoring children's progress that we run the risk of not giving them enough room to grow. When this happens, the support's there, but where's the challenge?

Marie Clay has cautioned against imprudently trying to transfer Reading Recovery practices, designed for tutorial situations with our most "at-risk" readers, to entire classes of children who don't need such supports. It's easy to see why this would be problematic. In classes of twenty-five-to-thirty children, it would be very difficult to find enough books at a specific level and to change them frequently enough to appropriately challenge every child. A Reading Recovery teacher meeting daily with a child can readily do this, but it's impractical for the classroom teacher. It could result in children being confined to levels they've mastered because there's no one to help them change books.

Children who are not at risk can handle texts with a wider range of difficulty if they have frequent opportunities to meet with their teacher, if they've been acquiring strategies to work out problems on their own, and if they have opportunities to read books again and again. Our goal is to help children become self-improving readers, but this can't happen if the children's books aren't challenging enough. Remember the Goldilocks standard: Books should neither be too easy nor too hard—but just right.

What about rereading?

Rereading is a powerful strategy. It allows young readers to read a text with more support the second and third time, and to work out different problems with each rereading. My emergent and early readers understand that they must learn to read the books in their bag, so they usually don't ask to remove them until they have done so. When they can read the words accurately, they work on fluency and phrasing.

More proficient transitional readers and fluent readers generally reread only those portions they have trouble comprehending. They may reread a paragraph, a page, or a chapter that they didn't get the first time. As Maky says: "When I was little, I read books over and over. Now that I read better, I do the same thing, but only the parts I don't understand."

Conversely, when a child doesn't like a book, I remove it from her bag. It's foolish to force her to read it when there are plenty of others to choose from.

Do the children ever take their book bags home?

No. I don't let children take their book bags home because the books we've worked so hard to collect are my tools for teaching reading and theirs for learning to read. I can't afford to have a child forget his bag at home.

However, since it's important that children read at home as well as in school, they often borrow books from the classroom and return them the following morning. I don't have any formal sign-out procedure. They just take the book they want to read. They're pretty good about bringing them back, and the parents oversee it.

How do you make book bags for children who can't read yet?

While this may seem quite challenging at the beginning of the year, it's not that difficult when we think about what children at a young age *can* do, instead of what they *can't*. Kindergarten children who aren't reading print yet can "read" pictures in books, so some of the first books in their bags might be books with engaging illustrations. They can also read simple caption books with an exact match of picture to text. A good collection of paperback alphabet books (they're lighter than hardcover) can be a great source of beginning books for nascent readers.

Even when a child can't read a book himself, he may be able to read one that has been read to him several times. Therefore, think of collecting multiple copies of your favorite read alouds (an idea from Liz Thompson, a friend and literacy consultant) to put into children's book bags, or small copies of Big Books you've shared. Children can also read copies of books they have written as a class, copies of class poems the children have learned, and their teacher's corrected transcription of their own attempts at writing. They may not be able to read the words, but they'll feel like readers, and begin to acquire some concepts about print.

At the start of the year, while you confer with children to match them with books, what are the children doing who still don't have any matched books?

At the start of the year, I approximate what a reading workshop will look like later. Since the children already have their reading folders (remember I purchased them over the summer and later asked parents to reimburse me), I can try to set them up with books starting from day one. I tell the children they should *read* while I'm having conferences. At first they don't know what a conference is, and many say they can't read, but usually, they humor me and go along.

During this time, I allow children to select books from the table book pots—but not the leveled book pots. Of course, they can't sustain their reading for very long this early in the year, and so there's a lot of commotion (more than I can easily tolerate) adding to my urgency to get the children matched with books. After thirty minutes or so of independent reading, we meet to process their reading, just as we'll do every day thereafter. (See Chapter 13 for how children reflect on their reading each day.) Then I give the children their writing folders and let them write for another thirty minutes. Children in our school have had writing workshop since kindergarten so there's seldom a question of not knowing what to write or thinking they "can't."

As more children confer with me and get their book bags, each new day is easier than the one before. By the end of the first week, I'll have conferred with each of the children at least once, and they'll each have a bag of books.

In addition, right from the first day of school, I ask the children to record the title and author of one book they read each day on their Weekly Reading Log. Emergent readers sometimes have trouble writing down the title and author, or even knowing where to look. So explaining this is certainly part of what I do at the end of the meeting time before I send the children off to read. I don't ask them to color the "genre box" in yet, as this requires many demonstrations.

What if more children need new books than you have the time for?

This happens sometimes, and then I wish there were two—even three—of me. When I say I can't meet with them right away, and ask are they all right with the books they have in their bags for just one or two more days, most children will say they are.

Occasionally, a child insists he's been reading the same books over and over, and he's bored with the books in his bag. If this happens and we're far enough into the year so that I'm reasonably sure the child knows the kind of book he should be reading, I send him over to the book pots to find one or two books to read until we can meet. Sometimes I ask the child to just walk past the conference table and quietly hold the books up so I can see what he's selected. Most of the time they're okay.

Conclusion

Matching children with books may seem a daunting undertaking at first. But just as you focus on what young readers can do, instead of what they can't, you need to build from the ground up with the resources you have.

It may be best to start by organizing your books into the four basic stages, and then gradually, as you learn more about them, refine your leveling. You may have to carve out a time, perhaps during your writing workshop or the first fifteen minutes of the day, to meet with one or two children. You may even put fewer books in each bag until you've built up your library. Providing ourselves and our children with the materials we need are challenging, but basic, tasks. Start small, but think big.

CHAPTER 12

Independent Reading: A Time for Practice

ONE MORNING AS SCHOOL WAS STARTING, A parent meeting in my classroom went on longer than expected. So as my children came up the stairs at 8:40, our principal Shelley Harwayne gathered them into her office and asked Pat Werner, who was doing coverages that day, to read to them until I finished. After a few minutes—what must have seemed much longer to the children—Jasmin left Pat's group and went to find Shelley in her office next door. "Shelley, Shelley," he pleaded, "Tell her to stop reading. She can read, I can't."

Out of the mouths of babes! Jasmin was used to coming in each morning and reading by himself for twenty minutes. It confused him to have someone do it for him when he's the one needing the practice. His appeal to Shelley was a spontaneous and compelling testimonial to the importance of independent reading: Children who can't yet read fluently need more time to read themselves. They need lots and lots of practice to learn new strategies by reading books that are just right for them. In fact, it's the only way they can improve.

I give my children plenty of opportunities to read in two independent reading sessions each day. They read for fifty minutes from 9:30 to 10:20, while I hold reading conferences or lead guided reading groups, in addition to the twenty minutes from 8:40 to 9:00 when they arrive.

The First Daily Independent Reading Time

The first independent reading session, described briefly in Chapter 3, is how we start our day. After the children put their work and messages from home in the "homework" and "notes" baskets, they select a book from the pots on the tables or from around the easel. They don't get their reading folder or their book bag. They don't need to record the title and author of a book they read, or process what worked well and didn't. Their only responsibility is to read books that interest them.

One morning as I sat alongside Mikey, I saw he was reading *Energy from Oil and Gas*, a book from the "Facts About" series. It's not a title I would have purchased, as the topic appears to have limited appeal, but it was part of a series the school had ordered. "Mikey," I asked, "Do you understand what you're reading?" I wondered because even I didn't understand the diagram of the offshore oil production platform that had his attention. "Mikey, do you understand this?" He pointed to the pictures and mumbled something inaudible. And finally, "Mikey, are you interested in offshore oil drilling?" I expected him to say "No" and be glad that I had intervened. But instead, he looked up at me and, in that disarming way only a young child can, answered: "I am interested in everything."

This first independent reading session gives children time to explore texts they're interested in, but might not get to see during the second independent reading time when the books are chosen to meet their needs. It isn't a problem if the books they select are too easy or too hard. If they're too hard, children might look at the pictures and read only the parts they can or chat quietly about it with a classmate. When books are too easy, it prepares them for the more challenging reading to come.

Then, during our 9:00 meeting, I ask if anyone has something to share related to school, our class, or topics we're investigating in science and social studies. Sometimes children offer books and artifacts they've brought from home. However, most of the time they share pictures or information from the books they've just read, jump-starting our day. I might point out text features that could help them access additional information. We're extending what we already know about these topics, setting up the expectation that we'll learn a whole lot more.

The Second Daily Independent Reading Time: More Than DEAR and SSR

You might ask: What's so new about giving children time to read? Don't most children have a daily DEAR (Drop Everything And Read) or SSR (Sustained Silent Reading) time to read books they've chosen?

My current practices for the second independent reading session have developed into something very different from the DEAR or SSR time of the past, when I wasn't fully aware of the purpose behind giving children time to read on their own. SSR was more of an add-on to an already too full day, rather than a *core* component of my reading program. The children got to read whatever they wanted after lunch (to quiet them down), or upon returning from a trip (when there wasn't enough time to start anything new). They simply took a book from their desk, which they may have brought from home or selected from the school or classroom library, to read for fifteen-to-thirty minutes.

In those days, I thought I needed to demonstrate that I was a reader, too. So I read for the first ten minutes before walking around the room to see how the children were doing. I'm not quite sure what I was looking for, since I had such poorly defined expectations. I felt little concern over whether or not the children were reading "just-right" books. I had no record of what they had read the day, week, or even month before. And there was certainly no talk of strategies. The children were reading, and I thought that was enough.

Now I know that it wasn't enough. The independent reading my children do today is an integral part of our day. It's where they get to *use* the strategies I've demonstrated. I even leave reminder notes in their assessment notebooks (see Figure 4–4 on page 41) of things they should try, and they know their books were carefully selected because of what they themselves can and can't do. Reading these books will help them improve, and they want that very much.

My role has changed too. I no longer read during independent reading. (The children know I'm a reader because I refer to the books I'm reading at home and model reading during read aloud and shared reading.) I'm much too busy conferring with children to see how they're doing, matching them with books, and demonstrating strategies one-on-one or in small groups. When a visitor happens upon this scene, I don't jump up out of fear he might wonder why I'm not standing in front of the classroom teaching. I know that I am teaching in the optimal way.

I've carefully prepared the environment and demonstrated ways for children to effectively engage with books, with their materials, and with one another. The children are reading under my close guidance.

Too Good to Be True?

Sounds good you say, but perhaps a little too good to be true. How can children who aren't working at centers, or doing pages of worksheets or answering comprehension questions on books they've read, remain engaged for so long?

Here is where planning and organization pay off, big time. I can ask this—and the children can do it—because everything about my teaching is designed to promote their independent work. The conceptual framework, my focus on strategies, my classroom organization, the reading folders, the assessment notebooks, the children's book bags, my demonstrations, their written responses, the strategy sheets to practice the featured strategies, the simple workshop structure provided, the processing they do afterward—*and how all these elements work together*—provide the groundwork for the children to work hard at their reading for sustained periods.

A Checklist for Sustaining Independent Reading

Here's a checklist (see Figure 12–1) of things to consider when reviewing how you manage independent reading:

Are you clear about your goals and how to achieve them?

My independent reading sessions are organized to support my beliefs about how children learn to read and my role in helping them.

FIGURE 12–1 Independent Reading Checklist

- ❏ Are you clear about your goals and how to achieve them?
- ❏ Do you communicate your expectations clearly and consistently to the children?
- ❏ Do your environment and materials support what you want to happen?
- ❏ Are your children reading books at their independent reading level?
- ❏ Are you offering your children a variety of real reading experiences?
- ❏ Is the amount of time you're asking children to read reasonable for their age and reading stage?
- ❏ Are the children held accountable for what they do?

Children need opportunities to practice working out problems that arise as they read, selecting appropriate strategies from their expanding repertoire. Since this is what they need, I must define my *specific* expectations and procedures to help us reach these goals. You must define yours for your classroom as well.

Are you going to allow some talking or none? Will you go for fifty minutes straight or divide your time into two shorter sessions, perhaps one "silent" and the other interactive? Will you permit children to walk around and change seats, or will you assign seats and insist they stay put? How will you provide opportunities for children to read books that interest them as well as those that support their developmental needs? How will they exchange their books when they need new ones? Knowing what you want to happen goes a long way to getting there.

Do you communicate your expectations clearly and consistently to the children?

Children do quite well when they understand *why* they're being asked to do things. When I discuss reading with children, I explain precisely what I expect and why. I leave no part of the procedure to chance. The children know how to get their book bags and return them at the end of the reading workshop. They know how to pass out the folders—one child taking

three and handing them out, and at the end, that same child collecting the folders and returning them to the plastic crates.

I prompt the children repeatedly to check the reminder notes in their assessment notebooks to see what they need to work on (see Figure 4–1 page 38), and to fill in their Weekly Reading Log (see Figure 3–6 page 28). I also remind them when there's only ten minutes left to complete their end-of-the-week response on the back of the log (see Figure 3–7 on page 29).

Every day before giving out the reading folders, I select one to inspect. I go through the "lucky child's" folder, commenting on how well he is carrying out his responsibilities. Did he record the title and author of his book each day? Is he taking enough care in the appearance of his responses? Is he reading a variety of genres as indicated by the color-coding on his log? Going through one folder each day keeps the children on their toes and reminds them all of what they need to do.

I don't allow talking during the workshop, unless it's related to the children's reading. There is noise enough as they read. Beginning readers can't read silently yet, and so they subvocalize. And a classful of children subvocalizing together creates quite a buzz, as any kindergarten or first-grade teacher can attest! In addition, children may be reading a book on tape or discussing the book they're reading with their partner, but this isn't the kind of talking that distracts them from their reading. It's what they're supposed to be doing.

Although I don't ask children to do a lot of *different* things during the independent reading time, I do set high expectations. To help children meet them, I keep the workshop structure simple and predictable so they can be flexible in their approach to problems they encounter as they read. In fact, I believe it's because our classroom and routines are so predictable that children do such amazing things!

Do your environment and materials support what you want to happen?

How we set up our classroom and prepare our materials impacts the relative ease or difficulty with which we teach and, therefore, the degree to which we enjoy our work. It also affects the way our children feel about school.

Think of dinner parties you've gone to where the hostess has attended to every detail, taking great care to make it a memorable evening. It's the same in the classroom. When materials are in place and working, when schedules provide large blocks of time for children to get involved in reading and composing text, when there are books to support our demonstrations and engage children, when time to read and write follow demonstrations of strategies and skills children can use, our chances of success are much greater than if we hadn't prepared our environment, schedule, and materials so carefully. And our children, appreciating the care we've taken to support their efforts, are more likely to take their work seriously and work hard.

Are your children reading books at their independent reading level?

If they're not reading "just-right" books—you need to do something to correct this. We have so little time to work with our children that having them read books that are too easy or too hard is a waste. We need to beg, borrow—anything short of steal—to get more books in our classrooms that meet our children's needs.

Imagine how you'd feel, having signed up for a beginning tennis lesson or ski class, and finding that you were put into an advanced group (or in a beginning group, if you were ready for advanced)—not by mistake, but because that was the only group there was. "Not for me" you'd say, and be on your way. Our kids can't say no or walk away, and so they suffer in silence.

Or do they? I'm convinced that one of the primary reasons children act out in class is that they're being asked to do things that are inappropriate. It's no wonder a child reading a book that's too easy might notice how perfectly his pencil fits into the mesh weave of the plastic crayon basket, and how if he turns it around and around he can make grooves on its side. It's no wonder a child who's scanning his "too difficult" text looking for familiar words notices each time a classmate leaves the room. We can't expect children to cooperate fully all day if we don't provide the supports and challenges they need to stay engaged.

Are you offering your children a variety of real reading experiences?

Children get better with lots of practice. If they spend their time filling in worksheets, coloring in pictures that match sounds the letters represent, writing the answers to comprehension questions posted on the board, then that's what they'll become better at. But is that what we want?

We need to offer children a variety of real reading experiences—where they're reading whole texts and using its features to work out the parts that give them trouble. This "whole-to-part" support is best exemplified in shared reading where the group reading the text together helps each child handle the parts that are problematic to him. These experiences carry over into independent reading when the child's ability to work out problems is enhanced by: knowing something about the topic or the author's style; previewing the front and back cover, the table of contents, and the illustrations; using what happens early in the book to figure out what might happen later; and asking what makes sense, sounds right, and matches the letters. But when reading is decontextualized, these supports aren't available.

Is the amount of time you're asking children to read reasonable for their age and reading stage?

This question deserves serious attention. We cannot ask children to do what is developmentally inappropriate and expect them to do it well. But at the same time, when considering what's a reasonable amount of time to ask children to read in one stretch, our criterion should be what they can do *under the right conditions*—not what they were previously able (or unable) to do in a less supportive setting. When children don't have enough books to read, when they don't know what strategies to try, when practices and procedures are random and inconsistent, their attention span is shortened.

On the other hand, when children have a bag of "just-right" books, when there are comfortable places for them to spread out or snuggle into, when they know what behaviors are expected of them because it's what they do day after day, when they process how things went after each workshop so they can do more of what's working and less of what isn't, then they can focus longer on their reading.

Kindergarten children may need two twenty-five-minute reading sessions instead of one longer one, as they are typically unable to sustain their independent reading—at least during the first half of the year—for fifty minutes. Having two shorter sessions helps them establish a "serious" outlook on this important time of day. Then you can realistically expect them to work successfully for the entire time, and during each session you can confer with two children or hold one guided reading group.

First graders may also need two separate, shorter sessions at the beginning of the year, but as they become more skilled they'll be able to extend their reading. Or you can organize one continuous fifty-minute session into two segments: in the first half, the children work independently (and "silently") on their own reading; and then, after twenty minutes or so, they read with partners, fill in their reading log, write a response, work on extension activities, or continue reading books from their bag. My goal would be for the two sessions to eventually become one, with children engaged in a variety of reading experiences throughout.

Second- and third-grade children can read for longer stretches right from the start. When they see independent reading as a key part of the reading workshop (taking the place of assignments, such as completing SRA task cards and answering comprehension questions) then they're likely to take it more seriously and stay with it longer.

Are the children held accountable for what they do?

It does no good to plan and then try to implement the very best independent reading time you can, and not hold the children responsible for their part. When I ask a child to write a response to one of his books and request a conference when he's done so I can read it, I expect him to follow through. If he doesn't, I ask why. Why did he ignore something we both agreed on as necessary?

Looking through Barbara's folder at the start of the workshop and scanning her reading logs, I learned from the number of the dates on which she recorded the same title, that it had taken three weeks to read a book that should have only taken one. I needed to know why! I said I couldn't meet with her that day (I had already scheduled conferences and this conversation was much too important to rush through), but we'd meet tomorrow so I could learn how this happened. Of course, Barbara, typically a hard worker, felt just awful about this and got to work right away reading and responding to other books in her bag. We did meet the following day, and when I asked: "Why?" "How?"—she said: "I was talking." End of conversation. Barbara knew her behavior was inappropriate and accepted responsibility for her actions. I continually reinforce these expectations with the children: It's important to work very hard at your reading; I expect it, and hold you accountable.

What the Children Do During Independent Reading

The question teachers most frequently ask in my staff development workshops on guided reading and reading conferences is: "What are the other children doing?" But I purposely didn't begin this chapter with a simple list of independent reading activities, because this would only have invited skepticism. For underlying this question of "What are the other children doing?" is a disbelieving "How?" How can you get your children to read for fifty minutes, when I have a hard time getting mine to read quietly for just a few? That's why I first described the organizational, environmental, and material supports I create for independent reading. Now, I'll relate some of the reading experiences in which my children engage:

They read books from their bags.

Most of the time, the children are reading books from their book bags that have been selected to meet their needs. At the start of the second independent reading session, they take their reading folder and their book bag, and find a spot—hopefully a quiet one—to read. The children don't have desks or assigned seats, so some of them sit around the tables or on the floor. Others sit on the sofa or in small carpeted areas around the room. I've tried to design our classroom space so there's room enough for them to spread out. Children need "quiet" to read, and I need "quiet" to teach.

Do they ever talk or fool around during this time? Of course they do— they're children. And I suspect that if adults were put into the same situation, we would respond in similar ways. "Taking breaks" after working for a stretch of time is how we function. Children can work hard for about fifteen minutes, then their minds, and sometimes their bodies, wander a little until something calls them back to the task at hand. Sometimes it's their own inner voice saying they aren't doing what they're supposed to be doing. Sometimes it's me, standing up and reminding them to get back to work. I take this "wandering" in stride, however, and know that it's as much my responsibility to refocus them as it is natural for them to stray.

They fill in their Weekly Reading Log.

Each day the children record the title and author of one book they've read on their Weekly

Reading Log. Except for those reading longer chapter books, most children read several volumes during each reading workshop, but I only ask them to record one. They color in the box alongside the title "red," "blue," or "yellow" to show whether the book is fictional, factual, or poetry (see Figure 3–6 on page 28).

Each Friday, children respond on the back of their log to the prompts: "This week I was successful at . . ." and "Next week I plan to . . . " More fluent readers and writers often respond specifically to what they've accomplished and intend to do the following week, as Griffin did in Figure 12–2, while those in the earlier stages respond more briefly about the strategies they're trying, as Daniel did in Figure 12–3. I remind the children at the start of the Friday workshop that they'll need to respond on the back of their reading log, and I give a ten-minute warning so they're able to finish. Eventually children learn to plan for this themselves, and some even start responding earlier in the week.

They respond to a book.

Children respond to *some* of the books they read on a response sheet or in their response notebook. Those who are just learning to read might use a response sheet to draw a picture of their favorite part of the book and write one or two sentences about it. More fluent readers respond in their notebooks, summarizing the text, describing a part they especially enjoyed, or relating it to other books and to their lives. (See Chapter 13 for more about how children respond to books and Figures 13–4A, B, C, and D on pages 169–170 for examples of different types of written responses.)

I don't ask children to respond to every book they read. That would take essential time away from their reading and might even lead them to

FIGURE 12–2

Back of Griffin's Weekly Reading Log

1. **This week I was successful at:**

• finishing Pirates Past noon
• Sitting next to Someone quiet
• getting Junie B. Jones and some Sneaky peeky spying
• getting to chapter 2 in Adam Joshua the Kid next door

2. **Next week I plan to:**

• Start Junie B Jones and some Sneaky peeky spying
• finish Adam Joshua the kid next door
• Start Junie B Jones and her big fat mouth

FIGURE 12–3

**Back of Daniel's
Weekly Reading Log**

1. This week I was successful at:

> This week I was
> successful at reading
> to myself.

2. Next week I plan to:

> Next week I plan
> to stretch the words
> out.

dislike it. How would we feel if we had to write a response to each book we read?

As a rule of thumb, I ask transitional and fluent readers (who also have an easier time writing) to write responses more frequently than less fluent readers. By the end of second grade, most children respond once a week. Younger readers, still working hard at acquiring the basic skills, generally respond twice a month. I no longer use writing to keep children busy, as I once did. Now I know they need to read more.

They read a Big Book.

Since all children don't need a turn reading Big Books during independent reading, each morning I post the names of two children who'd benefit most from reading them alongside the box where they're stored. Since these are books we've read together during shared reading, the children can read them more easily. They understand that they can read these books

for the first twenty minutes of the workshop, but then must read the books from their book bags. By the time I finish one guided reading group or hold two or three conferences, they should have made the transition. I find that the children can settle into the quieter reading that the rest of the class is engaged in more quickly, and sustain it longer, if they get their more interactive (and more supported) reading out of the way first, rather than leaving it to the end.

I store the Big Books we've read together during shared reading in a shallow cut-away box in the corner of the room near the tape player. I keep a couple of wooden rulers alongside the books so the children can point to the words as they read. Liz Thompson, who has lots of ideas for literacy centers, suggests making word frames from fly swatters. She cuts a 1″ × 3″ window on each fly swatter and lets the children use them to highlight words after the reading.

They listen to a book on tape and read along.

Diane Snowball is the first person I heard refer to the listening center as a "read-along/listening center." This makes perfect sense: We want children to read along with the books on tape not just listen to them.

I keep each tape and several copies of the book in a plastic bag and hang them on hooks attached to a cabinet near the tape player. Each tape contains several readings of a text—typically books we've read during shared reading or in guided reading groups—allowing the children to reread it several times, each time with a different purpose. For example, as the children follow the "reader's" prompts they may fill in the deleted words, look through the table of contents for specific poems and then read them, or sing along with the text put to music.

These tapes are especially helpful for emergent and early readers who are just acquiring the basic skills and need additional support. They're also wonderful for English-language learners who need to listen to a text several times before they're able to internalize its language structures.

As with the Big Books, each morning I post the names of the two-or-three children who will work at the tape player that day. They do this for the first twenty minutes of the workshop and then begin reading the books from their bags.

They read with a partner.

Although I have no formal partner reading where all the children in class are paired with a partner to read for a set time, there are occasions when a handful of children read with partners. Children in a guided reading group that's just ending have the same book in their bag and might read through the book one or two more times with a partner. And others might select the same title from the book pots to read together. Usually it's emergent and beginning early readers who benefit most, and the brevity of their texts lends itself to this practice.

Sitting alongside a child at the beginning of the year, I demonstrate partner reading to the whole class: The partners sit side by side, not facing one another, and each takes a turn reading the *entire* text. (When children alternate their reading, page by page, they lose the wholeness of the text and the support it gives.) As one child reads, the other follows along, ready to assist the reader if he has trouble with a word. The partner understands, however, that he should only suggest a strategy or offer the word after he's given the reader time to work out the problem on his own.

In addition to partnering children with similar needs, I sometimes ask a more fluent reader to assist an emergent reader for a few minutes at the start of the workshop. By receiving help with several of the books in his bag, the novice reader is better equipped to work independently for the remainder of the time.

I allow partners to read together for about ten minutes, usually at the beginning of the workshop. This allows each child to read through the text once or twice. Knowing when they start helps me monitor the time they spend reading together. By the end of the year, there are fewer and fewer children who will benefit from this practice, as most are able to read well enough on their own.

They work on a strategy sheet.

Although I introduce comprehension strategies such as making a Story Map, making a Character Map, or making a "Before and After" Chart during read aloud and shared reading, using enlarged versions of the graphics organizers found in Appendices G, H, and I, I usually introduce the strategy sheet itself during guided reading. I make it clear that they are intended to help the children practice a strategy *as* they read; they're not to be used as an instrument for responding to a text they've already read. Depending on the strategy I'm demonstrating, the children record on a strategy sheet, which they keep in their folder, what they're learning about the different story elements, what the character is like, or what they knew before and are learning now about the topic under investigation. Or I might also send them off to work on it independently after the group concludes for the day.

Sometimes children use a strategy sheet to support their independent reading. As I confer with a child, I might direct him to take a sheet from the metal file where they're stored and work on a specific comprehension strategy. Or I offer the strategy as one he might consider when reading longer, harder-to-understand texts. Children eventually learn to ask for a strategy sheet themselves.

After disbanding a guided reading group that read *Fancy Feet* by Patricia Reilly Giff and worked on a Story Map, the children asked if they could read more "New Kids of the Polk Street School" books and do a Story Map on their own. As it turned out, two children chose

Stacy Says Goodbye, two chose *B-E-S-T Friends*, and two chose *All About Stacy*. Each pair decided to sit side-by-side and help each other out with the parts they didn't understand. So in effect, these children ended up with double support—a Story Map and a partner.

Children may, in turn, use Story and Character Maps to help them plan out a story they're writing. See Figure 13–7 on page 178 for the Story Map Brittany worked on as she wrote her story *The Little Dutch Girl*.

Work on an extension activity.

After a guided reading group, I might give the children something to work on by themselves that relates to what they've done in the group. For example, emergent and early readers might write and illustrate their own page of text on 15″ × 18″ paper, patterning it after the predictable text they've been reading. (See Figures 7–10 on page 92 and 11–2 on page 142 for books with predictable patterns.) Or they might sort words they've cut from sentence strips that match the text in their guided reading book.

Sometimes a book or a discussion we're having during our meeting time prompts us to collect favorite lines from stories we've read together, tongue twisters, homophones, or idioms in a *blank* Big Book. (Younger children might also collect words beginning with different letters of the alphabet or make books of rhyming words.)

When working on our homophone book, an extension from our shared reading, the children wrote a sentence for each set of words and drew pictures describing them (see Figure 12–4). Each day two children volunteered to work on the book during independent reading time. Before starting, one child set our timer for fifteen minutes, knowing he'd need to finish within that time. When his time was up, the second child began. These two children shared their work during the next meeting, before the next two children were selected.

However, I'm careful not to overdo these extension activities. It's too easy to lose sight of what will help children the most: their own reading.

Living Without Reading Centers

My own teaching experience has led me to favor independent reading over centers. Although I am adept at organizing the classroom environment—the books, the materials, and the parts of the day—and understanding how all these facets of my teaching work together, I find it very difficult to organize children into groups to work at five or six literacy centers while I confer with readers or lead guided reading groups. How can I keep track of all the children or keep the center activities from becoming skill-oriented tasks that don't add up to powerful learning? How can I find the time to gather and organize the materials required to keep the centers vital and appealing?

With limited time to work closely with the children, I don't want to divert any of my efforts into shepherding them from center to center. Instead, I focus on conferring with children, demonstrating reading strategies one-on-one and in small groups, and matching them with books. I don't want to spend an hour each night, or three or four on the weekend, maintaining my centers. Instead, I spend my time thinking about the children's reading and planning ways to address their needs.

When I taught kindergarten, I did, in fact, have *developmental* centers—with sand and water tables, blocks, and dress-up clothes galore. But my role at that time was to work alongside the children, not use the centers to keep the children busy while I did other important work. The centers were my work, and I certainly would have them again if I were teaching kindergarten today! The social interaction and oral language skills they promote play a huge part in children's development.

And I do appreciate the value of literacy centers when they are purposefully planned and thoughtfully implemented. A few well-designed centers, like a letter-writing center, a poetry center, a Big Book center, and a read-along/listening center can be an effective means to engage children during reading workshop. However, I doubt any center can match independent reading itself as a way to both involve children and lead to better reading.

Organizing Without a Task Board

I don't use a task board to organize the children's supplemental reading experiences. The scheduling of additional reading experiences follows from what the children are doing in other parts of their reading day and what they need, just as the reading conferences and

FIGURE 12–4

Page from a Homophone Book

guided-reading groups grow out of the children's specific needs and events occurring in the workshop.

At the end of the meeting time, I remind them of what they need to do. In reviewing one child's folder each day, I'm reminding them all to take their independent reading seriously, record the title and author of one book on their log, respond to the prompts on the back each Friday, and write occasional responses. (Each child knows what "occasional" means for him.)

Children working on strategy sheets need no reminder since they have their sheet in their folder to remind them. And every morning, I post the names of the children who can read Big Books and the books-on-tape.

At the start of the year, some children complain that "it's not fair" they never get to work with the Big Books or books-on-tape while others get to work with them a lot. I explain that we all need different things, and that the only way I can be truly fair is to try to give each of them what they need. This, they understand and accept.

Conclusion

Independent reading is one of the most important times of my day, although this wasn't always so. The turning point for me was realizing that I have to give children more time to read if I really expect them to read better. While I gave this notion lip service before, I didn't fully understand its power. Learning to read involves applying strategies and skills to real text, and that requires practice. Lots and lots of practice. In addition, the experience of reading has intrinsic rewards that lead children to want more. And the more they want it, the more they read, and the better they get.

A Time for Response

M Y APARTMENT BUILDING IN NEW YORK City has twelve attractive floors, but nothing compares to the penthouse for its bright sunlight and panoramic views. As I begin this thirteenth and final chapter, I can't help but compare these enviable views to the perspective children gain as they "respond" to text. Each child's reflection on his reading process, his oral and written responses to text and his personal writing, expand his vision as he experiences different viewpoints and learns new things.

By reflecting on and sharing their process with classmates, children validate their strategies and consider new ones. They extend their thinking by responding to texts they've read or ones that have been read to them. And when children write their own stories, poems, and informational pieces, they are inspired by authors and begin to understand the depth and breadth of the reading/writing process.

Exploring a text's meaning in greater depth is an opportunity to observe children's comprehension, but our primary purpose in asking them to discuss or write about it is not to assess, but to broaden their understanding. Seeing the whole and understanding the parts, these children really do have the best view.

This chapter discusses how children's oral and written responses to text, their reflections on their reading process, and their own writing enable them to become better readers.

Oral and Written Responses to Text

Just as the artist's work is realized in the observer's response, literature elicits a child's views, sentiments, and opinions. On this aesthetic level, there are no "right" or "wrong" answers, just a growing appreciation for the "interaction" between writer and reader and an awareness that she is expected, even entitled, to respond.

Oral Responses

During our meeting time, from 9:00 to 9:30, I read texts aloud—factual texts and poetry, as well as fictional pieces. My children respond orally right from the first day of school when I read to them and ask: "So, what do you think?"

It's not at all unusual for children to initially respond with short, generic statements, like "It was funny," and then for me to prompt them to be more specific. The conversation that ensues when I ask children to say more or explain their responses generates additional topics for discussion. It's usually the children's comments and questions, not mine, that spark a debate.

One morning, I read aloud Phyllis Reynolds Naylor's *Sweet Strawberries* about a cranky peasant who accuses others of having the very vices that he himself exhibits—his wife's a complainer, the young lass's impatient, the boy's lazy, the farmer's selfish, and the merchant's stingy. These accusations and the fact that he won't buy his good-natured wife the strawberries she craves, greatly anger her, but he mistakenly thinks that it is the townspeople, and not he, who have upset her. And so on their next trip to market, in an effort to prevent them from annoying her again, he acts more kindly toward the lass, the boy, the farmer, and the merchant, and then is amazed at how much they've changed in just one week. Although he never realizes the folly of his ways, he does alter his behavior, causing his wife to reaffirm: "He's not the nicest man in the world, but he's not the worst one either."

Figure 13–1 contains three excerpts from the conversation that followed my reading of the

163

FIGURE 13–1 Excerpts from Our Conversation About *Sweet Strawberries*

Excerpt One:

Teacher: What do you think about the book?

Jordan: When I saw the picture of the ducks following the girl, it reminded me of a movie I saw. The movie was called *Fly Away Home.* The ducks always followed her.

Brittany: I didn't really understand it because the wife forgot how he acted last week and how she acted too.

Teacher: Say more about what you're not understanding.

Brittany: At the end, she said he wasn't the nicest man but he wasn't the worst one either. But he was still being mean. He still woke the boy up.

Sophia (to Brittany): At first he was being selfish and stuff and called all the people names, and he started to be a lot more better to be with because if he was still the old way you wouldn't want to be with him ever. He kept trying to cheer her up, but she was still upset because of what he had said to all the people who were passing through and stuff.

Teacher: And even though he still woke the boy up so he could open the gate, at least this time he woke him up by singing. That was nicer than yelling at him like the last time.

Daniel: When the lady was going to the wagon when the story just began, it reminded me of my grandma. She says: "Get in the car," and me and my brother go in the car and she takes like an hour to get ready.

Teacher: Let's get back to what Brittany was asking. Did the husband change at the end?

Excerpt Two:

Chelsea: I noticed that he's calling everybody what he is. He's saying stuff to other people that they aren't, but he is.

Teacher: You mean he's calling other people lazy and stingy, when he is?

Chelsea: That's what I mean.

Sophia: Chelsea's right. He's calling everybody what he is.

Maky: Almost everything is opposite, just like Chelsea said. He's the one that's really stingy and grumpy. He's really selfish and lazy.

Tiffany: Yeah, he wants the shade to himself.

Thomas: The wife even called him all the things that he called the other people.

Excerpt Three:

Sophia: He didn't really care about anybody but himself until he realized what he was doing.

Teacher: Do you think he realized at the end?

Sophia: Probably.

Teacher (restating the previous question): Do you think he understood at the end that he's been mean to the townspeople?

Georgie: He thinks they've changed, but he's the one that changed. He acts nicer and so they act nicer to him.

Alexis: Why did he turn nice?

Teacher (to the class): Why do you think he turned nice?

Chelsea: Because he didn't want his wife to be upset again.

Georgie: He wanted to be nice because he didn't want to get the people angry. He didn't want them to upset his wife. He thinks that they got her upset. That's what I think.

Fiona: They weren't the ones being mean anyway. He was.

Sophia: At first he was blaming everyone else. He thought they made her unhappy, but really he did. So at the end, he thought they were being mean. He said isn't it wonderful how they have changed in just a week. But it wasn't them who changed. It was him.

text and outlines our progression from making general observations about the book to focusing on why the husband changed his behavior.

IMPROVING CHILDREN'S ORAL RESPONSES

Here are several suggestions for improving children's oral responses to text:

- **Provide time for responses.** In the pressure of the curricular agenda, it's often tempting to read a book and then move directly to the next activity. Giving children the opportunity to respond may sometime seem too much of a luxury. However, the time we spend nurturing children's responses to text is important. It sets the stage for an interactive classroom where the children know they're expected to participate and enjoy the exchange.

The conversation related in Figure 13–1 took time. There's no way around that. But it's time well spent hearing the children's responses or helping them clarify their thinking. Brittany's secure admission in Excerpt One that she didn't understand why the wife said her husband's not the "worst man" when he'd behaved so badly the week before, allowed Sophia to explain it to her, and in doing so, become more confident in her own ability to interpret text. Then later in Excerpt Three, I questioned Sophia's conclusion—that the man "probably" realized he'd acted poorly, helping her listen as Fiona and Georgie explained their more accurate account of what had happened.

Unless we make responding to books a regular part of the classroom routine, children will be suspicious of the occasional time when we do ask for a response. They'll think we're checking up on their reading, instead of initiating a dialogue about books.

- **Help children interact.** Just as children begin pre-school parallel playing, indifferent to what the child sitting next to them is doing, their early responses to books show little regard for their classmates' comments. Then, as their social awareness develops, they begin to listen more carefully, and can eventually talk *with one another* about books.

I support interactions by asking a child to speak directly to his classmate ("Georgie, would you look at Thomas and say that again?") or by referring with a hand gesture to the child who made the original comment, when another child inappropriately addresses a response to me. In

Figure 13–1 (Excerpt Two), both Sophia and Maky preface their remarks with reference to Chelsea's insightful statement regarding how the husband is "calling everyone what he is."

- **Improve our questioning technique.** There used to be times when I posed a question (or more accurately—a series of questions, one right after the other) and got no response. I wanted to throw up my hands and ask: What's wrong with these kids? Instead, I've learned to ask what's wrong with my technique.

It's intimidating to have questions fired at us, one after the other. When someone really wants to know how you feel, they look you in the eye, ask a direct question, and give you time to consider it. Good questioning techniques provide response time, and the best questions foster divergent thinking, not one right answer.

Although I opened the discussion with a general query: "What do you think about the book?" my subsequent questions and prompts helped the children extend their thinking. "Say more about what you're not understanding." "Did the husband change at the end?" "You mean he's calling other people lazy and stingy when he is?" "Do you think he understood at the end that he's been mean to the townspeople?" and restating Alexis's question, "Why do you think he turned nice?" Good questions help children stay on course; they don't stifle their thinking.

Written Responses

After a Saturday workshop at a neighboring school district, a young teacher approached me for advice. It was the end of April, and she had recently been hired to take over a first-grade class for the remainder of the year. She was terribly frustrated that the children were so far behind, and disheartened by their poor attitude. She asked what she could do in these remaining months to make a difference in their reading.

I suggested she focus on shared reading since it offers abundant opportunities for demonstration and response, while providing a lot of support for readers who are not yet fluent. She'd tried reading aloud and sharing Big Books with the children, but their overriding concern was always whether or not they had to write a response. Although she had repeatedly tried to assure them that they needn't worry—that they should just listen and enjoy—invariably, several pages into the book, a hand would go up and a small voice ask: "But do we have to write about it?"

It was easy to imagine what must have gone on in that classroom from September to April. The children were probably required to write a response each and every time their teacher read to them. If that was the routine, then it's no wonder they didn't enjoy reading. No wonder this new teacher was having such trouble engaging them in an experience that should be so agreeable and supportive. These children weren't giving themselves over so easily without first knowing what was coming down the pike. If it was more written responses to text, then count them out. They'd done enough of that already.

Although I was troubled by this story, a part of me understood why their previous teacher may have used this approach. She probably had the children write to keep them busy while she coped with other responsibilities.

Years ago, I frequently asked my children to write while I met with guided reading groups. "How else could I keep them occupied?" I reasoned. From a classroom management perspective, these assignments had "worked." It took many of them a long time to copy the questions from the board and even longer to respond. But from a reading standpoint, it did exactly the wrong thing. It kept children writing instead of reading. It kept their fingers clasped tightly around a pencil instead of holding a book.

RESPONSE SHEETS AND NOTEBOOKS

At the beginning of the year, before I ask them to start responding to books, I get the children in the habit of reading independently, filling in their reading logs, and processing what went well during the reading workshop. Furthermore, because I first need to demonstrate to the whole class the types of responses they might make, and the Response Sheets and notebooks we will use, I wait a month or so before asking them to write individual responses to books. Then I introduce the responses described in the following section one at a time.

Children usually read more fluently than they write. At first, it may take them a long time just to write one or two lines. Then, even as they become more adept in writing, it's still quite a challenge to handle content, spelling, grammar, punctuation, and handwriting simultaneously. With this in mind, we need to be wise about the frequency and types of responses we ask them to make.

Although there are no hard and fast rules, I encourage emergent and early readers to respond once every two weeks, and transitional and fluent readers to respond weekly. It generally takes between twenty-and-thirty minutes for a child to write a response. If it takes someone longer, I check to make sure that he's using his time well.

Response Sheets

Children at different developmental stages need different response tools. When emergent readers and those at the beginning of the early stage want to respond to texts they've read, they take a Response Sheet from our metal storage file. When they're finished responding, they keep them in their reading folders, and during reading conferences, I often check them to see how the children are doing.

There's a space at the top of the Response Sheet for a picture and lines at the bottom to record the title, author, and one or two sentences (see Appendix F). At the emergent stage, most children just draw a picture and record the book's title and author. Some find even this difficult. They are often unable to distinguish the author's name from the illustrator's. Many struggle just putting pencil to paper.

Jasmin's response in Figure 13–2 to *I Am Not a Dinosaur* by Mary Packard is typical of an emergent reader's response. Although he couldn't express his ideas in writing (the words on his Response Sheet were painstakingly copied from the text because he wanted to do what he saw the other kids doing), he drew a bird—see its little wings!—to represent each time the rhamphorynchus met a different kind of dinosaur and sadly realized that he was not one of them.

As children's skills develop, they begin to write a line or two about the book at the bottom of the Response Sheet. Although Teddy's response (see Figure 13–3) to *Lulu Goes to Witch School* by Jane O'Connor had little to do with the text itself and more to do with how much he liked witches, it did explain *why* he enjoyed the book. He even underlined the high-frequency words to mimic what we do as a class with our shared reading text each Friday. Several responses later, Teddy drew lines at the top of his Response Sheet (another personal innovation) to signal that he felt ready to write longer responses in a Response Notebook.

FIGURE 13–2

Jasmin's Response to
I Am Not a Dinosaur

Name _____ Date _____

Response Sheet

Title: I AM NOT A DINOSAUR

Author: MARY PACKARD

I do NOT ROAR

I WISH-I-special Tail

A special sail

I-do-Have WINgs!

Response Notebooks

Toward the end of the early reading stage, children start writing their responses in a response notebook, a composition-style notebook stored in their reading folder.

During the first couple months of school, the children and I collaborate on writing responses on chart paper to some of the books we read aloud. Focusing on one type of response at a time, we describe a favorite part, summarize a story, or relate the book to our lives and to other texts. We hang these charts in the classroom as models for the types of responses the children can make on their own. They can:

- **Write about a favorite part.** This is usually the easiest type of response for children to make since they're used to describing their favorite part of a book in whole-class discussions. They now need to know that they can communicate the very same ideas through writing. See Figure 13–4A for Jordan M.'s explanation of why he thought *The Monster in the Third Dresser Drawer* by J. L. Smith was funny.

- **Relate a book to your life.** As children read more widely, they're amazed that: "The same thing's happened to me!" Seeing characters in stories experience the same joys, frustrations, and challenges as we do is an important lesson. What hooks us on books is the realization that in reading about others, we learn about ourselves. In one of her first notebook entries, Maxine compares the fictional Kate and her sister in *Kate Skates* by J. O'Connor with herself and her one-year-old sister Edie (see Figure 13–4B).

FIGURE 13–3

Teddy's Response to *Lulu Goes to Witch School*

Name _____ Date _____

Response Sheet

Title: Lulu goes to wich school
Author: Emil arnold
I Love wichis.
they have a Boom
and a Rap. and they
have a black Hat.

When children read factual text, they discover new things or learn more about topics in which they're already interested. They sense how reading expands their thinking and enriches their lives. In Rafe's response to *Water Pollution*, a book he read in a guided reading group, he wrote:

> If we pollute water we pollute the fish and then biger fish eat the fish and than we eat the fish and get posand.

He concludes: "We shouldn't pollute water because we hurt ourselves."

- **Summarize what a book is about.** Learning to summarize is an essential skill, but it's hard for most children to distill a story's key elements. Either they try to retell it in detail, or they don't understand how to proceed.

Children need many oral and written demonstrations of what a summary is before they can write one of their own. Usually I don't ask a child to summarize a text until he's at the end of the early reading stage. Before that, most children lack the ability to conceptualize a book's overriding theme and communicate their ideas in writing. They're better able to recall a favorite part or describe how the book relates to their own experiences.

Taha, an early reader, summarized *Nate the Great and the Lost List* as follows:

> Claude and Nate could not find Clauds grosery list. Then Nate found it. Then Nate went back to his vacasin.

Although accurate, Taha's summary reveals only the story's basic structure. On the other hand, Fiona's summary of *Little Swan* by Adele Geras (see Figure 13–4C) conveys a more detailed account of the story.

The Monster in the third
dresser drawer
     My favorite part was
when Adam was turning
the light on because of
the monster but the
sitter kept turning the
lightoff. When the sitter left
his mom got rid of
the monster.

FIGURE 13–4A

Jordan M. Describes His Favorite Part of *The Monster in the Third Dresser Drawer*

Kate Skates   11/25/97
I Like Kate skates becaus I
like to skate. In the year
19-96 I took skating classes.
And lerned very well. I
now like to skate. I have
a little sister like her that
is one year old but she does
not no how to skate yet.

FIGURE 13–4B

Maxine Relates *Kate Skates* **to Her Own Life**

FIGURE 13–4C

Fiona Summarizes
Little Swan

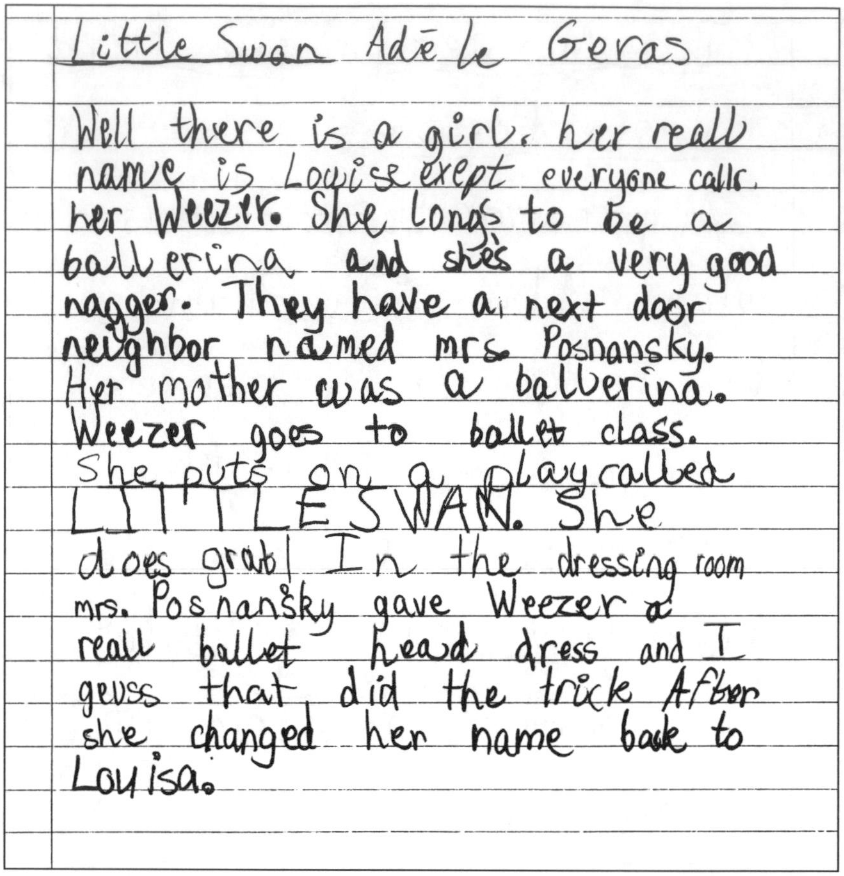

> Little Swan Adéle Geras
>
> Well there is a girl. her reall
> name is Louise exept everyone calls
> her Weezer. She longs to be a
> ballerina and she's a very good
> nagger. They have a next door
> neighbor named mrs. Posnansky.
> Her mother ewas a ballerina.
> Weezer goes to ballet class.
> She puts on a play called
> LITTLE SWAN. She
> does grabl In the dressing room
> mrs. Posnansky gave Weezer a
> reall ballet head dress and I
> geuss that did the trick After
> she changed her name back to
> Louisa.

FIGURE 13–4D

**Jack Compares "Mary
Marony" and
"Annabelle"**

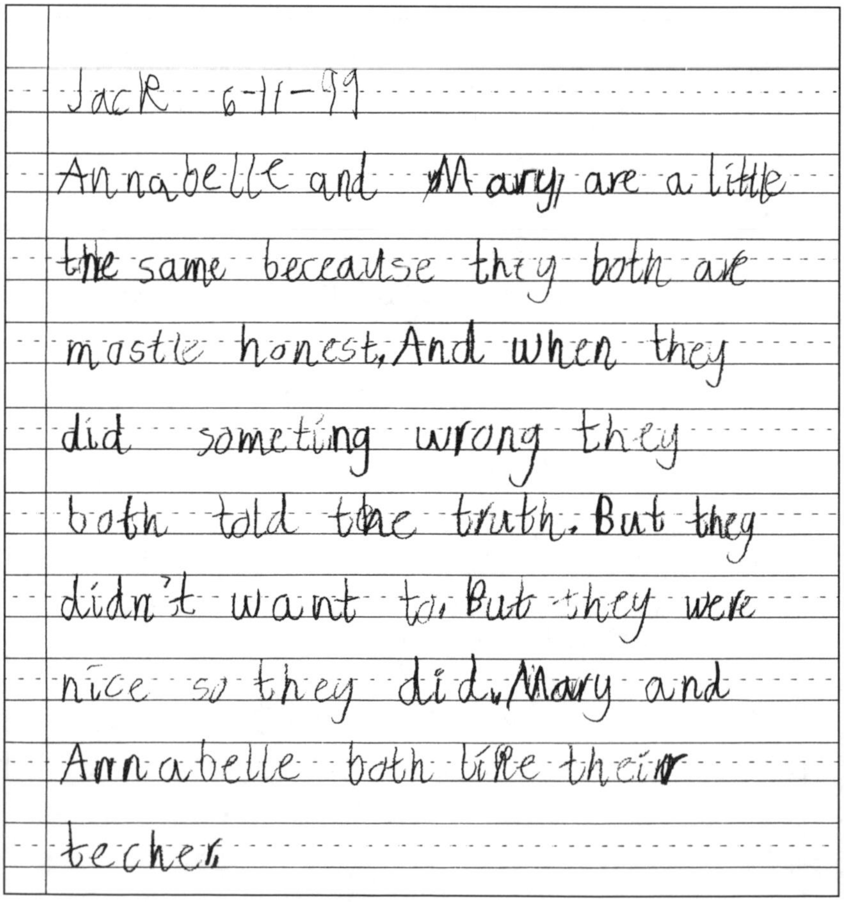

> Jack 6-11-99
>
> Annabelle and Mary are a little
> the same beceause they both are
> mostle honest. And when they
> did someting wrong they
> both told the truth. But they
> didn't want to. But they were
> nice so they did. Mary and
> Annabelle both like their
> techer.

Both summaries are typical of early and fluent readers. The qualitative differences between these responses don't mean that Taha understood his book less well than Fiona did hers. It only demonstrates that Fiona was willing and able to give a fuller written account of what happened.

- **Relate a book to other books** As children read more widely, they begin to note similarities between books. This involves a different kind of thinking than when their reflections are confined to one text. Not only do they have to understand the story's key concepts, they also need to recognize analogies in the structure, style, theme, and character's behavior. See Figure 13–4D for Jack's response in which he compares Mary in *Mary Marony and the Chocolate Surprise* by Suzy Kline and Annabelle in *Annabelle's Un-Birthday* by Steven Kroll.

I encourage children to respond to factual text and poetry just as they do to fictional text: highlighting favorite parts, relating what they've learned to their lives, summarizing the central theme, and comparing the book (or poem) to others they've read. They may also relate key facts that they've learned.

Although I demonstrate the different types of responses one at a time, children don't progress linearly from one form to the next. They're more eclectic, often combining several elements into one. Children might start out with a couple sentences that tell about the book and then describe a favorite part. Or, in explaining a favorite part, show how it relates to experiences they've had.

The Illusion of Control

We undermine the learning process when we ask children to respond to each and every book they read so that we can assess their comprehension. Yet this is often done out of a misplaced concern that, if we don't hold children accountable in this way, we won't know whether they understood the book, or even read it.

I've learned over the years that the sense of control I got by having children respond too frequency to most books they read was an illusion. It's not difficult to write a few lines or answer several questions about a book without understanding what you read or even reading it. In fact, I've heard this very complaint from teachers using commercial reading kits containing leveled cards, or computerized programs where their children read a book and then answer a se-

ries of comprehension questions before going on to the next book or level. The illusion is created by the appeal of logic and sequence, but I believe these programs put too much emphasis on the tool and not enough on the teacher.

On the other hand, it's no illusion to confer with a child about his reading to learn how well he understands what he's read. It's no illusion to generate a dialogue at the onset of a book or series to scaffold his comprehension. And it's no illusion to think long and hard with the child about the best way to proceed.

Be suspicious of reading programs that move children from book-to-book and level-to-level without teacher intervention. Ongoing assessment and purposeful demonstrations are key facets of teaching. We need opportunities to talk with children about how they're doing and plan ways to help them.

While I understand a teacher's desire to always know how her children are doing, this knowledge will *always* be approximate and provisional. We need to do our best to provide children with books that match their needs, strategies to unlock unfamiliar words and understand more complex text, and opportunities to practice those strategies. After all, the primary purpose of responding to books is to move children into a richer and a broader reading experience. And as children read more widely and more proficiently, they can respond more effectively.

Children's Reflections on Their Reading Process

When it's time for the children to share strategies they used at the end of the reading workshop, I interrupt their reading: "Boys and girls, put your books and pencils down and look at me. When I finish speaking, I'd like you to start cleaning up—pencils and crayons in the pots, paper off the floor, books in the pots facing out, chairs pushed under the tables, and book bags stored neatly in the baskets. Put your work back in your folder neatly, so you'll be able to get right to work tomorrow, and give your folder to the person that gave it to you. (This child then returns the three folders he passed out at the beginning of the workshop to the plastic crates.) And while you're doing this, think about your reading. Think about what worked so well today that you might try it again and again. And be ready to share it."

I don't give these instructions until all eyes are on me. And the children don't begin sharing until the room is in order. Even though I make these same housekeeping requests all year, I still remind the children each day, never assuming that just because I've said something once, twice, or even twenty times, they'll automatically remember to do it. And I'm clear and consistent about what I ask them to do.

The question I've prompted them to be thinking about—What did you do today that worked so well that you might try it again and again?—is one I ask from the first day of school to the last. It's one that the children have had time to think about throughout the workshop—actually before I even ask it—because I inquire about this each day.

I used to try to be creative in my questioning, thinking that the more thought-provoking and varied my questions were, the better. I've realized, however, that quite often just the opposite is true. The simpler the question and the more often it's asked, the more predictable it becomes, allowing children to consider it before it's expressly asked.

After the children have cleaned up, we reconvene at the meeting area. The children know that I'm going to ask them to be specific and give examples as they share what worked in their reading. Occasionally a child may keep a book with him for reference.

I ask the children, "Who would like to share?" And then, I call on several, one at a time, to sit on the rocking chair and describe the strategies they tried.

Sharing Strategies: Being Broad, Yet Specific

By asking children to share what worked in their reading, I'm helping them transform what was effective *once* into a strategy to apply to new situations. I'm also asking them to take a metacognitive stance—to look at and evaluate what they do as they read so they can do more of what's working and less of what isn't. This way, children begin to acquire a repertoire of strategies to employ at will. They know there are techniques they can try and approaches they can use to get better.

I help children reframe what they've learned about their reading, and themselves as readers into broader strategic terms. For example, when Tiffany shared that she reread Chapter 2 in *M & M and the Mummy Mess* because she didn't understand it, I helped her restate it as a

strategy: "Oh, you mean today you learned that when you have trouble understanding something, you can read it over to understand it better. What a smart thing to do! You could do that whenever you don't understand something." Or when Nick said he figured out the word "bottle" because he saw the "o-t" spelling pattern and then got the rest of the word, I said: "That's right. When you don't know a word, you can look for parts of the word you do know, and then use that to help you figure out the rest."

I also teach the children that it's not enough to simply name the strategy they used. They must learn to back-up their statements with examples and details. If a child says: "I sounded the word out," I ask her what the word was and I write it on the wipe-off board so she can show us what she did. Or if she says: "I stopped to think," I ask what book she was reading, what confused her at first, and how using this strategy helped her understand it better.

I'm skeptical when a child baldly states a strategy and is done, as this may indicate that she hasn't tried the strategy at all. She just wants her "moment of fame." I want her to be specific; the rest of the children do, too. Often it's the children who ask her to explain *how* she "got" the word or understood the text.

The Kinds of Strategies Children Share

Some strategies are more management-oriented. Even before children begin their daily reading, they make decisions that will either promote or impede their efforts. They have to decide where to sit and who to sit alongside—a friend or a quiet worker? They have to decide whether they can handle working in close proximity to other children or whether they're better trying to find a place where they can work alone. Sasha noted: "I realized that when I was sitting next to Chelsea, I didn't get much reading done. We talked too much. So I decided I shouldn't sit next to her any more." Chelsea immediately raised her hand and said she was thinking the exact same thing!

Others strategies are related to the reading process itself. They describe what a child does to figure out unfamiliar words and understand text that is giving her trouble. Sasha explains how writing responses helps her understand what she's reading: "I decided to write a response to *Little Witch Goes to School*. As I did it, I decided I should do this more. It helped me sort of understand the book more and I really needed that. It got my attention and made me really think about the book." Although these strategies are usually variations of ones I've demonstrated during whole- or small-group sessions, the children now describe how they use them as they read independently.

The following examples of strategies the children have shared give insight into their reading process and the decisions they make before, during, and after reading. My comments demonstrate some of the ways I prompt them to be more specific or to restate their experience as a general strategy. I also try to get the other children talking about similar experiences they've had.

STOPPING TO THINK

Scott: When I read a hard book, I stop to think about what's happening so I won't get mixed up and just have words flowing in my head. They have to go together.

Teacher: Explain more of what you mean. . . .

USING GRAPHOPHONIC CUES

Itamar: I came to a word that I didn't know. I looked in the word and saw the "i-p" spelling pattern. So I sounded out the rest and got "rippled."

Teacher: Looking for spelling patterns you know is a really good strategy that you could use a lot. Any comments or questions? . . .

USING CONTEXTUAL CUES

Jordan: Today in my guided reading group, when I was reading *The Best Older Sister*, I got a word wrong. I said "applaud," and it was really "adopt." But I knew that wouldn't make sense because Sunhi didn't want someone to *applaud* her brother, she wanted someone to *adopt* him. She was jealous of the attention he was getting.

Teacher: That's really wise to think about whether or not what you say makes sense. And you're right—if she was jealous of him, why would she want people to "applaud" him? . . .

USING CONTEXT TO FIGURE OUT THE MEANING OF A WORD

Sophia: I was reading *Girl Wonder and the Terrific Twins*. I saw a word—"puny." I didn't know what it meant. I didn't know

any other words like it. I looked closely at the whole sentence, and I used the whole sentence: "The bag was too 'puny' for a puppy." She wanted a dog and the bag was too *puny* to hold a dog. Now I know that "puny" means "small."

Teacher: Sophia did a really smart thing. She didn't know the *meaning* of a word and so she used the whole sentence to figure it out. How many of you have ever tried that? . . .

READING MAKES YOU A BETTER READER

Lauren: I learned that if I read more books and read easier ones, when I'm done, I could read harder ones. I mean, if you read an easier book like three times, and you keep on reading it, then you can read really really hard ones. When you read more books, you get used to all the words.

Teacher: That's right. The surest way to get better at reading is to read a lot. It's important to remember that . . .

PREVIEWING THE BACK OF THE BOOK

Molly: A lot of times before I start reading, I read what it says on the back of the book. Sometimes it helps me understand the book more.

Teacher: Can you give an example of a time you did that and how it helped? . . .

USING PICTURE CUES

Maxine: I came to a word and it was "powder." It was in *Amelia Bedelia*. At first I didn't know it, but I looked at the next page and saw that she was sprinkling powder on herself so I knew it was "powder."

Teacher: Good strategy. If you try a word and can't get it, one thing to do is check the picture. It might help . . .

Two Examples of Response Sequences

Usually when a child shares a strategy, two or three of his classmates ask a question or comment on how they've done something similar. Occasionally, however, a child sharing a strategy initiates a more sustained dialogue. Here are two examples. In the first, the focus is on strategies children use to figure out words they don't know. The second shows how you can use what you know about one story to help you understand another.

DANIEL'S RESPONSE AND THE CHILDREN'S FOLLOW-UP COMMENTS

Daniel: When I was in the guided reading group today, we were reading a book called *Grandpa Comes to Stay*. And I came to the word "absolutely" and I didn't know it. Then I said to myself "a" and "b" is /ab/, "s" and "o" is /so/, and "l-u-t-e-l-y" is /lutely/ and I put "a-b-s-" and "o" together and I put /lutely/ with that and I got "absolutely."

Teacher (restating Daniel's response as a strategy and writing "absolutely" on the wipe-off board to demonstrate what Daniel did): Daniel sounded the word out. He looked at the letters and sounded them out from the beginning of the word to the end. That's one strategy for figuring out a word.

Daniel: I did something else with another word. I came to "poured" and at first I didn't know it. Then I read on—almost to the end of the sentence—and I saw "milk." Then I said the word must be "poured." You can pour milk. So I said "poured."

Teacher: Nice! Here Daniel used a different strategy. He read past the word that was giving him trouble and then came back to it using what he'd learned in the rest of the sentence. Does anyone have any comments or questions for Daniel?

Sasha: When you were trying to read "absolutely," what was the rest of the sentence?

Daniel (looking in the book): "Absolutely not." Finley's mom said, "Absolutely not" when Finley asked about putting his feet on the sofa when Grandpa came for a visit.

Thomas: What's really weird is that when you read books like that they seem easy because the pictures make it look like the words are going to be easy, but there's really hard words.

Iana: It's kind of like today when I read this book that was factual. It's about a king in Egypt and I didn't know his name so I went to Jordan and she showed me a way to pronounce it. And she said: "Tu-tan . . ." (she was having trouble remembering the word).

Teacher: Jordan, could you help her out?

Jordan: The book's called *Tut's Mummy*. Well —it had the word and how you could say it

. . . uh . . . uh. (She tried to demonstrate the parentheses around the word with her hands.)

Teacher: A pronunciation guide?

Jordan: Yeah, I helped Iana pick the book 'cause I thought it was a really good book. Then later I showed her the pronunciation guide and I said "Too-tonk-AH-men" like the book.

Teacher: That helps. Good strategy. But let's get back to what Daniel shared about the conversation between Finley and his mom in *Grandpa Comes to Stay*. It says (reading from the book): "'You mean no television,' said Finley. 'Exactly,' said Mom. 'No feet on the sofa,' said Finley. 'Absolutely not,' said Mom." It's almost like you're expecting her to say something like "Absolutely not." Right?

Sophia: Yeah. Actually Daniel could have gotten the word "absolutely" from the sentence. Like when it says "Absolutely not." When you can't figure out that word you could just leave a blank and say "'_____ not' says Mom." And then you could get an idea that it could be "absolutely" because what else could they say in front of "not" that started with an "a?"

* * *

Daniel's use of different strategies for "absolutely" and "poured" demonstrate that he chooses from a variety of strategies and is flexible in their use. He didn't rotely skip the word "absolutely" (and then come back to it) when, for him, a better strategy for that word was to sound it out. And he wasn't locked into sounding out "poured" when it was better for him to read past the word and then come back and give it another try once he had the added support of the entire sentence.

Daniel's response also helped his classmates extend their thinking. Iana told about how she'd used the pronunciation guide; Thomas noted there are hard words even in books that look easy; and Sofia explained that she'd use the entire dialogue between Finley and his mother —not just the one sentence—along with the letter sounds to get the word.

RAFE'S RESPONSE AND THE CHILDREN'S FOLLOW-UP COMMENTS

Rafe: Well, I was reading this page in *The Mystery of the Blue Ring* (a book in the "Polka Dot Private Eye" series which is a spin-off from the "Kids of the Polk Street School" series) about how Dawn wanted to tell her father about the ring Emily lost, but she couldn't because then she'd have to tell him about the unicorn she stole. I read *Fish Face* before and I remembered when Dawn stole Emily's unicorn! *Fish Face* helped me understand this other book about Dawn.

Teacher: That's so interesting! We know that when you read books from a series, they're about the same characters, and sometimes things that happened in an earlier book show up in later books. And now you're saying that even books from different series about the "Polk Street Kids" can help you understand the others.

Georgie: In *Mary Marony and the Chocolate Surprise*, it's sort of like that cause she wanted to tell about the golden ticket.

Teacher: I don't understand what you mean.

Georgie: Mary took the golden ticket from Marvin, and Dawn took the unicorn from Emily.

Teacher: You're right. Something similar happened in both books—both girls took something that wasn't theirs. But think for a moment about what Rafe said—how reading one book can help you understand another. (Recalling some references in *Mary Marony and the Chocolate Surprise* to *Charlie and the Chocolate Factory*) I have a question for all of you about *Mary Marony and the Chocolate Surprise*. What book had the teacher, Mrs. Bird, just finished reading to the class?

Thomas: *Charlie and the Chocolate Factory.*

Teacher: How did that help us understand "Mary Marony" better?

Brittany: Because the kids in Mary Marony's class were kind of doing the same things as in *Charlie and the Chocolate Factory*. And it kind of helped me understand "Mary Marony" more because I read "The Chocolate Factory" before.

Teacher: That's something, isn't it? When you finish a book, let's say *Charlie and the Chocolate Factory*, you think "Well the book was great, but it's over." Then later, sometimes you find that book referred to in another book you're reading, and it helps you understand the new book.

Sophia: Even if it's not in the same series.

Teacher: Even if it's not in the same series. Like these two—*Fish Face* and *The Mystery of the Blue Ring*—are about the same kids so we might expect there to be a connection. But who would ever think there would be a connection between *Mary Marony and the Chocolate Surprise* and *Charlie and the Chocolate Factory*? But there is!

Thomas: They are doing a lot of the same things in both books. Like the five children who got a golden ticket in the "Chocolate Factory" could go and see the factory. And in "Mary Marony" the five children who got a gold ticket would have lunch with the teacher.

Nick: It's about "Mary Marony." When you were reading *Mary Marony and the Chocolate Surprise*, I knew that Marvin was going to steal Mary's chocolate bar, and he did.

Teacher: You're right. And do you know there's a whole book about Marvin? It's called *Marvin and the Mean Words*.

Sophia: *Mary Marony and the Chocolate Surprise* is related to *Charlie and the Chocolate Factory* because of the golden ticket thing. It's also related because they read the book and they were celebrating it in different ways.

Teacher: How were they celebrating it?

Sophia: By drinking lemonade called Fizzy Lifting Lemonade. . . .

So much happened in this discussion following Rafe's comment. The children saw the close relationship between books in the same series and how there may even be connections between seemingly unrelated books. But basically, they were learning that the more books they read, the better equipped they are to understand what they're reading.

In general, children's reflections and their sharing of successful practices shows them that their repertoire of strategies is not confined to this one experience, but can be applied to other reading efforts as well. They begin to appreciate that reading books, discussing them, and reflecting on "what worked" are all part of a complete learning process. Daniel can sound words out and read on whenever he has trouble with a word (in addition to the many other strategies he knows). Rafe now looks for connections between books, explaining: "I never knew that books were connected like that. But now I do."

Sharing their strategies increases children's awareness that others experience the same challenges they do, and that there are various ways to resolve their problems. It also helps them see reading as a process in which they are active participants.

Personal Writing As a "Response" to Reading

There is a synergy between reading and writing. Reading inspires and excites children about the possibilities awaiting them as writers and acquaints them with the structure of text and books and the conventions of written language. Writing allows them to use what they've gleaned from reading as they craft their own

stories, poems, and factual texts. And because of their writing efforts, children approach written text with a heightened awareness and understanding of print, text, and genre.

Applying Concepts About Print

Writing helps reinforce children's concepts about print. They write from left to right and top to bottom—the same direction as book print. They learn to leave spaces between words—just like in the books they read. In Figure 13–5, the dots Taha placed between words in this early piece of writing show he understands what a word is, and that there's a break between words in text.

FIGURE 13–5

Taha's Piece

Children become stronger readers through their writing experiences, becoming sensitized to print features because they also attend to them as they write.

Attending More Closely to Letter Sounds

As children write, they appreciate how important it is that the letters they use to represent words match the sounds in the words. Consequently, they pay closer attention to letter-sound relationships as they read.

When I met with Brittany for a writing conference and gave her feedback on the way some of her written attempts at spelling sounded, it helped reinforce a concept that we also focus on in reading. For example, in writing "presents" she failed to represent the /t/ sound near the end of the word. See Figure 13–6.

She even brought it up in a guided reading group when I was demonstrating how the children should make sure that what they read matches the letters, saying: "Sharon told me that about my writing, too." Our message is strengthened when children understand similar strategies apply to both reading and writing.

Examining How Text Structures Work

Children use complementary strategies to think about the structure of what they're reading and writing. They may use Story Maps to organize their thinking about the story they're reading or to plan the story they're writing. Just as thinking about how the past behavior of a character in a book helps them predict what he might do next, so can they also imagine how the characters in their own story will act and

FIGURE 13–6

Brittany's Piece

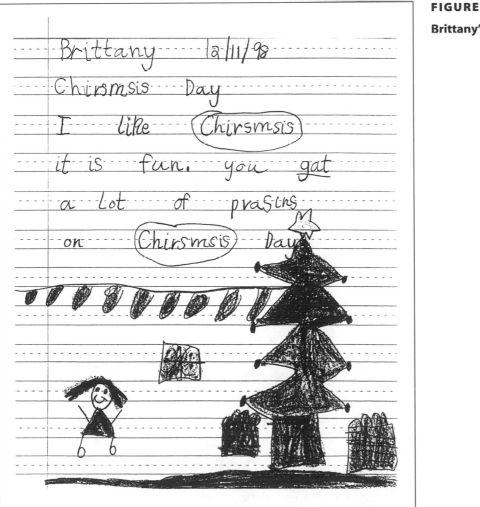

change. Likewise with factual pieces, reviewing what they already know about a topic before they begin helps them read and write more effectively. And reflecting on the elements and structure of a well-written text helps children make sense of their own writing.

For example, when Brittany began reading longer books, she had to think about the character, setting, main events, problem, resolution, and how these elements work together. And when she writes, she considers these same things, even using a Story Map to plan her story so that it makes sense to the reader. (See Figure 13–7 for the story map Brittany used to plan her story.) Using this same tool in both reading and writing strengthens both processes.

Understanding and Using Book Features

Children are apt to use features in their own writing like those they've seen in books. When Molly was writing her "Baby-Sitter's Club" series in response to several books she'd read from Ann Martin's series of the same title, she included a table of contents to help her readers (and herself) get a better sense of where the book was headed (see Figure 13–8).

She explained: "When I write a table of contents, it helps me think of what's going to happen in the story. It makes me think about it before I even start writing it." Having included a table of contents in her own writing, when Molly reads, she can't help be more attuned to tables of contents as a comprehension tool that give the reader more information, as well as help the writer plan.

Young writers like Molly and Brittany go back to reading with a heightened awareness of the thinking behind the books they read, and they can bring their experience as writers to their reading: Molly understanding the planning that goes into a piece, and Brittany appreciating how all the parts of a story fit together.

FIGURE 13–7

Brittanny's Story Map for a Piece She's Writing

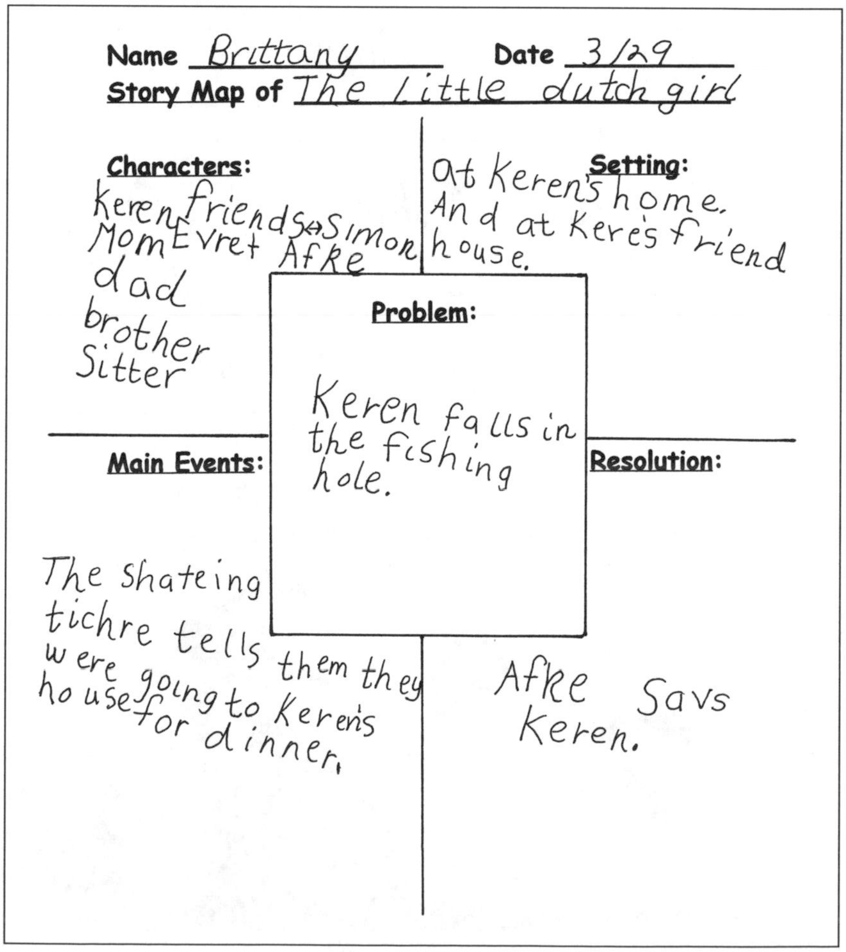

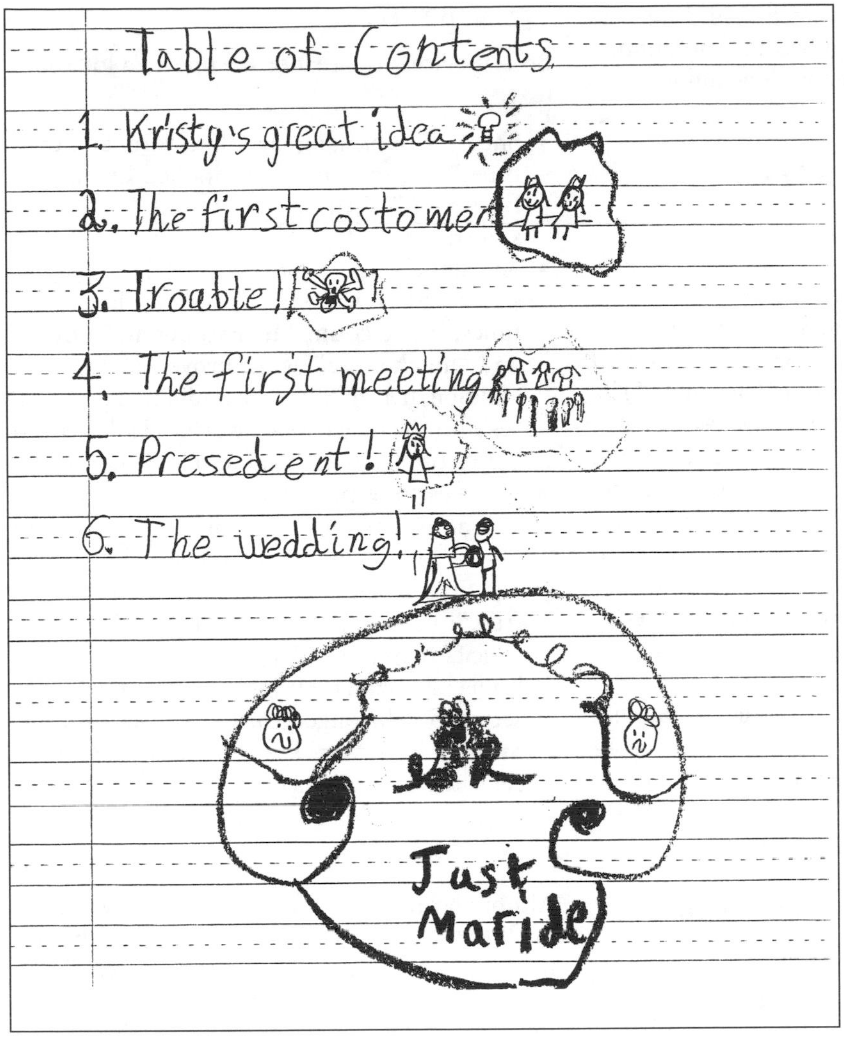

FIGURE 13-8

Molly's Table of Contents

Rereading Text for Sense

When children write, they reread their piece to make sure it makes sense. As children review their writing, it reinforces their understanding that their reading of a written text must also make sense and that they must self-correct when it doesn't.

As Jessica read one of her stories to the class, I could tell that she was making some last minute changes. After she finished, she said: "I did the same thing here as I did during reading time. When I was reading today I self-corrected to make sure that what I read matched the letters and made sense. And when I read my story just now, I made some changes because I realized that what I wrote didn't make sense. I changed it so it would." As a reader and a writer, Jessica understands that text must make sense.

Using Punctuation, Capitalization, Spelling, and the "Rules" of Grammar

Children read over what they write to check for spelling, grammar, punctuation, and capitalization. Doing this in writing helps them take note of these conventions in reading and understand how and why they're used.

When I conferred with Jena before she copied her piece over, I explained that she needed to add "'s" after "mom" and "sister" to show possession, as this language convention is expected in English but not in Jena's native Korean.

Jena still has much to learn about how spoken and written English works. And she will. As she reads more, writes more, and receives demonstrations of these features during the reading and writing workshop, she'll begin to use them correctly. Then as Jena reads, she'll assume an even stronger stance, understanding more of what she's reading because she's noting how the conventions assist with meaning.

Modeling Writing After Text You've Read

When writers are also readers, they're often able to internalize an author's mood, rhythm, or language, and take inspiration from her topics.

Mikey's poem demonstrates how he modeled "At the Beach," after Charlotte Zolotow's "The Shell" in *Snippets: A Gathering of Poems, Pictures, and Possibilities*, internalizing its mood, language, and theme. (See 13–9 for Charlotte Zolotow's and Mikey's poems.) Sophia was inspired by the topic and rhythm of Marilyn Singer's "Beaver's in November" and wrote her poem, "Beavers," in response. (See Chapter 7, page 90, for Marilyn Singer's poem and Figure 13–10 for Sophia's.)

It's unlikely that either Mikey or Sophia would have written such poems without being mentored by these poets. And now, in addition, they can read other poems with a greater awareness of what poets try to achieve.

FIONA: WRITING LIKE A READER AND READING LIKE A WRITER

Fiona, who is a strong reader, wrote "The Beaver" (see Figure 13–11). We'd been learning about beavers in connection with our study of mammals that inhabited the New York City area years ago. Fiona's piece illustrates how she's applied elements in her writing that she's learned from reading. And the flip side is that because she's a writer, she can read with an insider's view of the reading/writing process, helping her examine even more closely other authors' texts.

Writing Like a Reader

Because Fiona is a reader she knows a lot about text:

- She uses book language, like "Once upon a time," "... a dam which looked like a very fine dam," "All were shocked," and "He smiled."
- She understands conventional literary text structures—Swatter Tail asked for help three times, if you count Mr. Fast Swim, Zoomer, and "much more" as the proverbial three. In addition, her story has the traditional problem/resolution structure—Swatter Tail needed help from his friends, and then he got it.
- She uses conventions of language for emphasis and to enhance meaning, e.g., the ellipse ("I . . . I really will") adds suspense.
- She understands that fiction, although "untrue," must be believable. Thus Swatter Tail solicits help in building a dam, not a winter home in Arizona. He also smelled the dam to see who it belonged to. Even their names—Swatter Tail, Mr. Fast Swim, and Zoomer reflect what beavers do.

Reading Like a Writer

Although the effect of reading on our writing is much more apparent, the impact writing has on reading is nonetheless profound. When Fiona writes, she can't help but recognize that the authors of other texts have gone through a process similar to hers. She won't make the effort to consider how a character in her story is going to behave without understanding more deeply that other authors have pondered this same point. She won't reread her story again and again to confirm that it makes sense without knowing that all authors do the same thing. These insights transform her as a reader; they make her read differently.

FIGURE 13–9

Charlotte Zolotow's and Mikey's Poems

The Shell
    by Charlotte Zolotow
	At the Beach
	    by Mike Boruta

At the beach a little boy picks up a shell. It is twisted pink and grey and sandy inside. He wonders who lived in it before it was washed up from the sea.	At the beach, I found a seashell. I put the seashell to my ear. I could hear the ocean! I threw the seashell back to the sea.

FIGURE 13–10

Sophia's Poem

Beavers

by Sophia Nass

Beavers, beavers

Hard-working beavers.

Beavers, beavers

Busy beavers.

Very busy gnawing trees.

Fixing them

into a lodge.

Beavers, beavers

Hard-working beavers.

FIGURE 13–11 Fiona's Piece, "The Beaver"

The Beaver

Once upon a time there was a Beaver. His name was Swatter Tail because he always gave other beavers a wack. One day he said to himself: "This dam is geting too old for me. I will build another. I'll bet most beavers will help."

The next day he set off and came to a dam which looked like a very fine dam. He smelled the scent. It was Mr. Fast Swim. He said: "No."

Then he went to Zoomer. He said: "No." And he went to much more. They all said: "No."

I'll show them how strong I am. I . . . I really will. His tail was wagging. That meant that he was going to wack a beaver. So they all dunked underwater. He held his fire. All were shocked. He smiled. Then everyone pitched in. The end.

Conclusion

Frank Smith urges us to invite children to become members of "The Literacy Club" (1988). As members, children read and write alongside one another, sharing each other's challenges, frustrations, and accomplishments. They have mentors who serve as models for their own writing. Through dialogue with other writers and readers, they revise their thinking and their practices.

The surest path to fluency in reading and writing is to provide children many opportunities to read, to improve their reading through meaningful oral and written responses, and, ultimately, to write and read their own pieces. In this way, our children become better enjoyers and creators of text.

Epilogue

A FEW YEARS AGO, AT THE END OF A WEEK-long literacy institute I'd led, when all of us "more seasoned" teachers were pooped out, an enthusiastic young teacher asked me a long question on a topic I was certain I'd addressed earlier that week. I responded by saying: "I've just told you everything I know. I really don't know anything else." Although colleagues still tease me about this, I wasn't trying to be funny. I had, in that week, shared everything I knew. I feel that way now: I've just written down what has taken me years to learn.

Big changes don't happen overnight. Meaningful revision of our teaching requires more than modifying behaviors. It requires rethinking our understandings on many levels. When we find promising new practices at workshops or in professional books, it's tempting to think we can just add them to our already too-full day without taking anything away. This often results in our becoming overwhelmed and abandoning the new idea as impractical, because we failed to see that it needed a different or more supportive system to sustain it.

So don't try to take on too much at one time. Instead I urge you to take a step back and look at your current practice. Are you using your time well? Have you established goals and created the supports that enable you to be successful? Are you making connections among all the things you do? Does your day make sense for you and for your children?

In general, we shouldn't add something new unless we take something away, for we can't do it all. I'm most successful in my teaching when I limit myself. I try to do a few key things really well, things that will eventually add up to better teaching and learning. Gone are the days when I leave my classroom exhausted and overwhelmed by countless and often contradictory demands. I'm no longer worn out from "pushing and pulling" children through unconnected activities that others say are good for them. I know what I want to happen, and I'm clear about my role in helping children. And I assess my teaching and children's learning continuously, so I can do more of what's working and less of what isn't.

Perhaps the most important thing you can take away from this book is to view your teaching systematically. Everything I've described is part of a system—all the parts of my day and components of my teaching, all my goals for children and my role in helping them reach these goals, work together as a whole. In creating your own system, look for connections, explain them to children, encourage them to make their own.

Thinking deeply about what it means to teach and to learn is really at the heart of what I'm saying. I hope this book prompts you to revise and refine your teaching until a more effective and satisfying system replaces the old one, and you're standing on higher, more solid ground.

Appendices

Name _____   Week # _____

MONDAY

Title: _____

_____

Author: _____

TUESDAY

Title: _____

_____

Author: _____

WEDNESDAY

Title: _____

_____

Author: _____

THURSDAY

Title: _____

_____

Author: _____

FRIDAY

Title: _____

_____

Author: _____

Key: Poetry • Yellow   Fiction • Red   Non-Fiction • Blue

Name _____ Week # _____

This week I was successful at _____

_____

_____

_____

_____

_____

_____

_____

Next week I plan to _____

_____

_____

_____

_____

_____

_____

_____

_____

[The following describes how I use my Spelling/Poetry Folders. I don't recommend this folder for kindergarten, and I don't begin to implement Sections Two, Three, and Four until the second half of first grade. Second- and third-grade students can begin working with all sections at the start of the year.] Examples of folder contents are shown on page 187.

Section One—Poems, Songs, and Language-Experience Charts

At the end of each week, I photocopy the poem or song the children and I have worked on and put it into each child's spelling/poetry folder. The children may read through their folder during the reading workshop or take it home to read to their parents on the nights they have spelling homework. (I don't allow this folder to go home each night for fear the children will leave it there, and won't have it in class when they need it.)

Section Two—"If I Can Spell" Sheets

Every other week, I give the children this sheet to do for homework, reinforcing the work we do in class with spelling patterns. It's important that children understand that if they can read and spell one word, then they can read and spell others.

They select four words that contain four familiar, but different spelling patterns and write them in the boxes provided on the sheet. They may contain a dependable spelling pattern (e.g., the "-ame" in "name") from our word wall, or others they want to use. Then the children write four additional words they know that have the same spelling pattern. They can give four different words, or they can add inflectional endings, prefixes, or suffixes to the key word to make new words. Many times they find the key words from poems in section one. Sometimes a child's parent will help him with this exercise. That's well and good, for the purpose of this activity isn't to test children's knowledge of words but to demonstrate how they're connected.

Section Three—High-Frequency Words

At the end of each week, we go through our shared reading/writing text looking for words to add to our high-frequency word wall. From September through December, I simply add some of these words to the wall that I think will be most beneficial to their reading and writing. But in January I make a list of all the words we've collected so far and put a copy in each child's spelling folder.

I send a letter home to the parents explaining that these are some commonly used words that the children should begin to learn to spell. I tell them not to panic, for I don't expect them to know them all at once, but to begin learning them, a little each night. I'm looking for growth over time, not immediate mastery. (This book does not describe how I teach spelling, although helping children make the connection between what they know and what they're learning is one important strategy. For more about how to teach spelling, I highly recommend *Spelling K–8: Planning and Teaching* by Diane Snowball and Faye Bolton.)

Then at the beginning of each month from February on, I copy the new high-frequency words we added the month before and add them to the children's folders. Since they study these words at home (and in school) and read and write them daily, most children learn how to spell them by the end of the year.

Section Four—"Words I Want to Learn to Spell"

On the Monday of the first week in this two-week cycle, I fasten a sheet to the folder, containing five words (numbered one through five) which I've selected from our high-frequency word wall and lines for other words the children identify from their writing as those they want to learn. During week one of this two-week cycle, the children look for words they've misspelled on pieces of their own writing. Children who are fluent in reading and writing usually have no trouble identifying ten words. Others who are less fluent can select five more commonly used words with dependable spelling patterns instead. I may help them find the words during our writing conferences.

As they find a misspelled word, they copy it onto column one just as it's spelled in their writing. They do the same for the rest of the words. Then they have that week to try the words again, and find the correct spelling of the words. I tell the children that they may not put a word in the "correct" column unless they've seen it written down somewhere. They must *see* it in either a chart, a book, or a dictionary. This prevents them from entering guesses in the "correct" column. They work on this during the first week.

Then on the Monday of the second week, their homework is to correct any spelling words from the "First Try" column that are still misspelled, copy the "correct" list, and leave it at home to study for a spelling test on Friday. The children must bring their spelling folders back to school the next morning. The children are tested on their words on the Friday of the second week. (I assign them to work with partners, and they test each other.)

Goodnight, Sleep Tight

Goodnight, sleep tight.

Don't let the bedbugs bite.

And if they do, get your shoe

And hit them till they're black

and blue.

Anonymous

Name _Shiori_   Date _____

If I can spell
| Sun |

I can spell
1. bun
2. run
3. fun
4. hungry

If I can spell
| night |

I can spell
1. bright
2. tight
3. sight
4. might

If I can spell
| car |

I can spell
1. bar
2. far
3. garden
4. yard

If I can spell
| new |

I can spell
1. grew
2. chew
3. few
4. pewter

Name _____   January 1999

High Frequency Word List

as	end	into	one
a	each	in	own
are	from		or
and	for	keep	once
ago	four		our
about	five	love	
anyway	friend	like	play
always		liked	
an	go	let's	say
at	give		sit
	get	more	so
but	give	much	
by	good	make	thing
begin		my	there's
before	he	meet	two
	have		three
come	has	never	then
coming	how	now	there
can	had	night	that's
cold	his	no	they're
could	here		their
		on	time
do	is	out	to
dear	it	often	that

Name _____   Date _____

Words I Want to Learn to Spell

A-B-C

Notes:
1X on test

First Try	Second Try	Correct Spelling
		1. must
		2. been
		3. long
		4. where
6. Yestrdai	6. _____	5. many
7. tcaw-uped	7. tucrow-uped	6. yesterday
8. mach	8. _____	7. threw up
9. brthday	9. brithday	8. much
10. now	10. _____	9. birthday
11. samer	11. sumer	10. know
12. vakashon	12. _____	11. summer
13. perizent	13. _____	12. vacation
14. tidy	14. tedy	13. present
15. ber	15. bare	14. teddy
		15. bear

Name _____   Date _____

If I can spell

[ ]

I can spell

1. _____

2. _____

3. _____

4. _____

If I can spell

[ ]

I can spell

1. _____

2. _____

3. _____

4. _____

If I can spell

[ ]

I can spell

1. _____

2. _____

3. _____

4. _____

If I can spell

[ ]

I can spell

1. _____

2. _____

3. _____

4. _____

Name _____   Date _____

Words I Want to Learn to Spell

A-B-C

Notes:

D-E-F

Correct Spelling

1. _____
2. _____
3. _____
4. _____

First Try	Second Try	
6. _____	6. _____	5. _____
7. _____	7. _____	6. _____
8. _____	8. _____	7. _____
9. _____	9. _____	8. _____
10. _____	10. _____	9. _____
11. _____	11. _____	10. _____
12. _____	12. _____	11. _____
13. _____	13. _____	12. _____
14. _____	14. _____	13. _____
15. _____	15. _____	14. _____
		15. _____

Name _____ Date _____

Response Sheet

Title:

Author:

Name _____ Date _____

Title _____ Author _____

Story Map

Characters: Setting:

Problem:

Main Events: Resolution:

Name _____ Date _____

Title _____ Author _____

Character Map

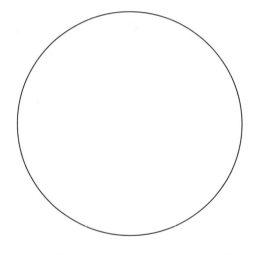

Name _____ Date _____

Title _____ Author _____

"Before and After" Chart

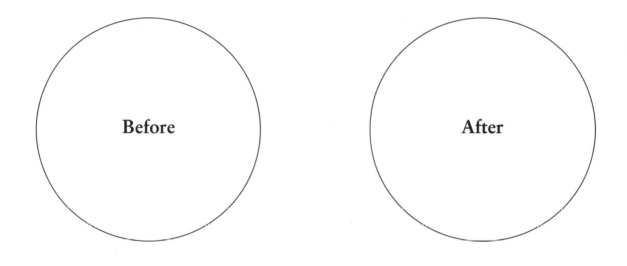

Take a few minutes to set or refine your goals for reading. This worksheet will help you organize your thoughts.

1. By the end of the year, I want my students to be able to:

    *

    *

    *

2. How can I use my greatest strengths as a teacher to help me reach my goals?

3. What changes must I make to my classroom and current reading program to support my goals?

4. What additional materials will I require?

5. Do I have colleagues who share my goals? If so, how can we work together?

6. During the year, how will I monitor success in reaching my goals?

7. What are some obstacles that could prevent me from reaching my goals? How can I avoid them?

Appendix K   **Ohio Word Test**

<table>
<tr><td colspan="4">**APPENDIX 1**   OHIO WORD TEST SCORE SHEET</td></tr>
</table>

TEST SCORE [ ] /20

Date: _____

Name: _____   School: _____

Recorder: _____   Classroom Teacher: _____

Record incorrect responses.
Choose appropriate list of words.   ✔ (Checkmark) Correct Response   • (Dot) No Response

	LIST A	LIST B	LIST C
Practice words	**can**	**in**	**see**
	and	ran	big
	the	it	to
	pretty	said	ride
	has	her	him
	down	find	for
	where	we	you
	after	they	this
	let	live	may
	here	away	in
	am	are	at
	there	no	with
	over	put	some
	little	look	make
	did	do	eat
	what	who	an
	them	then	walk
	one	play	red
	like	again	now
	could	give	from
	yes	saw	have

For Transitional Readers:

"Grandpa and Gus" series, by C. Mills (Farrar Straus & Giroux)

"Henry and Mudge" series, by C. Rylant (Trumpet Book Club)

"Mr. Putter and Tabby" series, by C. Rylant (Harcourt Brace)

"Poppleton" series, by C. Rylant (Scholastic)

"Nate the Great" series, M. W. Sharmat (Bantam Doubleday Dell)

"Jim and His First-Grade Friends" series, by M. Cohen (Bantam Doubleday Dell)

"Lionel" series, by S. Krensky (Puffin)

"Ronald Morgan" series, by P. R. Giff (Puffin)

"School Friends" series, by B. Chardiet and G. Maccarone (Scholastic)

"Dragon" series, by D. Pilkey (Orchard)

"Twiddle Twins" series, by H. Goldsmith (Mondo)

"Young Cam Jansen" series, by D. Adler (Viking)

For Transitional/Fluent Readers:

"Pee Wee Scouts" series, by J. Delton (Bantam Doubleday Dell)

"Grandpa" series, by R. Lewis (Mondo)

"George and Martha" series, by J. Marshall (Houghton Mifflin)

"M & M" series, by P. Ross (Puffin)

"Amelia Bedelia" series, by P. Parish (Harper & Trophy)

"Cam Jansen" series, by D. Adler (Viking)

"Junie B. Jones" series, by B. Park (Random House)

"New Kids of the Polk Street School" series, by P. R. Giff (Bantam Doubleday Dell)

"Kids of the Polk Street School" series, by P. R. Giff (Bantam Doubleday Dell)

"Polka Dot Private Eye" series, by P. R. Giff (Dell)

"Pinky and Rex" series, by J. Howe (Simon and Schuster)

"Triplet Trouble" series, by D. Dadley and M. T. Jones (Scholastic)

"The Littles" series, by J. Peterson (Random House)

"The Dog That Pitched a No-Hitter" series, by M. Christopher (Little, Brown & Co.)

"Arthur" chapterbook series, by M. Brown (Little, Brown & Co.)

"The Cobble Street Cousins" series, by C. Rylant (Simon & Schuster)

"Magic Tree House" series, by M. P. Osborne (Random House)

For Fluent Readers:

"Horrible Harry" series, by S. Kline (Puffin)

"Song Lee" series, by S. Kline (Puffin)

"Adam Joshua" series, by J. L. Smith (Harper Trophy)

"Ballet Slippers" series, by P. R. Giff (Puffin)

"Flower Girl" series, by K. Leverich (Harper Trophy)

"Best Enemies" series, by K. Leverich (Morrow)

"'Gator Girls" series, by S. Calmerson and J. Cole (Beech Tree)

"Marvin Redpost" series, by L. Sachar (Random House)

"Houdini Club Magic Mystery" series, by D. Adler (Random House)

"Jenny Archer" series, by D. Palmisciano (Little, Brown & Company)

"Little House Chapter Books" series, by L. E. Wilder (Harper Trophy)

"Mary Marony" series, by S. Kline (Dell)

"Nora" series, by J. Hurwitz (Penguin)

"Russell and Eliza" series, by J. Hurwitz (Puffin)

"Rip-Roaring Russell" series, by J. Hurwitz (Puffin)

"Flat Stanley" series, by J. Brown (Harper Trophy)

"Zach Files" series, by D. Greenburg (Grosset & Dunlap)

"Time Warp Trio" series, by J. Sciezska (Viking)

"Winky Blue" series, by P. Jane (Mondo)

"The Adventures of the Bailey School Kids" series, by D. Dadley and M. Jones (Scholastic)

"The Bailey City Monsters" series, by M. T. Jones and D. Dadley (Scholastic)

"Red Ribbon Rosie" series, by J. Marzollo (Random House)

"Boxcar Children" series, by G. C. Warner (Albert Whitman & Company)

"Amber Brown" series, by P. Danziger (Scholastic)

"Herbie Jones" series, by S. Kline (Puffin)

"Baby-Sitter's Club" series, by A. M. Martin (Scholastic)

"The Secrets of Droon" series, by T. Abbott (Scholastic)

"Henry Higgins" series, by B. Cleary (Avon Books)

"Starring Rosie" series, by P. R. Giff (Penguin)

"Ramona" series, by B. Cleary (Avon Books)

"The Many Troubles of Andy Russell" series, by D. A. Adler (Harcourt Brace & Co.)

"Annie Bananie" series, by L. Komaiko (Bantam Doubleday Dell)

Questions to Ask Children As the Year Goes On

1. *To find out the kinds of books children like to read:*

1. a. _____ How would you feel if you got books as a gift?

1. b. _____ Are there other books besides the ones we have that you'd like to see in our classroom? What are they?

1. c. _____ If you were going on vacation and wanted to take some books along, which would you select?

1. d. _____ If you were going to sleep over your grandma's for the weekend, what book would you bring?

1. e. _____ If you were a teacher, what book would you read aloud to the class?

1. f. _____ What book would you ask mom or dad to read to you?

2. *To learn about children's attitudes toward reading:*

2. a. _____ Do you like to read? Would you rather read than play outside? Go to the movies? Watch television? Play with a friend?

2. b. _____ What are the times in school when you are really happy? Is reading one of them?

2. c. _____ What are the times of day when you feel most confident? Is reading one of them?

2. d. _____ Do you notice other kids in the classroom get absorbed in their reading? Does that ever happen to you?

2. e. _____ Are there ever times when you're "lost in a book" and don't know what's happening around you? Tell me about them.

3. *To find out how children select books to read:*

3. a. _____ How do you select a book? Do you look at the title, read a few pages, get recommendations from friends?

3. b. _____ If you were buying a book for a friend, how would you go about choosing it? What would you do?

4. *To learn about a child's reading habits:*

4. a. _____ When is your favorite time of day to read? In class? In the morning before coming to school? Before dinner? At bedtime?

4. b. _____ Do you like to read in a room by yourself? Do you like to read where others are gathered?

4. c. _____ How many books do you read a week?

4. d. _____ Do you like to read one book at a time (finish a book before starting a new one) or do you like to read a couple at once?

Guided Reading Planning Sheet (____) for (____)   **Emergent Stage**

Some Strategies to Demonstrate:

- tracking print
- noting patterns in text
- using pictures to predict the story and words
- attending to graphophonic cues (especially the beginning and ending letters)
- looking through the word to the end

Guided Reading Planning Sheet (____) for (____)   **Early Stage**

Some Strategies to Demonstrate:

- noting spelling patterns
- monitoring and self-correcting
- using meaning, structure, and graphophonic cues together
- chunking words into phrases
- "Skip and Return"

Guided Reading Planning Sheet (_____) for (_____)   **Transitional Stage**

Some Strategies to Demonstrate:

- "Stopping to Think"
- making a Story Map
- making a Character Map
- using a "Before and After" Chart
- retelling chapters in writing
- rereading to clarify meaning

Guided Reading Planning Sheet (____) for (____)   **Fluent Stage**

Some Strategies to Demonstrate:

- "Preview and Predict"
- using text features to aid comprehension
- researching—taking notes—making data charts
- writing to deepen understanding of stories, factual texts, and poetry
- webbing "What I Knew/What I Know Now"

Guided Reading Groups   **Month of** _____

Book: _____

_____

Strategy: _____

_____

Dates: _____

Children:

1.

2.

3.

4.

5.

6.

Book: _____

_____

Strategy: _____

_____

Dates: _____

Children:

1.

2.

3.

4.

5.

6.

Book: _____

_____

Strategy: _____

_____

Dates: _____

Children:

1.

2.

3.

4.

5.

6.

Book: _____

_____

Strategy: _____

_____

Dates: _____

Children:

1.

2.

3.

4.

5.

6.

Works Cited

Professional Books

Adams, M. J. 1995. *Beginning to Read: Thinking and Learning About Print*. Cambridge, Mass.: The MIT Press.

Allington, R. 1994. "The schools we have. The schools we need." *The Reading Teacher*, 48: 20.

Bolton, F., and D. Snowball. 1993. *Teaching Spelling: A Practical Resource*. Victoria, Australia: Thomas Nelson Australia.

Bronowski, J. 1965. *Science and Human Values*. New York, NY: Harper & Row, Publishers.

Bruner, J. 1990. *Acts of Meaning*. Cambridge, Massachusetts: Harvard University Press.

Cambourne, B. 1998. *The Whole Story: Natural Learning and the Acquisition of Literacy in the Classroom*. Auckland, New Zealand: Ashton Scholastic.

Clay, M. 1991. *Becoming Literate: The Construction of Inner Control*. Portsmouth, NH: Heinemann.

———. 1992. *The Early Detection of Reading Difficulties*. Portsmouth, NH: Heinemann.

———. 1993. *An Observation Survey of Early Literacy Achievement*. Portsmouth, NH: Heinemann.

———. 1993. *Reading Recovery: A Guidebook for Teachers in Training*. Portsmouth, NH: Heinemann.

Clay, M., and P. H. Johnston. "Recording Oral Reading," in *Knowing Literacy: Constructive Literacy Achievement*. York, ME: Stenhouse.

Crevola, C., and Peter Hill. 1999. Presentation at the New Standards Conference in San Diego.

Cunningham, P. M. 1995. *Phonics They Use: Words for Reading and Writing*. 2d ed. New York, NY: Harper Collins.

Cunningham, P. M., and D. Hall. 1994. *Making Words*. Torrance, CA: Good Apple Publishing.

Educational Department of Western Australia, Researchers and Developers. 1994. *Reading Developmental Continuum*. Portsmouth, NH: Heinemann.

Foorman, B. R. 1995. "Research on 'The Great Debate': Code-Oriented Versus Whole Language Approaches to Reading Instruction." *School Psychology Review*, 24: 376–392.

Fountas, I., and G. S. Pinnell. 1996. *Guided Reading: Good First Teaching for All Children*. Portsmouth, NH: Heinemann.

———. 1999. *Matching Books to Readers: Using Leveled Books in Guided Reading, K–3*. Portsmouth, NH: Heinemann.

Fry, E. 1991. *Ten Best Ideas for Reading Teachers*. Menlo Park, CA: Addison-Wesley Publishing Co.

Goodman, K. 1965. "A Linguistic Study of Cues and Miscues in Reading." *Elementary English* 42: 639–643.

Harwayne, S. 1999. *Going Public: Priorities and Practice at The Manhattan New School*. Portsmouth, NH: Heinemann.

———. 2000. *Lifetime Guarantees: Toward Ambitious Literacy Teaching*. Portsmouth, NH: Heinemann.

Henrietta, D., M. Moustafa, and the staff of the Centre for Language in Primary Education. 1998. *Whole to Part Phonics*. Portsmouth, NH: Heinemann.

Holdaway, D. 1980. *Independence in Reading*. Sidney, Australia: Ashton Scholastic.

Holt, J. 1989. *Learning All the Time*. Reading, MA: Addison-Wesley Publishing.

Hornsby, D., J. Parry, and D. Sukarna. 1992. *Teach On: Teaching Strategies for Reading and Writing Workshops*. Portsmouth, NH: Heinemann.

Mooney, M. 1990. *Reading To, With, and By Children*. New York, NY: Richard C. Owen Publishing.

Moustafa, M. 1997. *Beyond Traditional Phonics: Research Discoveries and Reading Instruction*. Portsmouth, NH: Heinemann.

The National Academy of Education. 1985. *Becoming a Nation of Readers: The Report of the Commission on Reading*. Washington, DC: The National Institute of Education.

Peterson, B. 1991. "Selecting Books for Beginning Readers," in *Bridges to Literacy: Learning from Reading Recovery*. Ed. D. E. Deford, C. Lyons, and G. S. Pinnell. Portsmouth, NH: Heinemann.

Salch, J. H. 1996. *In the Company of Children*. York, ME: Stenhouse.

Smith, F. 1988. *Joining the Literacy Club: Further Essays Into Education*. Portsmouth, NH: Heinemann.

Stanovich, K. E. 1986. "Matthew Effects in Reading: Some Consequences of Individual Differences in the Acquisition of Literacy." *Reading Research Quarterly* 21: 360–397.

Stauffer, R. G. 1970. *The Language-Experience Approach to the Teaching of Reading*. New York, NY: Harper & Row.

Steinbeck, J. 1951. *The Log from the Sea of Cortez*. New York, NY: Viking Press, Inc.

Taberski, S. 1996. Video Series: *A Close-Up Look at Teaching Reading: Focusing on Children and Our Goals*. Portsmouth, NH: Heinemann.

Wylie, R. E., and D. D. Durrell. 1970. "Teaching Vowels Through Phonograms." *Elementary English* 47: 787–791.

Children's Books

Bailey, D. 1990. *Energy From Oil and Gas* ("Facts About" series). New York, NY: Steck-Vaughn.

Barrie, J. M. 1994. *Peter Pan* (The Young Collector's Illustrated Classics). Chicago, IL: Masterwork Books.

Berger, M. 1993. *The World of Ants*. New York, NY: Newbridge.

Blackman, M. 1991. *Girl Wonder and the Terrific Twins*. New York, NY: Dutton Children's Books.

Bliss, C. D. 1995. *The Shortest Kid in the World*. New York, NY: Random House.

[Bookshop, Stage 2]. 1996. *My Word Book*. Greenvale, NY: Mondo Publishing.

Brittain, B. 1983. *The Wish-Giver*. New York, NY: Scholastic.

Burnett, Frances Hodgson. 1987. *The Secret Garden* (The Young Collector's Illustrated Classics). Chicago, IL: Masterwork Books.

Butler, A. 1989. *A Zoo*. New York: Rigby.

Calmenson, S., and J. Cole. 1995. *'Gator Girls*. New York, NY: William Morrow & Co.

Catling, P. S. 1979. *The Chocolate Touch*. New York, NY: William Morrow & Co.

Chardiet, B., and G. Maccarone. 1999. *The Snowball War*. New York, NY: Scholastic.

Chew, R. 1971. *No Such Thing As a Witch*. New York, NY: Scholastic.

Choi, S. N. 1997. *The Best Older Sister*. New York, NY: Bantam Doubleday Dell.

Cleary, B. 1983. *Dear Mr. Henshaw*. New York, NY: William Morrow & Co.

Cohen, M. 1981. *Jim Meets the Thing*. New York, NY: Dell Publishing.

———. 1983. *Bee My Valentine*. New York, NY: Dell Publishing.

———. 1997. *Liar, Liar, Pants on Fire!* New York, NY: Scholastic Inc.

Cole, J. 1987. *Norma Jean, Jumping Bean*. New York, NY: Random House.

Cowley, J. 1987. *Just This Once*. New York, NY: Scott Foresman.

Coxe, Molly. 1997. *The Big Egg*. New York, NY: Random House.

Dahl, R. 1964. *Charlie and the Chocolate Factory*. New York, NY: Penguin.

———. 1970. *Fantastic Mr. Fox*. New York, NY: Knopf.

———. 1982. *The BFG*. New York, NY: Random House.

———. 1991. *George's Marvelous Medicine*. New York, NY: Puffin Books.

Donnelly, J. 1988. *Tut's Mummy: Lost and Found*. New York, NY: Random House.

Douglas, A. 1996. *The Lad Who Went to the North Wind*. Greenvale, NY: Mondo Publisher.

"Eyewitness" books (series). New York, NY: Alfred Knopf.

Geras, A. 1995. *Little Swan*. New York, NY: Random House.

Giff, P. R. 1984. *The Beast in Ms. Rooney's Room*. New York, NY: Dell Publishing.

———. 1984. *Fish Face*. New York, NY: Bantam Doubleday Dell.

———. 1985. *Snaggle Doodles*. New York, NY: Dell Publishing.

———. 1986. *Watch Out, Ronald Morgan!* New York, NY: Viking Press.

———. 1987. *The Mystery of the Blue Ring.* New York, NY: Young Yearling.

———. 1988. *All About Stacy.* New York, NY: Young Yearling.

———. 1988. *B-E-S-T Friends.* New York, NY: Bantam Doubleday Dell.

———. 1989. *Stacey Says Goodbye.* New York, NY: Doubleday Bantam Dell.

———. "New Kids of the Polk Street School" series. New York, NY: Dell Publishing.

Greydanus, Rose. 1980. *Animals at the Zoo.* New York, NY: Troll Associates.

Hanzl, A. 1986. *Silly Willy.* Greenvale, NY: Mondo Publishing.

Henkes, K. 1988. *Chester's Way.* New York, NY: William Morrow & Co.

———. 1990. *Julius: The Baby of the World.* New York, NY: William Morrow & Co.

———. 1991. *Chrysanthemum.* New York, NY: William Morrow & Co.

Hest, A. 1984. *The Crack-of-Dawn Walkers.* New York, NY: Mac Books.

Hoff, S. 1959. *Sammy the Seal.* New York, NY: Harper Trophy.

Hong, M. 1995. *Friends.* Greenvale, NY: Mondo Publishing.

Howe, J. 1983. *Celery Stalks at Midnight.* New York, NY: Simon & Schuster.

Huck, C. 1993. *Secret Places.* New York, NY: Greenwillow Publishing.

Jane, P. 1996. *No Way, Winky Blue.* Greenvale, NY: Mondo.

Kline, S. 1995. *Mary Marony and the Chocolate Surprise.* New York, NY: Bantam Doubleday Dell.

———. 1996. *Mary Marony and the Snake.* New York, NY: Bantam Doubleday Dell.

———. 1997. *Marvin and the Mean Words.* New York, NY: Putnam Publishing.

Kraft, E. 1998. *Chocolatina.* Bridgewater Books.

Krensky, S. 1987. *Lionel in the Fall.* New York, NY: Puffin.

Kroll, S. 1991. *Annabelle's Un-Birthday.* New York, NY: Macmillan Publishing.

London, J. 1995. *Like Butter on Pancakes.* New York, NY: Viking.

"Look Closer" books (series). New York, NY: Alfred A. Knopf.

Moon, C. "Once Upon a Time Books 1–4." Bothell, WA: The Wright Group.

Moore, H. H. 1996. *Beavers.* Greenvale, NY: Mondo Publishers.

Nayer, J. 1997. *A Week With Aunt Bea.* Greenvale, NY: Mondo.

Naylor, P. R. 1999. *Sweet Strawberries.* New York, NY: Simon & Schuster.

O'Connor, J. 1986. *Lulu Goes to Witch School.* New York, NY: Harper Trophy.

———. 1995. *Kate Skates.* New York, NY: Grosset and Dunlap.

Osborne, M. P. 1993. *Mummies in the Morning.* New York, NY: Random House.

Packard, M. 1997. *I Am Not a Dinosaur.* New York, NY: Simon & Schuster.

Palmer, T. S. 1994. *Rhino and Mouse.* New York, NY: Puffin.

Park, B. 1994. *Junie B. Jones and the Sneaky Peeky Spying.* New York, NY: Random House.

———. 1995. *Junie B. Jones and the Yucky Blucky Fruitcake.* New York, NY: Random House.

———. "Junie B. Jones" series. New York, NY: Random House.

Parrish, P. 1992. *Amelia Bedelia.* New York, NY: Harper Collins.

Phillips, J. 1986. *Tiger Is a Scaredy Cat.* New York, NY: Random House.

Platnick, N. 1995. *Tarantulas Are Spiders.* Greenvale, NY: Mondo.

Pollack, Y. (retold by). 1995. *The Old Man's Mitten.* Greenvale, NY: Mondo.

Rosenbloom, J. 1985. *Deputy Dan and the Bank Robbers.* New York, NY: Random House.

Ross, P. 1985. *M & M and the Bad News Babies.* New York, NY: Penguin.

———. 1985. *M & M and the Big Bag.* New York, NY: Puffin.

———. 1985. *M & M and the Mummy Mess.* New York, NY: Penguin.

———. 1988. *Meet M & M.* New York, NY: Puffin.

———. 1991. *M & M and the Halloween Monster.* New York, NY: Penguin.

Rylant, C. 1993. *Henry and Mudge and the Wild Wind.* New York, NY: Simon & Schuster.

Sachar, L. 1989. *The Wayside School Is Falling Down.* New York, NY: William Morrow and Co.

Scott Foresman Reading Systems. 1971. *Cats and Kittens.* New York, NY: Addison Wesley Educational Publishers.

Seuss, Dr. (T. S. Geisel). 1960. *Green Eggs and Ham.* New York, NY: Random House.

———. 1981. *One fish two fish red fish blue fish.* New York, NY: Random House.

————. 1987. *The Foot Book*. New York, NY: Random House.

Sharmat, M. W. 1975. *Nate the Great and the Lost List*. New York, NY: Bantam Doubleday Dell.

————. 1984. *Nate the Great and the Snowy Trail*. New York, NY: Bantam Doubleday Dell.

————. 1989. *Nate the Great and the Halloween Hunt*. New York, NY: Bantam Doubleday Dell.

————. 1991. *Nate the Great and the Missing Key*. New York, NY: Bantam Doubleday Dell.

————. "Nate the Great" series. New York, NY: Putnam Publishing.

Silverman, M. 1992. *My Tooth Is Loose*. New York, NY: Scott Foresman.

Singer, M. 1989. *Turtle in July*. New York, NY: Simon & Schuster.

Smith, J. L. 1981. *The Monster in the Third Dresser Drawer (and other stories about Adam Joshua)*. New York, NY: Harper Trophy.

————. 1990. *The Turkeys' Side of It: Adam Joshua's Thanksgiving*. New York, NY: Harper Trophy.

————. 1995. *The Adam Joshua Capers: The Kid Next Door*. New York, NY: Harper Trophy.

Spyri, J. 1996. *Heidi* (The Young Collector's Illustrated Classics). Chicago, IL: Masterwork Books.

Stein, R. L. "Goosebumps" series. New York, NY: Scholastic.

Stevens, C. 1989. *Anna, Grandpa, and the Big Storm*. New York, NY: Viking Press.

————. 1993. *Lily and Miss Liberty*. Little Apple.

Stevens, J. 1995. *Tops and Bottoms*. New York, NY: Harcourt Brace.

Stille, D. R. 1991. *Water Pollution* (a New True Book). New York, NY: Children's Press.

Taberski, S. 1996. *Morning, Noon, and Night: Poems to Fill Your Day*. Greenvale, NY: Mondo Publishing.

Vandine, J. 1995. *I Eat Leaves*. Greenvale, NY: Mondo Publishing.

Weinman, M. S. 1982. *Nate the Great and the Missing Key*. New York, NY: Putnam Publishing Group.

Wells, R. 1973. *Noisy Nora*. New York, NY: Dial Books.

White, E. B. 1952. *Charlotte's Web*. New York, NY: Harper Collins.

Wilder, L. I. 1997. *Pioneer Sisters* (adapted from the "Little House Books"). New York, NY: Harper Collins.

Wooley, M., and K. Pigdon. 1997. *Finding Out About: Birds of Prey*. Greenvale, NY: Mondo Publishing.

Ziefert, H. 1985. *A Dozen Dogs*. New York, NY: Random House.

Zolotow, C. 1993. *Snippets: A Gathering of Poems, Pictures, and Possibilities*. New York, NY: Harper Collins.

Index